Also by Jay Sexton

*Debtor Diplomacy: Finance and American Foreign Relations
in the Civil War Era, 1837–1873*

The Global Lincoln (coedited with Richard Carwardine)

The Monroe Doctrine

Doctrine

Empire and Nation in Nineteenth-Century America

Jay Sexton

ılı *Hill and Wang*
A division of Farrar, Straus and Giroux
New York

Hill and Wang
A division of Farrar, Straus and Giroux
18 West 18th Street, New York 10011
Copyright © 2011 by Jay Sexton
Map copyright © 2011 by Jeffrey L. Ward
Printed in the United States of America
First edition, 2011

Library of Congress Cataloging-in-Publication Data
Sexton, Jay, 1978–
    The Monroe Doctrine : empire and nation in nineteenth-century
America / Jay Sexton.
        p. cm.
    Includes bibliographical references and index.
    ISBN 978-0-8090-6999-6(alk. paper)
      1. Monroe doctrine.   2. United States—Foreign relations—19th century.
I. Title.

JZ1482.S49 2010
327.7304—dc22

                                                        2010023382

Designed by Jonathan D. Lippincott

www.fsgbooks.com

5   7   9   10   8   6   4

For my parents

Contents

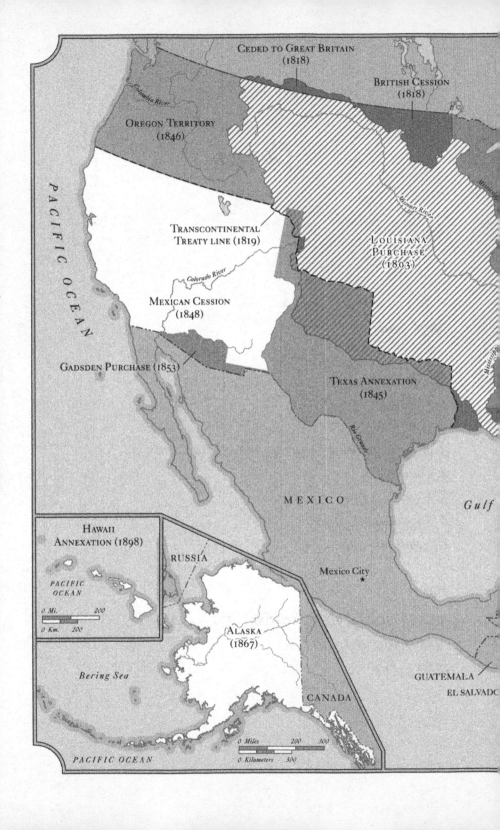

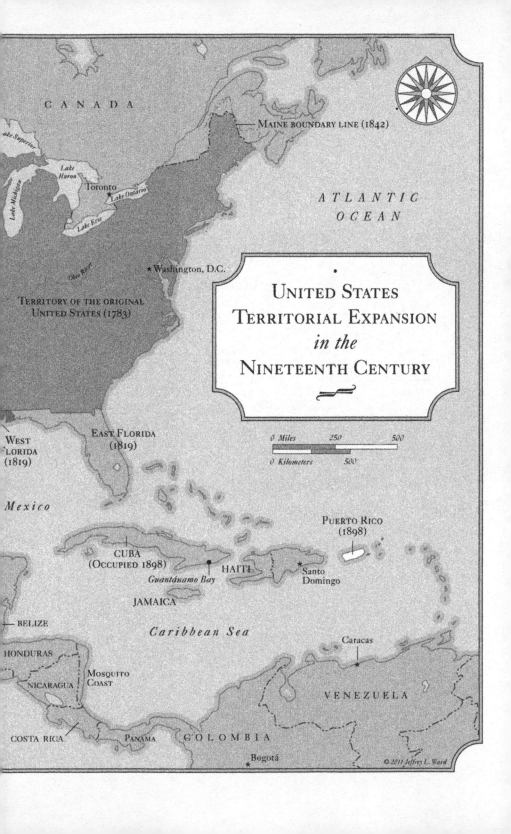

CANADA

MAINE BOUNDARY LINE (1842)

lake Superior

Lake Huron

Lake Michigan

Toronto

Lake Ontario

Lake Erie

ATLANTIC OCEAN

Ohio River

★Washington, D.C.

TERRITORY OF THE ORIGINAL UNITED STATES (1783)

UNITED STATES TERRITORIAL EXPANSION *in the* NINETEENTH CENTURY

WEST FLORIDA (1819)

EAST FLORIDA (1819)

0 Miles   250   500

0 Kilometers   500

Mexico

PUERTO RICO (1898)

CUBA (OCCUPIED 1898)
Guantánamo Bay

HAITI

Santo Domingo

JAMAICA

— BELIZE

Caribbean Sea

Caracas

HONDURAS

NICARAGUA

MOSQUITO COAST

★

VENEZUELA

COSTA RICA

PANAMA

COLOMBIA

Bogotá

★

© 2011 Jeffrey L. Ward

The Monroe Doctrine

Introduction

President James Monroe convened his cabinet in the autumn of 1823 to discuss how to respond to a perceived national security crisis. The Monroe administration feared that European powers were seeking to recolonize the newly independent states of Spanish America, an act that might endanger the United States itself. The cabinet's deliberations resulted in Monroe's December 2 message to Congress, the textual basis of what later became the "Monroe Doctrine." In it, the President declared that the Western Hemisphere was no longer open to European colonization and political intervention, which the United States would deem a threat to its security. The 1823 message unilaterally asserted that "the American continents, by the free and independent condition which they have assumed and maintain, are henceforth not to be considered as subjects for colonization by any European powers."

Despite its straightforward prose, Monroe's message was an ambiguous and paradoxical document. The message proclaimed American opposition to European colonialism, but within it lurked the imperial ambitions of the expansionist United States. It sought to further America's independence from Britain, yet its achievement resulted from the fact that Britain's Royal Navy deterred the European powers from intervention in Latin America. Though it was part of the administration's diplomatic strategy, Monroe addressed the message not to foreign governments, but to "Fellow-Citizens of the Senate and House of Representatives." The message articulated a national policy aimed at strengthening the union of states in North America; yet the members of the cabinet who drafted it—principally John Quincy Adams of Massachusetts, South Carolinian John C. Calhoun, and Virginians William Wirt and Monroe—had the interests of their own states, sections, and political positions in mind. Most important, the Monroe cabinet stated what European powers could not do, but stopped short of announcing any specific policy for the United States. The 1823 message placed no constraints or limitations on American statesmen.

The open-ended nature of the seemingly direct 1823 message foreshadowed the elasticity and political utility of what became known in the mid-nineteenth century as the Monroe Doctrine. Generations of Americans would proclaim that Monroe's message embodied fundamental principles of American statecraft. But they would disagree with one another over its meaning, purpose, and application. There would be as many Monroe Doctrines as foreign policy perspectives. When even the flexible language of the 1823 message proved restrictive, Americans would attach "corollaries" to it to extend legitimacy to new policies. The creation of the Monroe Doctrine was not a single event in 1823, but rather a contested process that lasted throughout the nineteenth century. The construction of the Monroe Doctrine was like a never-ending building project: upon the foundations of the 1823 message, Americans built larger, more elaborate structures, only to have political opponents or subsequent generations renovate or even demolish and rebuild what lay before them.

The Monroe Doctrine evolved in relation to the shifting dynamics and internal politics of the union. It also was the product of t1e larger geopolitical context of great power expansion, rivalry, and contraction from which the American nation and empire emerged. There was nothing inevitable or preordained about the rise of the United States, even if the Monroe Doctrine boldly called for a new world order premised upon American principles. Though the North American republic was blessed with many advantages, it was vulnerable from within and without. Nor did nineteenth-century Americans agree on the form and purposes that their nation and empire should assume. This book uses the Monroe Doctrine to examine how the state that emerged as the preeminent global power of the twentieth century was the product of the protracted, contentious, and interconnected processes of anticolonial liberation, internal national consolidation, and imperial expansion.

"Imperial Anticolonialism"

Unique in the nineteenth-century world, the United States transformed itself from a group of colonies to a global empire. The transition from colony to empire was not linear. American statesmen did not first focus on consolidating their independence from Britain before then setting about building their empire. They did not decide in 1823 that their colonial past had been put to rest and their imperial future now lay before them. Nor were anticolonialism and imperialism irreconcilable opposites in the context of nineteenth-century America. The key to understanding the nineteenth-century Monroe Doctrine is the simultaneity and interdependence of anticolonialism and imperialism. The historian William Appleman Williams perhaps summed it up best when he labeled American statecraft "imperial anticolonialism."[1]

The fusion of imperialism and anticolonialism shaped both the domestic and foreign policies of the United States in the nineteenth century. In part because of their experience under

British colonial rule, Americans embedded anticolonial principles into their two foundational documents of 1787: the Constitution and the Northwest Ordinance. These documents established a decentralized political structure that stood as an alternative to the colonial model of the Old World, in which central authority exercised control over far-flung dependencies. The foreign policy of the United States was anticolonial in that American statesmen opposed the colonial expansion of the European powers in the Western Hemisphere. These anticolonial principles and objectives were inextricably intertwined with the construction of the nineteenth-century American empire. The anticolonial political system of the United States facilitated the colonization of much of the North American continent. This imperialist process entailed not only voluntary white settlement and migration, but also the removal of native populations, the expansion of slavery (until 1861), and the conquest of territory held by other nations, particularly during the Mexican War in the 1840s. The United States also proved adept at projecting power in regions not formally annexed to the union, such as Mexico and the Caribbean. As the nineteenth century progressed, many Americans went further, arguing that the world should be remade in the image of the United States. Though rooted in traditional anticolonialism, this impulse fueled interventionist foreign policies and, in the aftermath of the War of 1898, would lead many Americans to embrace their own colonial expansion.

Central to this "imperial anticolonialism" was the United States' ongoing struggle to consolidate its independence from Britain. Though the thirteen colonies achieved their political independence during the American Revolution, the United States remained within the webs of an expanding and increasingly powerful British Empire. The young American republic continued to be an economic satellite of Britain; its intellectuals decried the predominance of British literature and ideas in its culture; its statesmen feared that British power could destroy the union itself. Americans' struggle against the British Empire lasted far longer than the military encounters of the American Revolution. This anticolonial process is impossible to separate from early American imperialism. The exercise of control over Native Americans, the acquisition of new territories, the attempt to control the economic system of the Western Hemisphere—all these imperialist acts were bound up with the effort to consolidate independence from the British Empire.

Nineteenth-century Americans were obsessed with the British Empire. They yearned to escape the shadow of their former colonial master, yet they remained reliant upon British investment, commerce, and power. Indeed, nationalist objectives more often necessitated the co-option than the negation of British power. The Monroe Doctrine became American shorthand for a hemisphere (and, ultimately, a world) cleared of the British Empire. Yet this did not stop generations of American statesmen from harnessing the power of their former colonial master, nor from looking to the British Empire, particularly the forms it took in Latin America, as a model when devising policies to advance their Monroe Doctrine. The *New York Herald* captured the irony of American thinking when it declared in 1882 that "we are a good enough England for this hemisphere."[2]

American statesmen formulated increasingly interventionist foreign policies as the nineteenth century progressed. The history of the Monroe Doctrine, however, is not simply the narrative of this development. The United States did not move from a policy of pure nonintervention to a strategy of consistent intervention. There were interventionist aspects of the allegedly noninterventionist foreign policies of the early nineteenth century, just as elements of nonintervention and anti-imperialism persisted in the late nineteenth and early twentieth centuries. Even as new "corollaries" extended the scope and purpose of the Monroe Doctrine at the turn of the century, the 1823 message remained a symbol for those opposed to expansionist and interventionist policies. It would be championed not only by the architects of the American empire as we now know it, but also by those, such as the defenders of slavery, who ultimately lost political battles at home to determine the nature of the American imperial project. The Doctrine also became a favored symbol both for internationalists, who argued that it was a foundation of international law, and isolationists, who contended that it demanded detachment from the rivalries of the Old World.

Examination of the Monroe Doctrine provides a way of charting the American relationship with the wider world over the course of the nineteenth century. It reveals how Americans envisioned themselves in relation to other nations and peoples. The Doctrine divided the globe into spheres. Most straightforward was the ideological bifurcation between the republics of the New World and the monarchies of the Old that found expression in Monroe's 1823 message. Throughout the nineteenth century, American statesmen also made the opposite, latitudinal division: between the "civilized" and "uncivilized" states that Theodore Roosevelt identified in his 1904 corollary, or, to use today's parlance, between the global north (Europe and the United States) and the global south (Latin America, Africa, and Asia).

The Creation of an American Nation

The Monroe Doctrine illuminates another process fundamental to nineteenth-century America: the development of the United States as a nation. The American Revolution alone did not create a nation. Rather, it established the political independence of thirteen separate states, loosely federated under the ill-fated Articles of Confederation. To be sure, there were powerful centripetal forces in the early republic: the states were connected to one another by their colonial past, networks of trade and communication, and the bonds forged by collectively fighting the British.

The peoples of Britain's former North American colonies were also brought together by a republican ideology conceived in opposition to the Old World's monarchical political system and aristocratic social structure. The name that nineteenth-century Americans most often used for their country—"the union"—evoked a passionate and even mystic attachment to the novel republic they established upon the ashes of their colonial past.[3]

Yet it would be a mistake to project our modern understanding of the American nation back onto the early history of the United States. Early inhabitants of the United States most often thought of themselves in terms of the state (Virginians and New Yorkers, for example) or region (Westerners and New Englanders) from which they hailed. They referred to their union in the plural, as "these United States," rather than in the singular form used today. The term "union" invoked not only a set of nationalist ideas of great potential power, but also a conception of a limited federal entity in which individual states retained sovereignty. "In the early days of the country, before we had railroads, telegraphs and steamboats," Ulysses S. Grant wrote in his 1885 memoirs, "the States were each almost a separate nationality." Indeed, one historian recently suggested that the negotiations between the American states at the 1787 Constitutional Convention in Philadelphia closely resembled the international peace conferences of the era such as the 1815 Congress of Vienna that ended the Napoleonic Wars.[4]

Nation building in the United States was a process that lasted throughout the nineteenth century. It entailed political compromise and constitutional adaptation, economic integration and religious awakenings, territorial expansion and technological innovation, the destruction of slavery and the development of a racialized, nationalist ideology. Ultimately, the fate of the United States hinged upon the outcome of one of the bloodiest conflicts in the nineteenth-century world, the American Civil War. But the

North-South divide was only one of many ways in which the United States might have fragmented. The thirteen original states might have formed several regional confederacies; new states in the West, such as Texas and California, might have maintained their distance from the United States, as would Canada; and the American union might have fallen victim to ideological and political divisions, such as those unleashed by the French Revolution, that did not exactly overlap with geographic regions.

The insecurity of the United States in the nineteenth century was twofold: it was weak relative to the Old World powers that dominated international affairs, and it was internally vulnerable, its union in danger of dissolution. The greatest fear of American statesmen was that these internal and external vulnerabilities would merge, transforming their independent union into factious colonial dependencies. Viewed from the perspective of the juiced-up American nationalism of our own era, this dreaded outcome appears curious and far-fetched. Yet the potential overlap between internal divisions and foreign threats was a very real and persistent fear of nineteenth-century statesmen. This doomsday scenario threatened to materialize at several points—never more so than during the Civil War in the form of a possible British alliance with the Confederacy. Proponents of the Monroe Doctrine thus advanced a series of nationalist principles of statecraft to preempt this possibility. The framers of the 1823 message, as well as later proponents of the Monroe Doctrine, concluded that only by controlling the entire Western Hemisphere—and, consequently, the new states of Latin America—would the United States be able to survive, develop, and ultimately replace the empires of the Old World.

The American conception of national security in the nineteenth century thus looked both inward and outward, particularly in the years before 1865, when federal authority remained weak and contested. Recognizing that the United States had legitimate security concerns, however, is not to contend that American statesmen were right to see foreign threats behind every tree. What is most remarkable about the nineteenth-century conception of threat is the gap between perception and reality. The Holy Allies were not on the verge of intervening in Spanish America when Monroe delivered his message in 1823; the British and French did not stand in the way of the vast American territorial annexations of the 1840s when President James K. Polk invented what he called "Monroe's doctrine"; German imperialists did not seek to trigger a scramble for Latin America in the early twentieth century when President Theodore Roosevelt announced his interventionist "Corollary of the Monroe Doctrine." To be sure, some of the fears held by American statesmen were legitimate. After all, the United States and Britain did engage in a protracted struggle for continental and, later, hemispheric mastery. Slaveholders in the South had reason to fear foreign powers, particularly the British after they embraced abolition in 1833. The French did intervene in Mexico in the 1860s. Yet relative to the chronic rivalries in the snake pit of nineteenth-century Europe, or the imperial scrambles in the Near East, Asia, and Africa, there is no question that the United States was the beneficiary of hospitable geopolitical circumstances.

The American nation and empire took root in fertile soil. To understand the nineteenth-century conception of threat therefore requires more than just re-creating the diplomatic jockeying of the era. It is also necessary to examine the contexts and manner in which American statesmen perceived threat. The ongoing struggle to consolidate independence from the British, as well as the contested nation-building project at home, made many Americans hypersensitive to foreign powers. Important, too, was the fact that American statesmen viewed international affairs through an ideological lens that presupposed rivalry between republics and monarchies. The anxiety of some statesmen resulted from how they calibrated foreign threats in relation to fixed policy objectives such as territorial expansion. Furthermore, many American statesmen exploited fears of foreign intervention in order to mobilize domestic political support for particular foreign policies. The American conception of national security was the product of both perceptions of threat and imperial ambitions, though the proportions of these two ingredients varied greatly among individual statesmen.

Though Americans came to celebrate the Monroe Doctrine as the nineteenth century progressed, they endlessly argued about when, where, how, and why it should be applied. There was no consensus on what specific passages of the 1823 message constituted the Doctrine, let alone how those passages should be interpreted and translated into specific policies. Americans spilled much ink on the Monroe Doctrine in the nineteenth century. Yet the instances when they directed it at foreign governments were few and far between—not to mention largely counterproductive in diplomatic regards. A remarkable feature of the Monroe Doctrine in the nineteenth century is that Americans most often invoked it against one another. They wrote pamphlets to establish their Monrovian credentials; they placed Monroe Doctrine planks in party platforms during election years; they questioned their political opponents' devotion to the dogma of 1823. Monroe did not create a "doctrine." That job would be done by later Americans who competed with one another to lay claim to the mantle of 1823.

The contested nature of the Monroe Doctrine reflected the discord and conflict that accompanied the larger project of national consolidation in nineteenth-century America. The nationalism of the Doctrine made it a potent political instrument that competing groups of Americans exploited to advance their particular agendas. As the nineteenth century progressed, the Doctrine became a ubiquitous symbol, particularly in election years, used for sundry purposes by politicians from across the spectrum. Americans invoked the Monroe Doctrine against one another for several reasons. Some sincerely feared that their political rivals were not committed to nationalist principles and policies. Others sought to advance the specific interests of their state, section, or political party under the guise of a national tradition. And many statesmen packaged expansionist and interventionist foreign policies as an outgrowth of the imagined tradition of unalloyed anticolonialism that the Monroe Doctrine symbolized.

The Monroe Doctrine provides a means to examine three interrelated processes central to nineteenth-century America: the ongoing struggle to consolidate independence from Britain, the forging of a new nation, and the emergence of the American empire. What follows is a history of the Monroe Doctrine that takes into account both the external relations of the United States and its internal dynamics and politics. This book charts how the reactive message of 1823 became a defining symbol of American statecraft that was invoked on behalf of policies that went far beyond the limited and ambiguous course articulated by Monroe himself.

I

Independence

The American Revolution was the first of what would be many struggles for independence from colonial rule in the Western Hemisphere. This "age of revolutions," as it has been called, witnessed the gradual breakdown of the colonial empires that Old World powers had constructed in the preceding centuries. This process lasted throughout the nineteenth century (and, in some places, deep into the twentieth). It not only entailed the achievement of political independence from a colonial master, but also concerned the political arrangements that would replace centuries of colonial rule, which often were born out of the struggle for independence. In a broad sense, the dissolution of colonial rule in the Western Hemisphere also involved the much slower erosion of economic structures and cultural forms that had upheld colonial regimes, as well as their neocolonial successors. The multifaceted and protracted process of decolonization dominated the Western Hemisphere in the nineteenth century.[1]

The origins of what later became the "Monroe Doctrine" lay not just in the deliberations of the Monroe cabinet in 1823, but in this larger geopolitical context. The message of 1823 was rooted in the policies and principles of statecraft that early American statesmen formulated to guide their young republic through the rocky waters of the dissolution of the European colonial order. These principles and policies looked both inward and outward. American statesmen aimed to bind together the various states, sections, and factions of their union that had been established during the era of the American Revolution. They also looked beyond their borders, seeking to consolidate their independence from an increasingly powerful British Empire, as well as to advance their interests in regions of the crumbling Spanish Empire. The interrelated processes that defined the Monroe Doctrine all shaped American statecraft long before 1823: the ongoing struggle of the United States against persistent British power, the nation-building process within the American union, and the projection of American power over peoples excluded from their constitutional arrangements.

The Rising British Empire

Early Americans were not bashful about proclaiming their ambitions for their fledgling republic. George Washington spoke of "our rising empire"; Thomas Jefferson boasted of the expanding American "empire of liberty"; and Tom Paine predicted that American principles "will penetrate where an army of soldiers cannot; it will succeed where diplomatic management would fail . . . it will march on the horizon of the world and it will conquer." In the twentieth century, American power would transform global politics, though perhaps not in the ways foreseen a century and more before. The global preeminence of the United States in our own time has given early American statesmen an aura of clairvoyance for predicting what one historian has called the "rising American empire." Yet there was nothing preordained about the global rise of the United States. Though Americans predicted future greatness for themselves, they also were consumed with their vulnerabilities in an era in which their young and untested union faced challenges from within and without.[2]

The empire that was most dramatically rising in the nineteenth century was not the American but the British. Despite having lost her most important North American colonies in the 1783 Treaty of Paris that ended the American Revolution, the height of the British Empire lay in the future. The British Empire was larger and more powerful in 1820 than it had been in 1776. During the intervening decades, it tightened its grip on India; its resources and people poured into its settler colonies in Canada and Australasia; it acquired strategic way stations such as the African cape and Singapore; it increased its commercial and naval presence in distant markets in East Asia and in Latin America; its naval power became unrivaled; industrialization at home fueled economic growth and the expansion of overseas commerce; it developed a sophisticated and flexible financial system capable of both underwriting international trade and funding wars of unprecedented cost; and its political system weathered the ideological storm unleashed by the American and French revolutions. Even within North America, the British retained a position of great strength, holding Canada and the strategically important Caribbean islands of the British West Indies and maintaining relations with Native American tribes. Following the defeat of Napoleon's France after nearly a quarter of a century of conflict (1793–1815), Britain stood atop the global hierarchy, a position of preeminence that it would consolidate as the nineteenth century progressed. By the early twentieth century, the British governed two-thirds of the world's colonial territories and three-quarters of its colonial population. To be sure, Britain's position of strength brought with it great anxiety stemming from the need to secure its many interests scattered around the globe, particularly as rivals emerged later in the century. This anxiety could serve as the rationale for retrenchment (as would be the case in North America) or could fuel further expansion (as would occur in Africa in the late nineteenth century).

The nineteenth-century British Empire was a multifaceted and dynamic entity. It included formal colonial possessions such as India and, in the late nineteenth century, large portions of Africa, governed through governmental structures originating in London. Settler colonies in Canada and Australasia functioned as a virtual "British West," as the historian James Belich has recently put it, attracting capital and migrants from the home country much like the American West of the same period. The inhabitants of the settler colonies enjoyed increased self-government during the nineteenth century, though they increasingly viewed themselves as members of a "Greater Britain."[3] In Latin America and East Asia, the British largely refrained from formal colonial rule, instead pursuing their interests through the informal projection of commercial and cultural power. Central to the British Empire in both its formal and informal manifestations were so-called collaborating elites, the native peoples whose self-interest led them to associate with the British. Recent historians have emphasized the interconnectivity and dynamism of the British Empire, arguing that its power rested on the fusion of its component parts. The integration of formal colonial possessions, settler colonies, and a global commercial empire constituted an expansive and adaptable "British world-system," as it has recently been called.[4] The decentralization of the British Empire contributed to its power and, as the nineteenth century progressed, paradoxically fueled its integration. Far from being the product of simple military might, the nineteenth-century British Empire rested upon the interconnected foundations of commercial and financial power, naval supremacy, communication networks, technological innovation, and political cooperation with indigenous elites.

The expanding British Empire cast a long shadow over nineteenth-century America. The young United States remained entrapped in the webs of the British world-system long after achieving its political independence during the Revolution. "In the year of grace 1776, we published to the world our Declaration of Independence. Six years later, England assented to the separation," wrote the American nationalist Henry Cabot Lodge in 1883. "These are tolerably familiar facts," Lodge continued. "That we have been striving ever since to make that independence real and complete, and that the work is not yet entirely finished, are not perhaps, equally obvious truisms." The persistence of "colonialism in the United States," as Lodge called it, threatened to keep the United States in a position of subordination to its former colonial master.[5]

The forms of British power in nineteenth-century America were as pervasive as they were enduring. When American statesmen consulted world maps, they found ever more territories colored red (the traditional color of British possessions); the national ledger books showed increasing indebtedness to British banks; English novels took up most of the space on American bookshelves; schoolchildren in the United States continued to be taught with British textbooks deep into the nineteenth century; popular songs—even Francis Scott Key's "Star-Spangled Banner," which later would become the national anthem—were set to old British tunes. It would not be until 1828 that Noah Webster formalized the spellings of "American English," and even then his dictionary served as much as a reminder of the links as of the differences between the two peoples. Nineteenth-century Americans were consumed by the question of how best to consolidate their independence from the British. The ongoing struggle to free themselves from the yoke of British imperialism united the disparate sections and peoples of the United States. It also created political divisions that endangered the union itself. British power was an inescapable reality that paradoxically threatened and benefited the young American republic.

Nowhere did British power exert itself more in the United States than in the material world of economics. If anything, independence brought with it a closer economic relationship than had existed before 1776. British merchants and financiers quickly recovered their leading position in the American economy, elbowing aside their opportunistic Dutch and French rivals who had sought to replace them during the Revolution. For most of the nineteenth century, Britain would be the United States' greatest source of foreign investment, its largest source of imports, and its most important foreign market. To be sure, this economic connection was symbiotic; just as Britain was central to the American economy, the United States was important to the British. But there is little doubt that the United States was the subordinate partner in the relationship. The young republic was a classic "developing economy" with vast resources at its disposal but lacking the means of exploiting them. The majority of American exports to Britain were raw materials and agricultural goods (especially, as the nineteenth century progressed, cotton), whereas most of Britain's exports to the United States were finished goods. Moreover, as Americans would discover in the run-up to the War of 1812, Britain's diplomatic and naval might could be turned against their republic, closing off the international connections upon which their economy relied.

In the eyes of many Americans, this unequal economic arrangement threatened the very independence of the United States. As the Kentucky statesman Henry Clay put it in 1820, the United States was in danger of remaining a "sort of independent colonies of England—politically free, commercially slaves."[6] The frequent financial panics that originated in London rippled through the American economy; banks in London had a habit of recalling loans when credit was tight in the United States; British manufacturers, exploiting the cheap labor at their disposal, undercut upstart American rivals; reliance on British capital necessitated unpopular compromises in foreign policy to reassure foreign bondholders. The American economy, in short, drifted in winds that originated across the Atlantic. As the Virginian John

Taylor put it, "The English who could not conquer us, may buy us."[7]

Yet for all the potential dangers of economic dependence upon Britain, the United States greatly benefited from this relationship. The British market provided the chief outlet for America's farmers and cotton planters. If the period of international instability in the early nineteenth century demonstrated the dangers of reliance upon the British market, the ensuing century of Pax Britannica and unilateral British tariff reductions revealed the advantage. Even as the British lowered their tariffs, the United States remained free to protect its industries, an option it would take full advantage of later in the nineteenth century. British capital played an important role in the dramatic economic takeoff of the United States in the nineteenth century. Investment channeled to the United States by London banks, such as the powerful Baring Brothers firm, kept down interest rates in the capital-starved republic. British investment underwrote important aspects of the "transportation revolution" of canals and railroads, as well as financing the debts of municipalities, state governments, and the federal government itself. By the mid-nineteenth century, nearly half of the United States' national debt was held abroad, chiefly in Britain. Funds provided to the federal government by Baring Brothers also underwrote American territorial expansion. Both the 1803 Louisiana Purchase (which acquired extensive territory in the interior of North America from France) and the Mexican indemnity payment of 1848 (which compensated Mexico for lands conquered by the United States) were made possible by loans from the English bank.

These benefits notwithstanding, how to break the cycle of economic subordination to the British was a principal issue in early American politics. Though Americans in the early republic agreed that the status quo was undesirable, they disagreed over the means that would best establish their economic independence. From this debate emerged the political coalitions of the first party system of Republicans and Federalists. Led by Thomas Jefferson, Republicans sought to construct a liberal international order cleared of preferential trading systems. This commercial vision, which aimed to entrench republicanism at home and advance the interests of agricultural exporters, challenged the structures of the British Empire. When Britain would not acquiesce to American demands for open trade and the respect of neutral rights, Jeffersonian Republicans advocated economic retaliation (either in the form of tariffs, which Jefferson advocated as a temporary measure at various points in the 1790s, or, as in 1807–1809, in the form of an all-out embargo). In opposition were the Federalists, led by Alexander Hamilton, who viewed Britain as an indispensable economic partner as well as a model to emulate. The Hamiltonian program called for the consolidation of the union's finances through the creation of a national bank and the federal assumption of state debts. The Federalists were prepared to make diplomatic compromises with their former colonial master to achieve their objectives, thus further widening the partisan divide at home. Most notable was the 1795 Jay Treaty, which averted war with Britain in the short term by addressing several leftover issues from the Revolutionary period, but outraged Republicans for aligning the United States with its old nemesis and for its failure to protect neutral rights on the high seas.

If Republicans and Federalists disagreed on the means of establishing their independence, they were of one voice in identifying Britain as their greatest economic rival in the long term. For all their differences, both parties agreed on the fundamental objective of establishing American economic independence. Though the Federalists were pro-British elites, they differed from "collaborating elites" in Britain's empire by rejecting associations with the old country that infringed upon American sovereignty. Economic and political exigencies at times blurred the lines between the two parties. For all their heated rhetoric, when in power, both parties found it difficult to implement their policy visions. Federalists and Republicans were also united by the ironic fact that both parties advocated policies that perpetuated short-term British economic hegemony. The Federalist policy of federal assumption of state debts increased American dependence on British credit; likewise, Jeffersonian opposition to barriers to international commerce furthered reliance on British manufactured goods. It would not be the last time that American politicians used British power as a means of achieving their nationalist objectives.

In the arena of diplomacy, British power similarly presented the United States with both threats and opportunities. The young United States remained vulnerable to its former colonial master. The Union Jack continued to be raised each morning in the years following 1783 in seven British posts within U.S. territory that would not be relinquished until 1796. British traders maintained links with Native American tribes, who were understandably hostile to the expansionist republic that had seized their land in the 1783 treaty, in which they were unrepresented. British statesmen pursued policies detrimental to the United States when necessary, as often was the case during their protracted conflict with France, which would not be resolved until 1815. The War of 1812, which arose from the clash between British control of the seas and the American demand for the respect of neutral rights, proved that though the United States could maintain its independence militarily, it remained vulnerable to British power (indeed, most government buildings in Washington lay in ashes at the war's end).

But as much as Britain threatened the young republic, its power also provided opportunities for American statesmen. At points during the European turmoil of 1789–1815, the chief threat to the United States was its former ally France. The Federalists of the 1790s concluded that aligning themselves with the British was preferable to strengthening ties with the French, with whom they soon engaged in the naval "Quasi-War" of 1798–1800. Even a stalwart Anglophobe like Thomas Jefferson conceded that if France choked off American access to New Orleans, "from that moment we must marry ourselves to the British fleet and nation."[8] The two English-speaking states collaborated so closely during this period that one historian has dubbed the 1795–1805 period "the first rapprochement." The United States also found advantage in Europe's distress. Though the United States eventually became entangled in the European conflicts of this period, this did not prevent it from capitalizing on several diplomatic opportunities. With the European powers' military might focused in Europe (and, in the New World, in the Caribbean), American statesmen were able to consolidate their strategic position in agreements such as the Pinckney Treaty of 1795, which secured from Spain access to the Mississippi River, and the Louisiana Purchase of 1803.[9]

A great dilemma for early American statesmen was how to take advantage of opportunities presented by British power without becoming a pawn of their former colonial master. American leaders also faced a domestic political challenge: the deeply Anglophobic political culture that was a product of the Revolution made it difficult to align openly with the British even when it was in the national interest to so do. Few walked this tightrope better than did George Washington, whose foreign policy tilted toward the British, especially with the 1795 Jay Treaty. Yet in his famous 1796 "Farewell Address," Washington glossed over this fact, emphasizing instead the alleged "great rule" of having "as little political connection as possible" with the Old World and the need "to steer clear of permanent alliances." Washington's farewell not only obscured the way his administration had allied itself with the British, but it also undermined the pro-French views of his political opponents.[10]

Nineteenth-century Americans were not uniformly opposed to all things British. American nationalism drew power from both

Anglophobia and Anglophilia. Britain served as an important negative self-reference, yet many Americans admired and reproduced British practices and culture. Such contradictory impulses can be seen in Americans' ambivalent views of the British monarchy. Despite all the fulminations against monarchy in Fourth of July orations, many Americans were fascinated by Britain's royal family. As the nineteenth century progressed, celebrations of the anniversaries of British monarchs in the United States became more common and open, giving rise to the curious appellation of "Victorian America" (named after Queen Victoria, who reigned from 1837 to 1901). "Had Queen Victoria been on the throne, instead of George III," Secretary of State William Evarts declared in 1878, "or if we had postponed our rebellion until Queen Victoria reigned, it would not have been necessary."[11] Such admiration of the British monarchy tapped into increasing racial identification between the self-proclaimed "Anglo-Saxon" peoples of America and Britain. The pride Americans took in their independence from Britain did not prevent many of them from viewing themselves, as the nineteenth century progressed, as part of a master "Anglo-Saxon" race in which they stood alongside their former colonial master atop a global racial hierarchy.

Union and Independence

If the conclusion of the American Revolution in 1783 did not end Americans' struggle against the powerful British, it also left unanswered fundamental questions about the nature and form of their union at home. Both centripetal and centrifugal forces swirled in the political vacuum of North America. The potential for unification among Britain's thirteen former colonies was strong. The American states were connected to one another by networks of trade and communication, a republican ideology, and the experience of collectively fighting the British during the Revolution.

Union between the states also brought with it the means to exert control over Native Americans, as well as to expand westward across the North American continent, exploiting its vast natural resources in the name of economic development and integration.

Yet much divided the thirteen states that, upon attaining political independence, were only loosely united under the Articles of Confederation. Small and large states argued over the form of political representation; Atlantic seaboard states worried about their status in a westward-expanding union; Southern slaveholding states and those increasingly opposed to the institution in the North looked upon each other with great suspicion. The extent to which certain states and individuals were committed to the national project was an open question. Leaders in independent Vermont toyed with reentering the British Empire; renegade frontiersmen schemed to detach various parts of the trans-Appalachian West; sectional interests and identities opened the prospect of the establishment of regional confederacies rather than a single union. The histories of other areas emerging from colonial rule—such as Spanish America, which fragmented into multiple nation-states in the nineteenth century, or South Asia, which divided into three separate states after attaining independence from Britain in the mid-twentieth century—make clear that independence from colonial rule often results in political fragmentation.

That the North American states remained united until they would be torn asunder by secession and civil war in 1861 owed much to the interlocking relationship between union and independence.[12] Even before the Revolution, American leaders feared that independence would result in a cluster of unstable and weak states or federations that would invite further European meddling. In this scenario the American states would have traded formal colonialism for an even less desirable position as pawns of the European powers, pitted against one another in conflicts waged to maintain the balance of power in the Old

World. The nationalist John Jay feared that "every state would be a little nation, jealous of its neighbors, and anxious to strengthen itself by foreign alliances, against its former friends." The newly independent states could only be secure if bound together in a strong union. "Weakness and divisions at home would invite dangers from abroad," Jay later asserted when making the case for a stronger central government; "nothing would tend more to secure us from them than union, strength, and good government within ourselves." The benefits of union far outweighed the costs, even in the minds of South Carolinians who, though aware of the proliferation of antislavery doctrines in the Northern states, concluded that a more powerful central authority could best secure slavery on their vulnerable periphery. Not only would union preempt future conflicts between the states and foreign intervention, but it also provided the means for territorial expansion, the exercise of control over Native Americans, and the economic development and integration of the vast resources of the North American continent. "We have seen the necessity of the Union," James Madison wrote in Federalist 14, "as our bulwark against foreign danger, as the conservator of peace among ourselves, as the guardian of our commerce and other common interests."[13]

The U.S. Constitution of 1787 aimed to consolidate the achievements of the Revolution by creating a union powerful enough to maintain its independence. It sought to walk the tightrope of conferring new powers to the federal government while at the same time satisfying individual states by retaining elements of home rule. In time, contrasting interpretations of whether ultimate power resided in the federal government or within the states would fuel constitutional crisis and contribute to the coming of the civil war. In the 1780s, however, this balancing act was required to achieve both union and independence. Strong central authority might better counter British power, but it could prove fatal to the union from within; too much delegation of power to the states, on the other hand, might leave the United States incapable of maintaining its independence, a lesson learned under the inadequate Articles of Confederation. The interdependent goals of union and independence became the twin pillars of early American statecraft; they "were from the beginning . . . joined at the hip," as the historian David Hendrickson has recently put it.[14]

The centrality of union and independence is made clear by the terror invoked by their opposites: disunion and colonial dependence. The greatest fear among American statesmen was the possibility that Old World powers would exploit internal divisions by allying with sections or factions of the union, thus fusing internal and external threats. It "was the interference of other nations in their domestic divisions" that undid previous republics, a young John Quincy Adams concluded.[15] American statesmen were determined not to allow history to repeat itself. Herein lay the rationale behind the American diplomatic practice of standing aloof, so far as possible, from conflicts that occurred in Europe. The two most famous articulations of this theme—Washington's Farewell Address (1796) and Jefferson's First Inaugural Address (1801)—argued that a foreign policy of nonentanglement should be pursued in order to mitigate the threat posed by internal divisions. Washington's address dealt primarily with the menace of separatist movements in the American West and the entrenchment of ideologically opposed political parties. His "great rule" of diplomatic nonentanglement was a means of safeguarding against these internal threats to the union, not an end in itself. Similarly, Jefferson's call for "entangling alliances with none" was made in the context of an address that called for national unity—albeit one premised upon his political triumph in the election of 1800—after the divisive politics of the 1790s.[16]

The objective of steering clear of European alliances was rooted in perceptions of threat, not in some dogma of isolationism. American statesmen had no qualms about engaging with the powers of the Old World when U.S. interests demanded—indeed, America's political independence owed much to the 1778 alliance with France. Washington's farewell carefully kept the door open to "temporary alliances for extraordinary emergencies," as he called them. Jefferson tilted toward the French in the 1790s, but would later contemplate joint action with the British when circumstances demanded. Nor were early American statesmen in any sense isolationist when it came to commerce, which they hoped to liberate from the restrictions of European colonialism. An open commercial system that respected neutral rights would benefit the internationalist American economy. Americans also hoped that it would accelerate the breakdown of Old World empires by depriving them of their economic basis. Washington's farewell contained another qualification on this score: "The great rule of conduct for us in regard to foreign nations is in extending our commercial relations, to have with them as little political connection as possible." The American objective, as John Adams put it, was nothing less than "a reformation, a kind of Protestantism, in the commercial system of the world."[17]

The United States' campaign for the sanctity of neutral rights found little support abroad in an era of great power conflict. Both Britain and France violated neutral rights in order to prevent American exports from reaching each other during their titanic struggle between 1793 and 1815. The United States eventually became entangled in war with both parties, the "Quasi-War" with France in the late 1790s and the War of 1812 with Britain. These conflicts exacerbated internal divisions that proved to be just as great a threat to the union as that posed by foreign powers. Jefferson's embargo of 1807–1809, which aimed to keep the United States out of the Napoleonic Wars and to coerce the European powers into respecting neutral shipping rights, provoked fierce domestic opposition, particularly among New England Federalists who represented mercantile and shipping interests adversely affected by the policy. Dissatisfaction from this quarter would be even more pronounced during the War of 1812. New England opponents of the conflict convened in Hartford, Connecticut, in late 1814 to discuss ways of securing their interests. In the run-up to the convention, rumors swirled of New England secession and the negotiation of a separate peace treaty with Britain—that toxic combination of disunion and colonial dependence. Moderates ultimately prevailed at Hartford, quashing talk of secession and instead issuing a report detailing their grievances. Yet if the episode reveals the limits of New England separatism in this period, it also underscores the union's good fortune: the Madison administration concluded a peace treaty with Britain just as the Hartford delegates convened. Had the unpopular war dragged on, it is possible that matters would have played out differently in New England, where a follow-up conference was scheduled if the war with Britain continued.

The War of 1812 ushered in the high tide of early American nationalism. This "second war of independence," as Americans soon called it, did nothing to protect neutral shipping rights, nor did it expand the borders of the United States northward into Canada, as some Americans had hoped. Yet it created an upsurge in nationalism that forged a stronger union at home. Though the conflict was militarily inconclusive, Andrew Jackson's victory at New Orleans (which ironically occurred after the peace treaty was signed) provided Americans with a high note by which to remember the conflict. The partisan conflict during the war was replaced with an interregnum of single-party rule. If this "era of good feelings" was not as harmonious as imagined by some at the time, it did witness politicians from across the spectrum embrace legislation that promoted economic development and the integration of internal markets. Even Jefferson himself briefly embraced nationalist economic measures, such as a moderate tariff, to prepare the United States for what many presumed would be a resumption of conflict in Europe.

The War of 1812 was one of many diplomatic and military episodes in this period in which the United States secured and expanded its position in North America. The 1783 Treaty of Paris had granted the new republic generous borders. Few in Europe thought that the United States would maintain its grip on the lands east of the Mississippi, let alone expand further. The young republic proved able to achieve both objectives. American statesmen extended their 1783 borders to include the vast Louisiana Territory and Florida, which the United States partly seized in 1810 and then bullied Spain into ceding by treaty in its entirety during the Monroe administration. Other territorial adjustments included the 1818 Anglo-American Convention, which established the U.S.-Canadian border to the west of the Great Lakes, and the Transcontinental Treaty with Spain (ratified in 1821), which gave the United States a claim on the Pacific Coast.

Just as important as this expansion of territory was the consolidation of dominion over the lands already possessed. Migrants streamed across the Appalachian Mountains, settling in the fertile Ohio Valley and cultivating the rich soil of the Deep South. This "explosive colonization," as James Belich has called it, witnessed some of the most dramatic population movements in modern history. The populations of both the Old Northwest (the Great Lakes region) and the Old Southwest (the region of the southern Mississippi Valley) tripled in the single decade of the 1810s.[18] This population movement invariably brought white settlers into conflict with the Native American inhabitants of these territories. Statesmen in Washington hoped that tensions would be resolved by the "civilization" of Native Americans and the gradual and legal appropriation of their lands. But on the frontier, force often prevailed. The War of 1812 was not just an Anglo-American conflict; it also pitted the United States against Indian tribes. The military commander Andrew Jackson aggressively seized the opportunity to consolidate American power over Native Americans in the Southwest, forcing upon them a series of treaties that ceded vast tracts of territory to the United States. The conflict that advanced American independence from Britain paradoxically entailed the projection of power over peoples deemed to be subordinates.

There was no master plan hatched in Washington that dictated early expansion, even if American leaders made clear that they sought to control areas of strategic importance such as New Orleans, Florida, and Cuba. Statesmen exploited opportunities as they arose in a volatile international system, and also capitalized on population movements that often played into their hands. Yet if there was no blueprint for expansion, Americans developed a political logic for the process of adding new territories to the union. Rather than follow the traditional colonialist model of exerting central authority over distant territories indefinitely, American leaders, led by Thomas Jefferson, proposed that new territories enter the republic as equal members after an appropriate period of tutelage under a federally controlled territorial government. The Northwest Ordinance, passed by the Confederation Congress in 1787, outlined the process by which the federal government would oversee the administration of the Northwest Territory. The ordinance sought to secure this territory for the United States until a time in which republican state governments could be formed and trusted enough to be admitted into the union on equal terms. This model of anticolonial colonization aimed to advance individual liberty and the equality of new states in the long term, while reaping the benefits of controlling strategically important territories in the short term. The Northwest Ordinance also balanced the demands of the inhabitants of the Western territories, who wanted republican self-government and political equality, with the security concerns of the existing states, which used the federal government to control the territories until they proved loyal enough to enter the union as equal states.

As much as Jefferson and many of his contemporaries waxed lyrical about the virtues of an expanding "empire of liberty," their insecurities and perception of threat were just as significant to expansion as was ideology. Jefferson acquired Louisiana not out of regard for its inhabitants (whose support for entry into the union he did not bother to acquire), but because he viewed control of New Orleans as vital to national security and economic interests. The Louisiana Purchase prompted charges of executive tyranny from many in New England who grasped that the future addition of new Western states would change the balance of power within the union. Jefferson defended the acquisition of the Louisiana Territory on the grounds of both political theory and hardheaded diplomatic realism. "I know that the acquisition of Louisiana has been disapproved by some, from a candid apprehension that the enlargement of our territory would endanger its union," Jefferson stated in his second inaugural of 1805. "But who can limit the extent to which the federative principle may operate effectively? The larger our association, the less will it be shaken by local passions; and in any view, is it not better that the opposite bank of the Mississippi should be settled by our own brethren and children, than by strangers of another family?"[19]

Jefferson's Louisiana diplomacy reflected a fear widespread among American statesmen that the territories on their periphery threatened national security. The European threat loomed both in regions bordering the United States, such as Florida (still a Spanish possession), and in outlying territories of the trans-Appalachian West, where the loyalties of the inhabitants were open to question. Even members of the federal government such as Tennessee senator William Blount and Jefferson's former vice president Aaron Burr schemed to detach outlying regions from the union. The expansionist process outlined in the Northwest Ordinance aimed to counter the potential of Western separatism within American territories by having territorial governments answer directly to the federal government in Washington. Indeed, federal authority exerted itself far more strongly on the periphery of the union than it did in the preexisting states. Congress kept a watchful eye on the political activities on the frontier so that it could suppress disunionist plots. Nonetheless, the federal government lacked the power, and often the will, to coerce the white inhabitants of the Western territories into complying with its wishes. "If they declare themselves a separate people," Jefferson wrote of Westerners in 1787, "we are incapable of a single effort to retain them."[20]

Federal coercion of white settlers was less effective than was enticing them into the union with generous incentives. Not only were white settlers promised self-government, but they also received, upon entering the union, political representation, in the form of two senators, disproportionate to their population. Moreover, they were the beneficiaries of the continued economic development and exploitation of America's expanding "empire of liberty." As further enticement, the federal government often bowed to local demands, frequently supporting white settlers, for example, in their struggles with Native Americans. The federal government also acquiesced to the entrenchment of slavery in the Southwest and Louisiana territories. Congress abandoned the idea of restricting slavery in the Louisiana Territory once it became apparent that it would antagonize the settlers in the region, possibly even leading them into the hands of a European power. This political compromise was necessary to secure the strategically important territories of the Deep South, yet it ironically sowed the seeds for disunion later in the century by enabling the expansion and consolidation of slavery in what would become the states of Alabama, Mississippi, and Louisiana.[21]

Early American expansionism thus resulted from a mixture of opportunity, ideology, insecurity, and the dynamics of its decentralized and anticolonial political structure. This formula proved remarkably successful, particularly in the context of the European turmoil of the Napoleonic Wars. By the 1820s, Americans had secured their major objectives on the North American continent: they had pushed the British out of their territory; they controlled places of strategic importance such as New Orleans and Florida; and they established supremacy over most Native American tribes east of the Mississippi River. Just as important, they strengthened the bonds between the new Western states and those of the Atlantic seaboard. Long-held fears of Western separatism diminished, particularly as a result of the War of 1812, which demonstrated, in John Adams's estimation, "that our trans-Alleghanian States, in patriotism, bravery, enterprise and perseverance, are at least equal to any in the Union."[22]

In the years after 1815, the North-South divide concerning the future of slavery replaced the old East-West split as the greatest sectional threat to the union. Indeed, the binding together of the East and West ironically fueled conflict between North and South, as the crisis surrounding Missouri's admission to the union in 1819–21 demonstrated. No longer paralyzed by the fear that Missourians would spurn admission to the union or ally themselves with a foreign power, a broad coalition of Northern politicians now sought to dictate that statehood be contingent upon a moderate plan of gradual emancipation. The prospect of a unified North using the federal government to impose antislavery policies upon Missouri alarmed Southerners, prompting them to speak openly of disunion and to rehearse the proslavery arguments that they would recite throughout the coming decades. Resolution to the crisis came only after protracted debate and the adept political leadership of moderate nationalists, particularly President James Monroe and the Kentucky congressman Henry Clay. The compromise saw Missouri enter the union as a slave state, counterbalanced by the admission of free-state Maine, and slavery prohibited in the Western territories north of parallel 36°30' (and allowed south of that latitude).[23]

The Missouri crisis profoundly shaped the subsequent statecraft of the Monroe administration. The controversy made clear the internal dangers of continued territorial expansion. Though

Monroe and his secretary of state, John Quincy Adams, remained convinced that it was "a settled geographical element that the United States and North America are identical" (as Adams put it), they opted not to press claims to Texas during the negotiations with Spain that would lead to the Transcontinental Treaty. "It is evident," Monroe wrote to Jefferson in 1820, "that the further acquisition of territory, to the West and South, involves difficulties of an internal nature which menace the Union itself." Monroe believed that the United States could take Florida, acquire Texas for "some trifle," and expel Spain from North America. "No European power could prevent this," the President asserted, "but the difficulty does not proceed from these sources. It is altogether internal, and of the most distressing nature and dangerous tendency."[24]

The fallout from the Missouri crisis also can be seen in the Monroe administration's embrace of colonization, a fantastical scheme to resolve internal tensions by removing African Americans from the United States. The Monroe administration subsidized the activities of the American Colonization Society, as well as directing the U.S. Navy in 1821–22 to support the establishment of the ACS colony of Liberia. It was a result of this support that the capital of this West African colony was named Monrovia. The President who later sought to ensure domestic security by formulating a doctrine prohibiting external intervention in the New World in this case sought to promote the security of the union by removing African Americans from its borders.

The early American union was a complex and paradoxical political beast, notable both for its fragility and for its remarkable capacity to survive the trials it faced from within and without. Despite—or perhaps because of—the decentralized nature of its political system, nationalism was a powerful force in the early republic, particularly in the years following 1815. The triumph of compromise during the Missouri crisis, Clay contended, "ought to be mainly ascribed to those strong feelings of attachment to the Union . . . without it, our country would be exposed to the greatest calamities, rent into miserable petty states, and these convulsed by perpetual feuds and wars." Yet in darker moments, even a nationalist like Clay wondered if just such a contingency would unfold, confessing his fear to Adams "that within five years from this time [1820], the Union would be divided into three distinct confederacies."[25]

The "Western Question"

As American statesmen delicately balanced their objectives of union and independence, they confronted the dissolution of other European empires in the Western Hemisphere, most notably the vast dominion previously held by Spain. As in British North America, the peoples of these territories resorted to force to achieve their independence. The revolutions in Spanish America, as well as the success of the Haitian Revolution and the erosion of Portuguese control of Brazil, created a power vacuum in an immense region of great strategic and economic importance. Considered as a whole, the early-nineteenth-century revolutions in what became known as Latin America created the "Western Question" that witnessed the powers of Europe, as well as the upstart states of the Americas, compete for power and influence in areas that Spain was no longer able to control.[26]

Having recently battled for their own independence from a colonial power, Americans instinctively identified with the Spanish American revolutionaries. "And behold!" Jefferson wrote shortly after the rebellions against Spain began, "Another example of man rising in his might and bursting the chains of his oppressor, and in the same hemisphere." Statements such as this reflected a current of thought fashionable at the time that divided the globe into distinct and politically diametric spheres of a republican "New World" and a monarchical "Old World." Yet as the Spanish American revolutions progressed, many Americans questioned such a bifurcation of the globe, as well as the links between their revolution and those occurring elsewhere in the hemisphere. Jefferson's anticlericalism and his view that Spanish colonialism was particularly retrograde left him doubting the capacity of Catholic Spanish Americans to live up to the North American example of 1776. "I fear [that] the degrading ignorance into which their priests and kings have sunk them," he confided, "has disqualified them from the maintenance or even knowledge of their rights, and that much blood may be shed for little improvement in their condition." Such thinking prompted the author of the Declaration of Independence to resign himself to the temporary continuation of Spanish authority until Spanish Americans proved capable of self-government.[27]

Jefferson's evolving views of the Spanish American revolutions shine an instructive light upon the ambivalence with which many Americans approached the dissolution of European empires. Nearly all Americans welcomed the collapse of the Old World colonial order, viewing it as validation of their own revolution and an opportunity to expand their interests. Yet many doubted the capacity of peoples other than themselves to establish stable governments and worried that the turmoil might adversely impinge upon their interests. Such misgivings were particularly pronounced in regard to Haiti, where a slave rebellion led by Toussaint-Louverture that began in 1791 succeeded in establishing independence from France in 1804. Racial attitudes in the United States, combined with the bloody nature of the rebellion, prevented most white Americans from identifying with the Haitians. Furthermore, anxiety about slave revolts at home, particularly in the wake of Gabriel's 1800 plot in Virginia, prompted the Jefferson administration to devise policies that quarantined Haiti from the United States. Nonrecognition would remain the heart of American policy toward Haiti until the Lincoln administration reversed course in 1862.[28]

Few in the United States advocated isolating the new states of Spanish America when the revolutions there climaxed in the late 1810s and early 1820s. The proponents of extending diplomatic recognition to the new states, however, had their work cut out for them. The Kentucky congressman Henry Clay was the chief advocate of this move. A nationalist who had been a "war hawk" in the run-up to the 1812 clash with Britain, Clay was not one to shy away from confronting Old World colonialism. The Kentuckian viewed the struggles in Spanish America as a reenactment of the American Revolution. His speeches in Congress that made the case for recognition are notable for the equal regard in which he presented the Spanish American revolutionaries. Clay contended that Spanish American leaders such as Simón Bolívar and José de San Martín were the "brothers" of North Americans, whose state papers were worthy of "the most celebrated that ever issued from the pens of Jefferson or Madison." Clay was confident that under such leadership the new states of Spanish America would become the ideological and political kin of the United States. He first used in 1820 the phrase "American system" to describe the convergence of interests and ideals between the peoples of the Americas. The Kentuckian went further, calling in 1821 for the creation of a hemispheric alliance system "in favour of National Independence and Liberty, to operate by the force of example and moral influence" that would serve as "a sort of counterpoise" to the colonial powers of the Old World.[29]

As much as Clay emphasized the ideological rationale for recognition, his case for an active Spanish American policy also rested on hardheaded realism. He argued that the economic benefits of cultivating relations with the new states were too good to pass up. Recognition would facilitate trade with Spanish America, Clay predicted, opening up a lucrative market that had been closed to the United States under the restrictions of Spanish mercantilism. These new markets would eagerly consume American exports, particularly those from Western states such as Clay's own

Kentucky. In return they would ship precious metals to the United States that could be used to pay off debts held across the Atlantic and to bolster gold reserves in the capital-starved American West. In this way, Clay contended, recognition would advance the economic independence of the United States as well as providing benefits for the developing states of the West.[30]

Clay's campaign for extending recognition to the new states of Spanish America ran into stiff opposition. The Monroe administration (in office beginning in 1817) repeatedly opposed the move, thanks in large part to the views of Secretary of State John Quincy Adams. Even within the more receptive House of Representatives, Clay met with little success. It was not until 1821 that one of his resolutions advocating recognition was approved by this legislative body (and even here the resolution was watered down and nonbinding).

Many of the opponents of recognition doubted the capacity of Spanish Americans to replicate the American Revolution. "You cannot make liberty out of Spanish matter," the Virginian John Randolph declared; "you might as well try to build a seventy-four [a type of warship] out of pine saplings."[31] Such statements reflect an emerging racism, as well as a widespread view that Spanish colonialism and Catholicism had degraded the peoples of Spanish America to such an extent that they were unprepared for self-government. "The people of South America," John Adams contended in 1815, "are the most ignorant, the most bigoted, the most superstitious of all the Roman Catholics in Christendom."[32] John Adams's son, the Secretary of State, had a more charitable view of Spanish Americans, but he, too, dismissed Clay's arguments. "As to an American system," John Quincy Adams wrote in his diary in 1820, "we have it; we constitute the whole of it; there is no community of interests or of principles between North and South America."[33] Views such as this challenged the division of the globe into distinct "New" and "Old" spheres. Some Americans went further, suggesting that the relationship between the United States and the new states of Spanish America would come to resemble that of superior and subordinate. "South America will be to North America," the aptly entitled *North American Review* asserted in 1821, "we are strongly inclined to think, what Asia and Africa are to Europe."[34]

Such views portended the imperialist mind-set of the late nineteenth century. But blocking Clay's calls for recognition in the early nineteenth century required arguments grounded in national interest as well as in race and religion. Adams doubted that recognition would lead to the economic benefits Clay trumpeted, contending that South American markets "cannot for ages, if ever, be very considerable."[35] The Secretary of State also expressed reservations about pursuing a foreign policy that might entangle the United States in conflict either within Spanish America or with European powers intent on upholding the old colonial order. His famous Fourth of July speech in 1821 countered the argument for recognition by contending that the very universality of the Declaration of Independence that Clay heralded undermined the case for an assertive foreign policy. Given that the Declaration "was the corner stone of a new fabric, destined to cover the surface of the globe," Adams argued that there was no need to pursue a risky foreign policy that might embroil the United States in war. Such a war inevitably would exacerbate internal divisions, posing as much danger to the union from within as from without. Rather than risk this result, Adams proposed that the United States instead applaud the cause of anticolonialism and independence from the sidelines. "Wherever the standard of freedom and Independence has been or shall be unfurled, there will [America's] heart, her benedictions and her prayers be," Adams proclaimed. "But she goes not abroad, in search of monsters to destroy . . . She well knows that by once enlisting under other banners than her own, were they even the banners of foreign independence, she would involve herself beyond the power of extrication, in all the wars of interest and intrigue, of individual avarice, envy, and ambition, which assume the colors and usurp the standard of freedom."[36]

Adams's oration would become a classic statement of American nonintervention, trotted out in future times by opponents of interventions in Vietnam and Iraq. Yet its implications were not so clear-cut at the time. The logic of the speech, which emphasized the righteousness of anticolonialism, put Adams on the path toward recognition of Spanish American independence.[37] Nor, despite his condemnations of the European colonial order, was Adams strictly opposed to venturing into the messy game of Old World power politics. One reason the Secretary of State opposed Clay's campaign for recognition was that it undermined his negotiations with Spanish minister Luis de Onís that sought the transfer of Florida to the United States, as well as a claim to the Pacific Coast. The Monroe administration also took into consideration the views of the British. As early as 1818, Monroe inched toward extending recognition, but he refused to act without assurances that the British would make the same move, thus providing cover for the United States in the event of Spanish reprisals. For not the last time, American statesmen were reluctant to act in Spanish America without British support. The British, whose economic interests were well served by the status quo of weak Spanish rule, rejected the Monroe administration's overtures.

Clay premised his argument for recognition on the ideological and economic ambitions of the United States. Yet in the end it was heightened perceptions of threat that compelled the Monroe administration in 1822 to recognize the Spanish American governments of Buenos Aires, Chile, Gran Colombia, Mexico, and Peru.[38] The move was prompted in part by the ratification in 1821 of the Transcontinental Treaty, in which Spain ceded Florida to the United States and gave the American republic a claim to the Pacific Coast. With this long-sought agreement in hand, Monroe and Adams could move more boldly on the issue of Spanish American independence. But recognition also stemmed from the identification of a new threat: the prospect that the new Spanish American states would not embrace the political and economic principles favored by the United States. Despite the analogies with the American Revolution made by Clay and his supporters, the reality on the ground was more complex. Monarchy remained an attractive political form, especially in Brazil and Mexico, where monarchists loyal to Emperor Agustín I emerged temporarily victorious in 1822. Many Spanish Americans looked toward the Old World rather than the United States for political inspiration and economic sustenance. There was no guarantee that the new states would be the ideological and political allies of the United States.

It was this very political gulf that prompted the Monroe administration to reverse its previous policy and extend recognition. Though several Spanish American states had consolidated their independence by 1822, the Monroe administration feared that they remained unstable and vulnerable to European intervention. Adams felt as if "their governments are Chinese Shadows[,] they rise upon the Stage, and pass off like the images of Banquo[']s descendants in Macbeth." To continue to delay recognition would play into the hands of hostile European powers. Monroe predicted that Spanish Americans would feel "resentment towards us" if recognition continued to be withheld, making them all the more susceptible to "the artful practices of the European powers, to become the dupes of their policy." The prospect of a monarchical Spanish America allied with European powers led the Monroe administration to fear for its own security. If surrounded by hostile states, the United States would be under siege: its preexisting internal divisions would be exacerbated and its decentralized political system might require alteration, such as increased taxation and military buildup, in order to confront these new threats. "There was danger in standing still or moving forward," Monroe asserted. By 1822, Monroe and Adams embraced moving forward, despite the risk that it would trigger European reprisals.[39]

The Monroe administration's reversal on recognition portended a new direction in its foreign policy. It was a bold move, particularly considering that the administration acted without British support. As the historian James Lewis has made clear, recognition prefigured the more celebrated presidential message of the following year.[40] The enlarged concept of national security that had prompted recognition necessitated more and more diplomatic involvement. Adams's instructions to his ministers to the new Spanish American states reflected a newfound desire to shape their political and economic practices, albeit using the powers of persuasion and example rather than intervention or force. "With relation to Europe," Adams informed his new minister to Buenos Aires, "there is perceived to be only one object, in which the interests and wishes of the United States can be the same as those of the South American nations, and that is that they should all be governed by republican institutions, politically and commercially independent of Europe." Already in early 1823, Adams was moving closer to Clay's "American system" ideas that he would champion as president in the future.[41]

In its first four decades, the United States transformed itself from a weak collection of former colonies to an increasingly united and expansive republic. It secured the lands east of the Mississippi and laid claim to portions of the faraway Pacific Coast. What had been uncertain in 1783—union at home and independence from an increasingly powerful British Empire—was closer to achievement in 1823, though still not an established fact. The success of the United States on these counts owed partly to shrewd statecraft, but more to the hospitable circumstances in which it was born. The European turmoil of this period provided many opportunities for American statesmen and provided enough threats to bind the union together, but none so great as to destroy it or even prevent the consolidation and extension of its domain.

As the second generation of American statesmen assumed

leadership in the years after 1815, they looked to the future with great confidence. "The truth is that the American union, while united," John Quincy Adams wrote to his father in 1816 (with a revealing qualification), "may be certain of success in every rightful cause, and may if it pleases never have any but a rightful cause to maintain."[42] The great exception to such optimistic predictions, of course, was the intensifying debate over slavery evidenced in the Missouri crisis, the "title page to a great tragic volume," as Adams portentously called it.[43] Yet even here, the glass could be seen as half full. The successful compromise to the crisis served as evidence of the strength of the bonds of union. If compromise had been achieved over Missouri, there were grounds for hope that future statesmen, cut from the centrist political cloth of Henry Clay and James Monroe, could continue to resolve sectional disputes. These conflicting impulses—the persistent danger of internal divisions and the potential power of nationalism—were on the minds of members of the Monroe cabinet when they convened in November 1823 to formulate a response to yet another crisis arising from the dissolution of the Spanish Empire.

American Systems

The Constitution states that the President "shall from time to time give to the Congress Information of the State of the Union." From this clause arose the custom of the President's annual message to a joint session of Congress, now known as the State of the Union address. Unlike today's State of the Union speech, in the nineteenth century a government clerk delivered the annual message in written form to Congress. Thomas Jefferson started this custom to differentiate the annual message from the yearly statements of Old World monarchs. Despite this uninspiring means of delivery, the annual message was the President's most important state paper of the year. It provided the executive with the opportunity to communicate priorities to Congress, to appeal directly to voters, and to outline positions to foreign governments. The importance of the annual message is revealed in the time spent drafting it: presidents and their cabinet members, who often composed the sections of the message pertaining to their departments, devoted weeks, sometimes even more than a month, to its composition.

James Monroe's 1823 message was 6,397 words long. It addressed issues ranging from the operations of the Post Office to the state of public finances to the repairs made to the Cumberland Road. But its three nonsequential paragraphs on foreign affairs would be what made it the most famous annual message of the nineteenth century. That later Americans would consider these 954 words a keystone of their foreign policy is somewhat surprising. Far from a triumph of American letters—a Declaration of Independence or a Gettysburg Address—Monroe's message was particular and prosaic, more closely resembling the preamble to the Articles of Confederation than the preamble to the Constitution. Furthermore, the 1823 message itself accomplished nothing. It was British statecraft, not Monroe's message, that achieved the immediate objectives of 1823.

Understanding what later Americans would see in this presidential message will be a task for later chapters. Here, the goal is to focus on the message itself and its immediate aftermath. The message of 1823 expressed at once the ambitions and insecurities of the United States. It reflected traditional distrust of Britain, but it also portended Anglo-American imperial collaboration. Most significantly, the statecraft of the 1820s illustrated how foreign affairs both could strengthen and endanger the American union from within. Reflecting the high tide of the nationalist "era of good feelings" that followed the War of 1812, the statesmen of the Monroe cabinet settled after much debate in 1823 upon a compromise course of action. But this consensus proved fleeting when the administration of John Quincy Adams attempted to complement the negative principles of the 1823 message with a series of proactive policies that aimed to counter British power and cultivate relations with the new states of Latin America. Different conceptions of national interest and statecraft—or competing "American systems," to use the phrase of the time—thus emerged in the aftermath of the compromise of 1823.

The Compromise of 1823

In the summer and autumn of 1823, the Monroe administration confronted a series of ominous foreign policy developments. Czar Alexander I issued a unilateral *ukaz* (edict) that asserted Russia's claim to a stretch of the Pacific Northwest and prohibited foreign vessels from using waters within one hundred miles of the coastline. In the Mediterranean, Greek rebels fought to free themselves from the oppressive rule of the Ottoman Empire, a cause that attracted much sympathy among Americans raised on the classic texts of ancient Greece. Americans saw similar dynamics playing out elsewhere in Europe, where the forces of liberalism also clashed with established orders. The reactionary monarchies of Europe—France, Austria, Russia, and Prussia—federated under the banner of the Holy Alliance to oppose any such constitutional or political reform. In the Troppau Circular of 1820, the Holy Allies (minus the French at this point) asserted the right to suppress any revolutionary movement in Europe that they deemed a threat to their security. To the horror of the United States, France acted on the Troppau principle in April 1823 when it intervened in Spain to suppress constitutionalists and restore the monarchy of Ferdinand VII. This move set off alarm bells in Washington that Spanish America might be the next target of the Troppau doctrine. If the French, with the support of the Holy Allies, could intervene in Spain, what would stop them from undertaking a similar action in Spain's rebellious American colonies?

The crisis of 1823 was another chapter in the long story of the dissolution of Spain's American empire. What gave it a new twist was the diplomacy of the British, whose interests and ideals nudged them away from the reactionary European powers and closer to the republican United States. British foreign secretary George Canning also viewed the French intervention in Spain with horror. He, too, worried about the future of Spanish America, where he hoped to expand British influence and secure new markets for his nation's burgeoning industries and commerce. Canning feared that the Holy Allies would close off this market if they assumed control of Spanish America. These considerations prompted him to present the American minister to London, Richard Rush, with an intriguing offer to issue a joint declaration warning the Holy Allies to stay out of Spanish America. Given the convergence of interests between the two English-speaking governments, Canning asked Rush, "why should we hesitate mutually to confide them to each other; and to declare them in the face of the world?"[1]

Canning's offer caught Rush by surprise. But it did not come out of the blue. In the years following the War of 1812, these recent adversaries reached a series of compromise agreements on vexing territorial, naval, and commercial disputes that paved the way for a warming of relations. The increasingly reactionary positions of the Holy Allies further highlighted the harmony of interests between the two English-speaking countries. Britain's influential *Edinburgh Review* had gone so far as to call for an Anglo-American alliance against the Holy Allies back in 1820. Canning's objection to the French intervention in Spain convinced even Secretary of State John Quincy Adams that Britain "now for the first time has seceded from the political system of the European alliance."[2] The Massachusetts diplomat Alexander Hill Everett went so far as to contend that Anglo-American relations had evolved "into a situation of virtual alliance and amity, so deeply and broadly founded in the interests of both, and in the established political system of Christendom, that it cannot well fail to supersede all the old motives of contention, and to endure as long, perhaps, as the national existence of either."[3]

American statesmen proved surprisingly predisposed to accept Canning's offer, a fact largely explained by their heightened perception of threat. We now know that the Holy Allies had no intention of intervening in Spanish America. But this was not clear at the time.[4] The fact that Canning approached the United States for assistance led most American statesmen to fear for the worst. Thomas Jefferson, whose counsel Monroe sought, thought the whole situation was "the most momentous which has ever been offered to my contemplation since that of Independence." Such fears led Jefferson to recommend acceptance of Canning's offer despite its provision of the nonannexation of Cuba (which he viewed "as the most interesting addition which could ever be made to our system of States"). Jefferson also saw long-term benefit in using the crisis to harness British power on behalf of American interests: "by acceding to her proposition," he wrote, "we detach her [Britain] from her bands [the Holy Alliance], bring her mighty weight into the scale of free government, and emancipate a continent at one stroke." James Madison went even further. Though suspicious of Canning's motives, Madison argued that Monroe should seize the opportunity to enlist Britain's power on behalf of the cause of republican government in Spain and Greece as well as Spanish America.[5]

In the Monroe cabinet, the President and Secretary of War John C. Calhoun favored acceptance of Canning's proposal on grounds similar to Jefferson's. John Quincy Adams emerged as the great opponent of this move within the Monroe cabinet. The Secretary of State argued against cooperation with the British in a series of cabinet meetings that took place in November 1823. Yet even Adams appears initially to have entertained the possibility of association with the British. Adams informed a British diplomat in Washington that it was his "deliberate and decided impression that a time will come, and is probably not far distant when Great Britain and the United States—'the Mother and the daughter'—will feel it incumbent upon them to stand forward and to make a broad declaration of their principles in the face of the world."[6]

Adams soon changed course and argued against the immediate acceptance of Canning's offer. Unlike Monroe and Calhoun (whom Adams thought "moonstruck" by the prospect of a Holy Alliance intervention), the Secretary of State doubted that European intervention was imminent. Even if it was, he was certain it would fail: "I no more believe that the Holy Allies will restore the Spanish dominion upon the American continent than that the Chimborazo will sink beneath the ocean," he asserted.[7] Given the unlikelihood of a successful European intervention in Spanish America, Adams maintained that there was no need to ally with the British.

The Secretary of State emphasized the potential costs of accepting Canning's offer. The wily British statesman declined to extend recognition to the new states of Spanish America (indeed, it was this issue that proved the stumbling block in Canning's initial discussions with Rush). Adams feared that Canning's refusal to commit to Spanish American independence portended a duplicitous reversal in British policy that would leave the United States standing alone against the Holy Alliance. Canning drove a hard bargain with the Americans in another way: his proposal included a joint pledge prohibiting both states from the future annexation of territories in Spain's crumbling empire. Adams was loath to preclude any future additions to the union, particularly those of strategic importance such as Cuba and Texas. A pledge of nonannexation would be no loss to Canning, he argued, as Spanish Americans would never volunteer to join the British Empire. But Adams thought it likely that the people of Texas or Cuba "may exercise their primitive rights, and solicit a union with us." Finally, Adams argued against Canning's offer on the grounds that a joint declaration would give Britain the lion's share of the credit for protecting Spanish America from the Holy Allies, thus giving the British a leg up in the race for these markets. "It would be more candid, as well as more dignified," Adams concluded, "to avow our principles explicitly . . . than to come in as a cock-boat in the wake of the British man-of-war."[8]

Adams seized the opportunity to promote an independent

policy. He fended off Calhoun's push for the acceptance of Canning's offer and encouraged Monroe to use the forum of the annual message to Congress (conveniently scheduled for December 2) to announce American opposition to further European colonization and intervention in the Western Hemisphere. This move would address the related issues of threatened European intervention in Spanish America, Russian claims in the Pacific Northwest, and Canning's offer. It also would proclaim to the world that the American principles of anticolonialism and nonintervention applied to the Western Hemisphere. "The whole of the papers now drawn up," Adams recorded in his diary, "were but various parts of one system under consideration."[9] The Secretary of State did not dictate policy to the President, but he nonetheless played a central role in the creation of what later became the "Monroe Doctrine." Of the three paragraphs of the Doctrine, Adams solely authored one (the noncolonization paragraph) and deeply influenced the other two (the nonintervention paragraphs).[10]

The course of action pursued by the Monroe administration advanced American interests and principles at minimal cost. The 1823 message shrewdly exploited British power, which Adams hedged would be deployed against the Holy Allies in the case of an intervention, without signing up to the restrictive terms of Canning's offer. Years after the fact, Adams contended that the diplomacy of 1823 went further than simply hitching a free ride on the Royal Navy: the noncolonization clause, he asserted, was nothing less than "a warning to Great Britain herself."[11] This was akin to the hitchhiker dictating directions to the driver. Adams's arguments during the cabinet debates of November 1823 would become an American legend (it helped that his diary is the only source for the cabinet's deliberations). Statesmen and historians in the late nineteenth century would view it as the foundation of American unilateralism and the clarion call of American independence in international affairs. "The Monroe doctrine bore witness to the strong foreign policy of an independent people," Henry Cabot Lodge asserted in 1883. Historians in the twentieth century interpreted the episode similarly, dubbing the 1823 message America's "diplomatic declaration of independence."[12]

Though the 1823 message reflected traditional distrust of America's former colonial master, it did not rule out cooperation with Britain. The Monroe administration never rejected Canning's offer. As Adams formulated his arguments, Canning himself backpedaled from the joint declaration proposal after he secured an assurance of nonintervention in Spanish America from the French ambassador in London. Word of Canning's change of heart, which Monroe labeled a "most unpleasant circumstance," arrived in Washington on November 16, right in the middle of the cabinet's monthlong debate.[13] The President's continued fear of a Holy Alliance intervention led him to resume the flirtation with the suddenly reticent British. Monroe went so far as to instruct Adams to modify his new instructions to Rush "so as not to refuse co-operating with Great Britain even if she should yet demur to the recognition of South American independence."[14] In the dispatch to Rush written just after the 1823 message, Adams informed Rush that the President was "anxiously desirous" for a general "cordial harmony in the policy of the United States and Great Britain" and alluded to the possibility of a "further concert of operations" if circumstances required. Far from believing that the December 2 message settled matters, the Monroe administration hoped that the British would reinforce it with a similar proclamation of their own. "It will now remain for Great Britain to make [her position] equally public," Adams wrote in the instructions to Rush. Monroe even dispatched an envoy to Europe so that the United States would be represented in the event of a European congress on the Spanish American question.[15]

Monroe's 1823 message to Congress was a unilateral pronouncement, much to the satisfaction of John Quincy Adams. Yet the full story behind it is more complex than Americans later in the nineteenth century would remember. Monroe and his cabinet did not set out to pronounce a binding foreign policy doctrine, nor to declare their diplomatic independence. To be sure, the statesmen of 1823 boldly proclaimed the principles of republicanism, anticolonialism, and nonintervention. But the background to the message reveals that they proceeded with great caution. They had reservations about collaborating with the British, but they also were wary of acting without the support of their former colonial master. The Monroe administration considered a number of different policy options, several of which remained open after the December 2 message.

The 1823 message itself is also less straightforward than is often assumed. The message paradoxically expressed both the confidence and anxiety of American statesmen. For all their caution and realism, the Monroe cabinet remained certain that American ideals and practices would transform global politics. Adams viewed the reactionary doctrines and interventions of the Holy Alliance as the last gasp of a defunct political system. "The influence of our example has unsettled all the ancient governments of Europe," he wrote with characteristic certitude shortly after the French intervention in Spain. "It will overthrow them all without a single exception. I hold this revolution to be as infallible as that the earth will perform a revolution around the sun in a year."[16] Such ideological optimism underlay the 1823 message. With the spirit of the Declaration of Independence spreading around the world, the United States did not need to mimic the interventionist tactics of the Holy Allies. Rather, it simply needed to embed in the fabric of international relations certain principles and structures—namely, republicanism, nonintervention, and commercial liberalism—that would usher this process along. The 1823 message disclaimed any intent to dictate the political practices of the new Spanish American states, expressing instead confidence that "our Southern brethren" would never voluntarily embrace the political system of the Holy Allies.

The ideological confidence of the statesmen of 1823 sat paradoxically beside their anxieties about the future of the union at home. For as much as the Monroe cabinet thought about constructing a new international system, their thoughts returned time and again to how best to preserve and strengthen their union. This was clear in the 1823 message itself, which was written not out of concern for the new states in Spanish America, but because the Monroe administration deemed European intervention in the Western Hemisphere to be "dangerous to our peace and safety." "There never was a period since the establishment of our Revolution," stated the opening paragraph of the message, "when . . . there was greater necessity for . . . patriotism and union." If members of the Monroe cabinet disagreed on the likelihood of a successful intervention by the Holy Alliance, all were of one mind in viewing such an act as a threat to national security. That the Monroe administration's conception of national security encompassed potential European actions thousands of miles from the borders of the United States might come as a surprise, especially considering the almost complete absence of American interests in places such as Buenos Aires (which, incidentally, is farther from Washington than is Moscow). One can be forgiven for asking why American statesmen regarded the installation of a Bourbon prince in Buenos Aires or the monopolization by Russia of the maritime rights off the Alaska coast as a threat to national security.

The answer to this question resides in part in the ideological lens through which the Monroe administration viewed potential threats. The reactionary doctrines promulgated by the Holy Allies reinforced the old view that the American republic was engaged in an ideological struggle with the monarchies of the Old World. "The political system of the allied powers is essentially different . . . from that of America," the 1823 message asserted. Similar to the Cold War thinking of the twentieth century, the protagonists in this struggle viewed each other's political system as inherently expansionist, thus necessitating strategies of containment. Monroe's message countered the Holy Allies' Troppau Circular: just as the Continental monarchies asserted their right to oppose revolutionary forces in Europe, the Monroe administration declared that European colonization and political intervention in the New World constituted a threat to the United States.

When the members of the Monroe cabinet considered a single European intrusion in the New World, they ended up envisioning multiple interventions. It was taken as a given that a move by one power—France installing a puppet monarch in Buenos Aires, for example—would set in motion a series of interventions and landgrabs throughout the Western Hemisphere. John Quincy Adams recorded in his diary the administration's doomsday scenario: "Russia might take California, Peru, Chili [*sic*]; France, Mexico—where we know she has been intriguing to get a monarch under a prince of the House of Bourbon, as at Buenos Ayres [*sic*]. And Great Britain, as her last resort, if she could not resist this course of things, would take at least the island of Cuba for her share of the scramble. Then what would be our situation—England holding Cuba, France Mexico?"[17]

Surrounded by hostile states with antagonistic political and economic systems, the Monroe administration feared that it would have no choice but to alter its own domestic practices. Increased taxation, a standing army, the centralization of political power—all of these and more would be required to counter such a threat. But these actions would in themselves endanger the union by running counter to established political practices, perhaps even leading disillusioned Americans into the arms of Old World powers. Old concerns about Western separatism resurfaced during the Monroe cabinet's discussions. Adams feared that the French still "had a strong party" in Louisiana, which might turn

against the United States in the event of a conflict with the Holy
Allies. In this way, the presence of European puppet monarchies
in Spanish America, particularly in neighboring Mexico, would
inflame domestic conflict and threaten the union from within.
"Violent parties would arise in this country," Calhoun prophesied
in a cabinet meeting, "one for and one against them, and we
should have to fight upon our own shores for our own institutions."[18]

The Monroe administration's perception of threat in 1823
thus linked foreign dangers to internal vulnerabilities. The differ-
ing views within the cabinet on the likelihood of a successful
Holy Alliance intervention, however, led to different conceptions
of what constituted the greatest threat. Calhoun's fear that the
Holy Allies could succeed in establishing puppet monarchies in
Spanish America—Adams recorded him as saying in a cabinet
meeting that "he had no doubt" that the Holy Allies could retain
South America "in subjection by military force"[19]—led him to
argue that the United States should prevent them from acquiring
a foothold in the New World at all costs. This former "war hawk"
of 1812 was prepared to ally with the hated British, as well as to
give a pledge not to annex the two territories he viewed as central to national security, Texas and Cuba. The future advocate of
states' rights from South Carolina went even further, contemplat-
ing increased powers for the federal government to deter the
Holy Allies from intervening in Spanish America. "Our country
ought to omit no measures necessary to guard our liberty and
independence against the possible attacks of the Armed Alliance," Calhoun argued. "They are on one side, and we the other
of political systems wholly irreconcilable. The two cannot exist
together. One, or the other must gain the ascendency [*sic*]."[20]

Adams, in contrast, contended that the greatest threat to the
union was precipitate action to forestall a phantom threat. Convinced that the Holy Allies could not succeed in establishing
control of Spanish America, Adams argued against the actions

proposed by Calhoun. Above all, Adams sought to avoid war with the Holy Allies. Such a conflict should be avoided, he argued, because it would place "different portions of the Union in conflict with each other, and thereby endangering the Union itself." The United States thus "should retreat to the wall before taking up arms." Rattling the saber too loudly might provoke the Holy Allies into taking actions that they otherwise would not and lead to a counterproductive war that would expose the union's internal vulnerabilities.[21]

The first draft of the 1823 message, written by Calhoun and Monroe, distressed the Secretary of State. It condemned the French intervention in Spain, recommended extending diplomatic recognition to the Greek rebels, and called upon the American people "for their most vigorous energies and the closest union." Adams feared that the draft message "would take the nation by surprise and greatly alarm them. It would come upon them like a clap of thunder." Even worse was that it "would be a summons to arms—to arms against all Europe, and for objects of policy exclusively European—Greece and Spain." "If an issue must be made up between us and the Holy Alliance," the Secretary of State argued, "it ought to be upon grounds exclusively American." Here lay the basis of the "separate spheres" clause of the 1823 message, which drew a line between Europe and the Americas. Adams advocated the separate spheres to avoid a war that might result from bearding the Holy Allies in their own den. Realism, not isolationism, lay behind the separation of the spheres in 1823. Close readers of the message noted that it carefully qualified noninvolvement in European affairs to "matters relating to themselves." The recent Napoleonic Wars demonstrated that conflicts between European powers had a way of involving the United States.[22]

Despite their many differences, both Calhoun and Adams endorsed the final draft of the 1823 message, for it was a compromise that addressed both of their concerns. This compromise of

1823 had several components. It kept the door open to joint action with the British without bowing to the conditions of Canning's offer. The message informed the Holy Allies that the United States would consider any intervention in Spanish America as a threat to its own security, but sugarcoated this warning by pledging not to interfere in European affairs as well as to respect functional colonial arrangements established before December 2, 1823. The message expressed sympathy for the Greek rebels but stopped short of recommending recognition. Finally, it articulated a conception of national security that, despite their differences, both Calhoun and Adams held. Premised upon a curious mixture of imperial ambitions and perceptions of internal vulnerability, the national security of the United States required more than just the safety of its borders—it required an entire hemispheric system conducive to its political system and economic practices.

The message of 1823 articulated this extensive conception of national security in direct language. The noncolonization clause maintained that "the American continents, by the free and independent condition which they have assumed and maintain, are henceforth not to be considered as subjects for colonization by any European powers." The nonintervention clause declared that the Holy Alliance could not "extend their political system to any portion of either continent without endangering our peace and happiness." Despite their cautious diplomacy and ongoing flirtation with the British, the statesmen of 1823 boldly articulated their position. The message of 1823 unilaterally declared that the principles of anticolonialism and nonintervention governed the Western Hemisphere. Though future Americans would dispute exactly what constituted the Monroe Doctrine, most would see these two clauses as its basis.[23]

As is the case in most political compromises, the statesmen of 1823 sidestepped the most contentious issues. The Monroe administration framed the message in negative terms: they stated what European powers could not do, but dodged the question of what the United States would do. During the November cabinet debates, Attorney General William Wirt raised an issue that Adams deemed "the only really important question to be determined": How would the United States respond if the European powers ignored the message and intervened in the Western Hemisphere? Given that Canning had recently backpedaled from his offer of joint action, this was no small question. Yet the Monroe cabinet never answered it.[24]

The Monroe administration also avoided an explicit statement on the important issue of territorial expansion. The statesmen of 1823 certainly sought to keep open the possibility of future territorial acquisitions. The possible annexation of Cuba and Texas loomed large in the cabinet debates regarding Canning's offer. The pretensions of the Russians in the distant Pacific Northwest even concerned the administration. During the cabinet deliberations, American statesmen viewed the expansion of their borders in terms of anticolonial self-determination: the peoples of Texas and Cuba would voluntarily choose to enter the union. Adams later would come to a different conclusion regarding the acquisition of these two territories, but in 1823 it is clear that the cabinet drafted the message with future expansion in mind.

Monroe could have endorsed the annexation of Texas or Cuba, as did many other nineteenth-century presidents. Yet the message of 1823 stopped short of an explicit call for territorial expansion, opting instead for implicit endorsement. The final paragraph of Monroe's 1823 message—which is rarely considered part of the Monroe Doctrine—celebrated the American tradition of expansion: "[The] expansion of our population and accession of new States to our Union have had the happiest effect on all its highest interests. That it has eminently augmented our resources and added to our strength and respectability as a power is admitted by all." Expansionism also appeared between the lines of the noncolonization clause, which prohibited only "European powers" from acts of colonization in the Western Hemisphere. British observers read this as a loophole intended to reserve the New World for American expansion. "The plain *Yankee* of the matter," a British newspaper asserted, "is that the United States wish to monopolize to themselves the privilege of colonising . . . every . . . part of the American Continent."[25]

That the Monroe administration stopped short of an explicit call for territorial expansion testifies to the cautious nature of its statecraft. A call to annex Cuba would have antagonized the British at a time when the administration sought their support. American statesmen also had fresh memories of the domestic turmoil surrounding the recent admission of Missouri as a slave state. The lack of an endorsement of expansion in the message of 1823, in other words, was the result of diplomatic and political considerations rather than some change of heart on the issue. It is nonetheless important that the message neglected to embrace expansion, for this ambiguity would allow anti-imperialists later in the nineteenth century to read it as forbidding the acquisition of new territories.

Collaborative Competition

The 1823 message played no role in the decision of the Holy Allies not to intervene in Spanish America. To be sure, European statesmen thought the message haughty and provocative. "In their indecent declarations," Prince Metternich of Austria declared, "they have cast blame and scorn on the institutions of Europe most worthy of respect."[26] But the Holy Allies had decided against intervention in Spanish America long before Monroe's message reached them. France, the putative ringleader of such a venture, had misgivings about the project from the beginning. French statesmen particularly feared provoking their old enemy, the British. Canning scored a diplomatic triumph in October 1823 when he obtained a pledge from the French ambassador, the Prince de Polignac, not to intervene in Spanish America. This "Polignac Memorandum," not Monroe's message, was the key diplomatic episode of the international crisis. Ironically, the Monroe cabinet's lengthy debates occurred after the threat of European intervention had passed.

Yet the work of the Monroe cabinet was not without purpose. Far from ending great power rivalry in the New World, the diplomacy of 1823 kicked off what would become a near-century-long struggle for hemispheric ascendancy between Britain and the United States. A peculiar dimension of this Anglo-American competition was that both states agreed on the general rules of the game. Indeed, the Polignac Memorandum outlined a series of principles that anticipated Monroe's message of two months later. In both documents, English-speaking statesmen opposed European intervention in Spanish America and disclaimed any intent to dictate the political systems of the new states. Upon receiving Monroe's message in early 1824, the London *Times* applauded it on the grounds that it articulated "a policy so directly British." Later, the London *Economist* contended that "the Monroe doctrine might quite as fairly be called the Canning doctrine."[27]

The two powers, of course, had different visions for the political future of Latin America. Just as Americans boasted about the superiority of republican government and the inevitable spread of the Declaration of Independence, the British viewed their constitutional monarchy as the ideal political system that occupied the middle ground between the extremes of American republicanism and the reactionary monarchism of the Holy Allies. "The great danger of the time," Canning declared, "was a division of the World into European and American, Republican and Monarchical; a league of worn-out Govts on the one hand, and of youthful and stirring Nations, with the Un[ited] States at their head, on the other. We slip in between; and plant ourselves in Mexico . . . and we link once more America to Europe."[28] Despite their respective ideological objectives, Britain and the United States in fact pursued very similar foreign policies in Latin America. Ideological considerations did not prevent the United States from recognizing monarchical Brazil in 1824. Nor would they keep Britain from recognizing republican governments in Latin America. Both sides employed ideological appeals as a means of gaining support within Latin America. But the ultimate prize was less the form that these new governments would take than the significant commercial and strategic benefits that they would provide.

Throughout the nineteenth century, Britain and the United States engaged in a collaborative competition for ascendancy in Latin America. This rivalry was collaborative in that both states opposed the formal reconquest of Latin America and sought to profit from the economic development and exploitation of the new states. American and British merchants and traders also worked closely together. Yet the two English-speaking states simultaneously competed for market supremacy and strategic superiority. They both also sought to establish clients and allies within the new Latin American states. To be sure, not all of the rules of this collaborative competition were agreed upon, nor were they consistently followed. Both sides would resort to intervention in Latin America and, on some occasions, to outright conquest. The United States would demand unilateral domination of much of North America. Occasional war scares between the two powers threatened to end any semblance of collaboration. But, in general terms, the two states collaborated even as they competed to gain the upper hand in the Western Hemisphere.

One dimension of this Anglo-American competition was that of public diplomacy, or the battle for the hearts and minds of the peoples of Latin America. With both the British and Americans disinclined to engage in outright colonialism, they needed to establish supporters within the new states of Latin America. Members of the Monroe cabinet expressed concern about the image of the United States in Spanish America during the cabinet debates of 1823. Monroe and Adams saw in a unilateral message to Congress the key advantage that it would enhance the United States' reputation in Spanish America at Britain's expense. Similarly, the "separate spheres" of the 1823 message grouped Britain with the reactionary powers of Europe in order to invoke suspicion of the British in Latin America. When meeting with Spanish American ministers, Adams lost no chance to remind them that while the United States had extended recognition, the British continued to drag their feet. In his final annual message of December 1824, Monroe inflated his role in protecting Spanish America. The President declared that the Holy Allies "have appeared to acquiesce" to the demands of the United States the previous year. Thus was born the myth that the 1823 message had thwarted the intervention of the Holy Alliance.[29]

The Americans outfoxed Canning in the diplomacy of 1823. But the British foreign secretary was not about to let it happen again. Canning was a veteran of the bare-knuckled politics of the early-nineteenth-century British Parliament. He was not one to back down from his adversaries (indeed, Canning engaged political opponent Lord Castlereagh in a duel in 1809 despite never before having fired a pistol). Canning well understood the role of public relations and image in foreign affairs. He was the first foreign secretary to publish his diplomatic correspondence, including a famous dispatch that he composed in rhyming verse. A sympathetic biographer has even suggested that Canning be credited with establishing "open diplomacy," an honor Americans typically reserve for Woodrow Wilson. It is Canning the orator and manipulator of public opinion who is enshrined in the National Portrait Gallery in London. The portrait of Canning depicts his famous "Portugal speech" in which the triumphant British statesman, right hand held firmly aloft, dares his adversaries to stand in his way. The Portugal speech was a stunning performance—one that looked like an actor reciting his lines in front of a mirror, a critic mused.[30]

Canning recognized the propaganda value of Monroe's message in Spanish America. He scoffed at the Americans for thumping their chests about republican government while sheltered behind Britain's powerful Royal Navy. In March 1824, Canning fired back. He ordered the mass reproduction of the hitherto confidential Polignac Memorandum through the new technology of the lithograph. The foreign secretary deleted all references to the United States in this published version of the memo. British agents in Spanish America circulated this version to demonstrate their government's decisive role in thwarting the designs of the Holy Alliance. "Its date is most important," the foreign secretary wrote of the Polignac Memo, "in reference to the American speech which it so long preceded." Canning continued to trumpet Britain's role in supporting the independence of Spanish America. Though it was the United States that had first recognized the independence of the new governments from Spain, Canning boasted in 1826 that he himself had "called into existence the New World."[31]

Statesmen in both Washington and London pledged not to intervene in the new states of Spanish America. But this did not prevent their agents on the ground from meddling in Spanish American politics. Nowhere was this more the case than in Mexico, a nation whose factionalism provided ample opportunity for foreign interference. The U.S. minister Joel Poinsett allied himself with Mexican liberals; in opposition was the British diplomat Henry Ward, who sought the support of Mexican conservatives and the Catholic Church. The rivalry between Poinsett and Ward quickly took on a life of its own, with each diplomat drawing support from rival Masonic lodges in Mexico City. Both English-speaking diplomats aimed to promote the political fortunes of their Mexican allies in anticipation of a future payoff in the form of an advantageous commercial treaty. In their zeal to achieve this objective, they at times became pawns of their Mexican support base. Nonetheless, Ward eventually had a commercial treaty to show for his efforts (though the British-Mexican agreement was far from perfect in that it allowed Mexico to give commercial preference to the other Spanish American states). Poinsett, in contrast, failed both to acquire a commercial agreement and to renegotiate the border treaty of 1819 (a euphemism for U.S. acquisition of Texas). In 1829 a conservative Mexican government demanded the recall of its longtime American adversary. All the departing American diplomat had to show for his activities was the plant named after him, the poinsettia.[32]

The situation in Mexico made clear that Spanish America would not naturally fall into the hands of the United States. Yet American statesmen remained reluctant to commit themselves to active policies to achieve their goals. The failure of two congressional resolutions in early 1824 revealed that even token foreign policy gestures could invoke great disagreement. The first, the brainchild of the Massachusetts congressman Daniel Webster, called for the appropriation of funds for a commissioner to be sent to Greece upon the request of the President. Shortly after Webster introduced his measure, Henry Clay introduced a second resolution that announced that the United States would regard with "serious inquietude" any attempt made by the Holy Allies to forcibly intervene in Spanish America.

There was an element of grandstanding for domestic audiences in both resolutions, which did not go unnoticed at the time. Yet both Webster and Clay sought to extend congressional support for a more active foreign policy. Neither was successful. One of the strongest objections voiced in Congress was constitutional: many feared that a legislative endorsement of the 1823 message would give a blank check to the executive. Other congressmen objected to the resolutions on the grounds that they might start the United States down the slippery slope of foreign entanglements. Lurking behind both of these objections was a nascent proslavery critique of an active foreign policy. A group of Southerners led by the Virginian John Randolph objected to these resolutions on the grounds that they would increase the powers of the central government, which might one day turn against the South's peculiar institution. Randolph argued that the logic of the resolutions would lead to the recognition of the black republic of Haiti, if not to similar resolutions condemning slaveholding in the South.[33]

Randolph's speech portended future troubles. But sectional divisions on hemispheric policy at this point should not be exaggerated, for the New Englander Adams similarly shied away from making any commitments to the new Latin American states. When approached by representatives of Colombia and Brazil to enter into defensive treaties of alliance, Adams declined on the grounds that a treaty binding the United States to defend Latin America "would be inconsistent with the policy that the United States have heretofore prescribed to themselves." Adams made clear that Monroe's 1823 message did not bind the United States to defend the new nations against European intervention, something that would require an act of Congress. The fate of Clay's resolution did not give the Colombian and Brazilian governments any reason for optimism.[34]

Just as the United States backpedaled from commitments in Latin America, Britain moved in the opposite direction. In December 1824, Canning extended recognition to Mexico, Gran Colombia, and Buenos Aires. "The deed is done, the nail is driven," Canning crowed. "Spanish America is free; and if we do not mismanage our affairs sadly, she is English."[35] The move consolidated Britain's already strong position in South America, where it had developed trading links in the first years of the nineteenth century. The United States minister to Santiago, Henman Allen, informed Washington that Chile and Argentina were fast becoming "de facto colonies" of Britain. "The preponderating influence of England in the affairs of these countries,"

Allen reported, "is already seen and felt in almost every department." From Buenos Aires, John Murray Forbes reported that
whereas Fourth of July celebrations had to be carefully choreo-
graphed by American representatives, the people of Buenos
Aires, which included a sizable community of British expatriates,
spontaneously celebrated England's St. George's Day. Wherever
Americans looked they found evidence of British influence: the
establishment of a cricket club in Buenos Aires; pro-British newspapers; the outlawing of bullfighting in Argentina and Chile as
an act of deference to English sensibilities. Vehicular traffic in
Buenos Aires even moved on the left-hand side of the street, the
English practice, until 1889.[36]

Britain simply had more to offer South Americans than did
the United States. Spanish American leaders, such as Simón
Bolívar in Gran Colombia, were not fooled by the Monroe administration's claim that it had prevented the intervention of the
Holy Alliance. "The whole of America together," Bolívar wrote,
"is not equal to a British fleet; the entire Holy Alliance is power-
less against her liberal principles combined with immense
resources." Bolívar had been attracted to Britain since undertaking a diplomatic mission to London early in the Spanish
American revolutions. He admired aspects of the political systems of both Britain and the United States, but he saw the old
country's constitutional monarchy as better suited to the conditions of Spanish America than the pure republicanism of his
Yankee neighbors. "England is the envy of all Countries in the
world, and the pattern all would wish to follow in forming a
Constitution and Government," he asserted. Britain's constitutional monarchy and economic dynamism appealed to New
World aristocrats such as Bolívar and the Mexican conservative
Lucas Alamán. In Britain they found evidence that development and modernization could be achieved without the radical
overthrow of the established social order. As late as 1826, Bolívar called for a "union of the new states with the British
Empire."[37]

Economic considerations further pointed to a pro-British tilt in Spanish America. When a Chilean official dubbed Canning "the liberator of Chile," he did so in the context of the marketing of a bond issue in London. British merchants and investors, not those from the United States, were most responsible for the boom in South American port cities in the 1820s. By 1830, Britain's overall trade with Latin America was roughly double that of the United States. British investment in the region totaled £25 million (far from exporting capital, the United States was itself becoming increasingly indebted to Britain in this period). So, too, did Britain take the lead in the negotiation of commercial agreements with the new states, securing four treaties to the three of the United States.[38]

It was the British, not the Americans, who constructed a new system upon the ashes of the old Spanish empire. But as much as Americans condemned the extension of British power into the Western Hemisphere, they often were its beneficiaries. It was the British, of course, who continued to keep a watchful eye on the activities of the French. Britain's commercial success in Latin America also brought benefits to the United States. The British scoffed at the American campaign to enshrine total reciprocity in commerce, an objective first realized in the 1825 U.S.–Central American commercial agreement. Yet they cooperated with American traders in South American ports, often sharing contacts and extending credit to them. Without the drafts provided by the South American branches of London's Baring Brothers bank, American diplomats and traders would not have been able to do business in the region. Such cooperation stemmed from the fact that traders from the two English-speaking states rarely were direct economic competitors in this period: the British exported textiles and finished products, whereas the Americans largely sold foodstuffs.

Despite their subordinate position, American statesmen refused to cooperate with the British on an issue they considered fundamental to their national security: Cuba. The movement for independence from Spain on this strategic island met with little success in the early nineteenth century. The island remained Spain's most important foothold in the New World and served as the staging point for military operations against her former colonial possessions. By 1825, governments in Mexico and Colombia turned their attention to liberating Cuba, as well as neighboring Puerto Rico, on the grounds of military necessity. Statesmen in Washington and London feared that such a move might trigger an imperial scramble in the Caribbean. Canning proposed that the British, French, and Americans sign a tripartite pledge not to take the island in the future. The newly elected President John Quincy Adams once again wanted nothing to do with a British plot to prevent the future American annexation of the island and quickly rejected the offer.

The situation in Cuba, however, demanded a response. Adams and his secretary of state, Henry Clay, had no intention of annexing the island when it was certain to provoke the British and inflame sectional tensions at home. But they thought Colombia and Mexico too weak to protect Cuba from grasping European powers and had little confidence in the capacity of Cubans to exercise self-government. In contrast to his speeches advocating recognition a decade earlier that trumpeted the political capacity of Spanish Americans, the now secretary of state Clay took the opposite position. He argued that the "population itself, of the Islands, is incompetent, at present, from its composition and its amount to maintain self-government."[39] Above all, Clay feared that instability on this slaveholding island might devolve into a race war such as had occurred in Haiti some three decades earlier. The destabilization of slavery in Cuba would threaten the union both by inspiring slave revolts and by leading Southerners to demand controversial safeguards to protect their peculiar institution.

These considerations led the Adams administration to promote the continued Spanish possession of the island. "In the hands of Spain," Clay asserted, "[Cuba's] ports are open, its cannon silent and harmless, and its possession guaranteed by the mutual jealousies and interests of the maritime powers of Europe."[40] The means that Clay and Adams employed to achieve this goal were as surprising as the objective itself. In an early enunciation of what became known as the "no-transfer principle," the United States made clear that it would not allow Cuba to fall into the hands of another power. This articulation of the no-transfer principle had an important twist: it applied not only to European powers but also to the new Spanish American states. The Secretary of State went so far as to hint that a potential invasion of Cuba by Colombia and Mexico might lead the United States to ally itself with other European powers in upholding Spanish rule.[41] While they warned Spanish Americans not to intervene, Adams and Clay engaged in a diplomatic offensive in Europe, where they hoped to create a coalition of governments to press the Spanish to recognize the independence of its former colonies in Central and South America in exchange for diplomatic support for their ownership of Cuba and Puerto Rico. Surprised European statesmen soon received American diplomats who proposed ways to consolidate Spain's hold over Cuba. The scheme did not unfold smoothly, but the United States achieved its desired objective of perpetuating Spanish rule of these strategically important islands.

This curious episode witnessed the fervently anticolonial Adams administration take the side of a crumbling Old World empire. Technically, the administration's diplomacy did not repudiate the 1823 message, as the United States had not recognized Cuban independence. But Cuban nationalists then and later saw the affair as an act of betrayal and hypocrisy. "The lips that had just proclaimed that no European monarch could have slaves in America," the Cuban nationalist José Martí later lamented, "demanded that the armies of the South abandon their plans to redeem the American islands in the Gulf from the slavery of a European monarchy."[42] Two factors best explain the actions of the administration. First, Adams and Clay believed Cuba to be of such strategic importance that they decided against any change to what was an acceptable status quo. Second, the administration viewed the affair in relation to internal affairs. Domestic political considerations ruled out annexation, which would reopen the divisions from the Missouri crisis. They also contributed to the administration's opposition to the Mexican and Colombian liberation of the island. An increasingly vocal group of proslavery Southerners made clear that they considered such a move a threat to their security. The Adams administration would soon find domestic politics even more inhibiting to its foreign policy goals.

The End of the Consensus of 1823

The political genius of Monroe's 1823 message was that it did not call for any action. All Monroe did was declare what European powers could not do in the New World. The message dodged all of the important questions—Canning's offer of alliance, future relations with the new states of Spanish America, and the matter of if and how the United States would uphold the prohibitions it placed on European actions. Avoiding all commitments and costs, yet trumpeting the ideals of the United States, Monroe's message not surprisingly met with great popularity at home. Henry Clay predicted that the foreign policy of 1823 would "create no divisions of opinion among us . . . We shall, in regard to it, be 'all federalists—all republicans.' "[43]

Yet the consensus of 1823 proved short-lived. Without the menace of the Holy Alliance to bind them together, Americans found themselves deeply divided over foreign policy. A mere two years after Monroe's popular 1823 message, Latin American policy would be the subject of one of the most vitriolic congressional debates on foreign affairs in American history. The source of this discord was the proposal of now president John Quincy Adams to participate in the Panama Congress organized by Simón Bolívar. A former skeptic of Henry Clay's hemispheric "American system," Adams, with Clay as his secretary of state, now argued that the United States needed to take a leading role in hemispheric affairs.

The Adams administration was fortunate to receive an invitation to participate in the Congress of Panama. Bolívar initially opposed inviting the United States. He viewed the congress as an opportunity to federate the new Spanish American states, not as the beginning of a pan-American union. The United States received an invitation only after lobbying from officials in Mexico and Colombia (the Spanish Americans also welcomed unofficial observers from Britain and the Netherlands). Despite barely being invited, the Adams administration was not bashful about using the conference to advance its interests. Adams's only lament was that the United States itself had not set the agenda for the conference.[44] The conference offered the President the opportunity to advance all of the goals he had long sought: to enhance the security of the union, limit the reach of the British and Europeans in the New World, and promote the economic interests of the United States. In a series of messages delivered to the U.S. Congress in 1825–26, Adams outlined his objectives at Panama: reinforcement of Monroe's 1823 message through a "joint declaration" signed by the participating governments, the establishment of liberal commercial agreements enshrining the most-favored-nation principle, codification of neutral shipping rights, and the "advancement of religious liberty" in Spanish America.[45]

Adams's messages delineating his objectives at Panama provided a proactive complement to the negatively framed message of 1823. Whereas Monroe had declared in 1823 what the European powers could not do, Adams now presented a vision of what the United States would do. This hemispheric vision was intimately intertwined with the administration's domestic agenda of internal development and liberation from economic dependence on Britain. Adams first advocated participation in Panama in his landmark 1825 annual message to Congress, which outlined an ambitious set of measures such as federal assistance for internal improvements and the creation of a national university. Indeed, the phrase "American system" denoted not only a hemispheric diplomacy, but also a set of domestic policies aimed at strengthening the bonds of union through measures designed to counter Britain's economic hegemony. The foreign and domestic components of the American system were two halves of the same whole. Protective tariffs, for example, sought to end Britain's dominance in manufacturing. The subsequent increase in American manufacturing would necessitate the negotiation of trade agreements with Spanish America to provide markets for these new goods.

The "American system" of Adams and Clay fused anticolonialism, unionism, and nascent imperialism. Though the American system was not devised as a plan to dominate Latin America, its logic led in that direction. Just as independence from Britain had entailed control over Native Americans in 1812, liberation from Britain's economic control in the 1820s necessitated the establishment of economic supremacy in the Americas. "It is in our power to create a system of which we shall be the centre," Clay asserted, "and in which all South America will act with us."[46] Even as Clay denounced British economic imperialism, he used Britain's informal empire as a model for his vision of economic and political relations with the new American states.[47] While "American system" boosters emphasized their ideological solidarity with the new states of Spanish America, many of them racially and culturally identified with their former colonial master.

The Adams administration's plans to participate in the

Panama Congress provoked vituperative domestic opposition in Congress. Ostensibly at issue were the approval of the diplomats Adams nominated to attend the conference (in the Senate) and the appropriation of the required funds (in the House). Lurking behind these procedural matters were fundamental questions about the form and future direction of the American union.

Most ominous was the sectionalism unleashed by the administration's proposed participation in the Panama Congress. Given the recent Missouri crisis, this should come as no surprise. Back in 1823, divergent sectional interests had also popped up during the Monroe cabinet's discussions of how to respond to Foreign Secretary Canning's offer of a joint British-American response to the perceived threat of European intervention in the Western Hemisphere. It is perhaps not a coincidence that those most in favor of accepting Canning's proposal were all Southerners (Monroe, Calhoun, and Jefferson) who viewed Britain as a crucial export market, whereas the man opposed to the joint declaration proposition (Adams) came from the mercantile and nascent industrial center of New England, which increasingly regarded Britain as a great commercial and industrial rival. Despite this sectional divide, slavery appears never to have been discussed during the cabinet debates in November 1823. Neither the future proslavery leader John C. Calhoun nor the future antislavery leader John Quincy Adams explicitly called attention to the fateful topic during the monthlong debate on national security, despite the fact that their concerns about divisions within the union arose in part from awareness of the dangers lurking behind the slavery issue.

A group of proslavery Southerners in Congress made sure that slavery did not hide in the tall grass again. Southerners such as Robert Hayne (South Carolina) and John Randolph (Virginia) argued that the "American system" had an antislavery tilt: John Sergeant of Pennsylvania, one of Adams's nominees to represent the administration at the Panama Congress, had been an outspoken advocate of restricting slavery in Missouri a few years earlier; possible items on the agenda in Panama included cooperation with Britain to prohibit the international slave trade and the possible recognition of Haiti. Though slavery remained entrenched in Cuba and Brazil, Southerners also took note of its weakness in Latin America, where it was in the process of being phased out.

As the Panama debates progressed, proslavery Southerners ratcheted up the rhetoric and demanded ever more. The attempts of the Adams administration to placate the interests of slaveholders made little difference (not only did the administration's policy effectively preserve slavery in Cuba, but the President also explicitly informed Congress that he opposed the recognition of Haiti). Designed to strengthen the union, the American system of Adams and Clay had the opposite effect, triggering the sectional objections of a group of proslavery radicals. Southerners such as Hayne took the opportunity to proclaim that new rules must be followed if the union was to remain intact. "With nothing connected with slavery can we consent to treat with other nations," Robert Hayne asserted, before warning that any federal intervention within the South would prompt disunion.[48]

The proslavery opposition to the Congress of Panama was one of many such political controversies in this period that foreshadowed the dissolution of the American union. Yet the significance of the Panama debates lay not just in that they prefigured secession and civil war, but also, paradoxically, in how they demonstrated the potential for the shrewd exploitation of partisan conflict and racialized nationalism to hold the union together. The Panama debates played an important early role in the reconfiguration of American politics from the interregnum of the single-party "era of good feelings" to the second party system of Whigs and Democrats. The establishment of two cross-sectional parties would be instrumental in preserving the union in the coming decades (indeed, it is no coincidence that civil war came shortly after the collapse of the second party system in the mid-1850s).[49]

Ambitious party builders such as the New Yorker Martin Van Buren and James Buchanan of Pennsylvania seized the opportunity to unite the disparate critics of the Adams administration. They exploited recent memories of the "corrupt bargain" between Henry Clay and John Quincy Adams that allegedly had denied Andrew Jackson the presidency in the contested election of 1824. They capitalized on the popularity of Monroe's 1823 message and Washington's Farewell Address by contending that the administration's foreign policy violated the traditions of unilateralism and political nonentanglement.[50] "The moment we engage in confederations, or alliances with any nation," Jackson declared in 1826, "we may from that time date the downfall of our republic."[51] They argued that President Adams assumed powers in foreign policy that the Constitution reserved for Congress. James K. Polk, a young congressman from Tennessee, maintained that the 1823 message was "the mere expression of opinion of the Executive ... The President had no power to bind the nation by such a pledge" (though once he became President, Polk would come to a very different conclusion about the nature of the 1823 message).[52] The opponents of the Adams administration further claimed that the Panama Congress constituted a new, superfederal system that would infringe upon the sovereignty of the United States. And they used the Panama issue as a means of discrediting the larger "American system," which many, particularly proponents of free trade from the South and West, equated with corruption and centralization. The words "American system," Hayne declared, "when applied to our domestic policy, mean restriction and Monopoly, and when applied to our foreign policy, mean 'entangling alliances.' "[53]

The opponents of the Panama Congress articulated a racialized view of the American nation. Racist views of Latin Americans, of course, were not new. But they became increasingly pronounced as the 1820s progressed. When compared to the congressional debates a decade earlier on the recognition of Spanish American independence, the racist nature of the Panama debates immediately jumps out. Speaker after speaker on the floor of Congress pointed to the racial and religious inferiorities of Catholic Latin Americans. "I do not believe that there ever can be any cordial fraternity between us and them," the Virginian William Rives stated, before warning that Mexico was more likely to be an enemy than an ally of the United States. Even friends of the administration, though generally less virulent in their racism, portrayed Spanish Americans as "pupils in the school," struggling to adapt to the responsibilities of self-government.[54]

One manifestation of this thinking was the increased use of the phrase "South America." Prior to this period, it was common to refer to North and South America as a single continent, the singular "America" that found expression in Clay's hemispheric "American system." As time passed, the division of the continent into two entities became more and more common. The genesis of the English phrase "South America" is unclear (and it should be noted that the phrase was used well before this period), but it appears with increasing frequency as the debates on recognition and the Congress of Panama, which collectively became known as "the South American question," unfolded in the 1810s and 1820s. Webster's 1828 *American Dictionary* codified this linguistic development. In defining "America," Webster felt compelled to note that Darien (in modern-day Panama) divided "North America" from "South America." This latitudinal division of the globe separated the North American republic from the new states of Latin America. It contrasted the Old/New World bifurcation of Monroe's 1823 message, prefiguring the North/South divide of the late nineteenth century.[55]

Conceptions of Latin Americans that emphasized racial and religious difference would become an important foundation of

American imperialism. In the more immediate term, the racial thinking of the Panama debates contributed to the emergent nationalism that held the union together in the coming decades of the Jacksonian era. The British threat had long united the disparate elements of the American union. Now party builders in the nascent Jacksonian coalition exploited racist conceptions of Latin Americans as a means of bringing together their constituencies in the North and South. Opponents of the Panama Congress particularly emphasized the racial inferiority of black Haitians and the undesirability of diplomatic engagement with that state, a message that united slaveholders and nonslaveholders alike. Racialized nationalism diminished sectional identities and united white Americans from across the union.

After months of repetitive debate, both houses of Congress approved participation in the hemispheric conference. It was a Pyrrhic victory for the Adams administration. Neither of its representatives arrived in Panama in time to take part in the deliberations. The reports of the British diplomat Edward Dawkins, who observed the proceedings in Panama, suggest that little would have been achieved had the American delegates attended the congress. Dawkins found the Spanish American representatives "to be much less republican than I had anticipated" and concluded that "the general influence of the United States is not, in my opinion, to be feared."[56] The Panama Congress itself accomplished little, and the follow-up meeting, scheduled to convene the next year in Tacubaya, Mexico, never assembled, thus ending this initial experiment in what later would be called "pan-Americanism."

The opponents of the Panama Congress emerged even more victorious in the longer term. Though they failed to block congressional support for participating in the conference, they fatally undermined the idea of hemispheric cooperation within the United States until the late nineteenth century. The coalition that opposed the Panama Congress—comprised of many disparate elements, but most notably Southern slavers, Midwestern expansionists, and Northeastern radicals—soon coalesced into the Democratic Party. Following Adams's unsuccessful single term in the White House, three of the next five presidents had opposed the Panama Congress: Andrew Jackson (1829–37), Martin Van Buren (1837–41), and James K. Polk (1845–49).

These Jacksonian Democrats formulated policies antithetical to the "American system" of Adams and Clay. President Andrew Jackson maintained that the institutions and programs of the American system reeked of corruption and cronyism. He vetoed the extension of the charter for the Second Bank of the United States, a privately run depository of federal funds, as well as blocking federal aid to local internal improvement projects such as the proposed Maysville Road in Henry Clay's state of Kentucky. Though he opposed Adams's measures of political economy, Jackson was just as committed a nationalist, whose devotion to the union was also rooted in traditional anticolonialism. "Without union our independence and liberty would never have been achieved," he asserted in his second inaugural address; "without union they never can be maintained."[57] Jackson had little patience for those he perceived to be enemies of the union, whether they were foreign governments or domestic political adversaries. When radicals in South Carolina moved to nullify a federal tariff, Jackson asserted national sovereignty and threatened force against them, thus gaining time for a compromise tariff to be hammered out in Congress.

Jackson parted ways with the Adams administration on foreign policy. Both Adams and Jackson prioritized commercial expansion. But whereas Adams intransigently pursued the principle of most-favored-nation status and reciprocity, Jackson proved more willing to cut deals, most notably in an 1830 agreement with Britain that opened the British West Indies to American goods, though it limited American shipping access to these ports. Adams had rejected a similar deal on the grounds that it discriminated against American shippers and enabled Britain to preserve elements of her discriminatory trading system in the New World. In Jackson's eyes, the benefits of opening British markets were well worth compromising on points of principle held most strongly by his political opponents in the Northeast. Reflecting his own position as a Southwestern planter, Jackson's commercial agenda prioritized the interests of the agricultural exporters of the South and West, whose prized market remained Britain.

Adams and Clay contended that national interests necessitated diplomatic engagement with the new states of Spanish America. Jackson, in contrast, proposed disengagement from the new states and the unilateral pursuit of more narrowly defined interests, particularly the consolidation of control over the North American continent. Latin America might have been most important to Jackson as a dumping ground for spoils system diplomatic appointments. Selected as a reward for their political support, many of Jackson's representatives to the region spoke no Spanish and achieved little apart from alienating Latin American governments. Not surprisingly, the gap between Britain and the United States in the race for the markets and sympathies of Latin America widened during the Jackson years.[58]

Jackson appears to have said little about Monroe's 1823 message, hardly a surprise given its close association at this point with his political rivals. His actions suggest that he saw no need to enforce the 1823 message, unless its tenets were violated in an area of strategic importance such as Texas or Cuba. In 1833 the British seized the Malvinas/Falkland Islands, then claimed by Buenos Aires. Argentine statesmen appealed to the message of 1823 in an attempt to procure American support for their claims. Jackson, however, looked the other way. Despite its legendary Anglophobia, the Jackson administration calculated that British ownership of the islands was preferable to their being in the hands of Buenos Aires, which had blocked American fishing and sealing rights off the islands the previous year. Not unlike the paradoxical views of Britain held by "American system" advocates, Jackson, too, found that he had reason to break bread with the hated British.[59]

Portents of the future "Monroe Doctrine" of the Democratic Party are most visible in Jackson's program of Indian removal. The forced removal of Native Americans from the "Five Civilized Tribes" in the American Southeast demonstrated the lengths to which Jacksonians would go in order to achieve their objective of continental supremacy. Native Americans were doomed to a subordinate place, if any place at all, in the white supremacist world of Jacksonian America. Jackson feared that Native Americans could be manipulated by meddlesome Old World powers, particularly the British with their history of Indian alliances. Constitutional and realist arguments also underlay Jackson's policy of Indian removal. Federal acceptance of Indian sovereignty within a state (such as Georgia, home of the Cherokee people) posed awkward questions regarding states' rights and the nature of the American union. Jacksonians similarly feared that federal restrictions on the actions of white settlers would violate America's anticolonial tradition. It was in this way that the nakedly colonialist project of Indian removal could be presented as an extension of traditional anticolonialism and that the opponents of removal could be branded as imperialists for seeking to control the actions of white settlers and state governments. Finally, Jackson and his supporters claimed that removal would protect Indians from the fate they might face east of the Mississippi River. Yet for all their paternalistic rhetoric, there is no question that the interests of white Americans superseded those of the Indians. Most shocking was the inability of the United States to execute its objective humanely, an outcome predicted by its many opponents, who rallied together in opposition to Indian removal much as the Jacksonian coalition had assembled during the Panama debates. The treaties with Indian tribes that spelled out the terms of removal were the products of coercion and duplicity. Incompetent administration and inadequate provisions led to the deaths of some four thousand of the twelve thousand Cherokees force-marched on the "Trail of Tears" to their new home west of the Mississippi River.

With its imperialist ideology and racialized assumption that white Americans had a special claim to the land of North America, Indian removal anticipated the way Jackson protégé James K. Polk would interpret the 1823 message as a call for an aggressive and expansionist foreign policy. But just as the "American system" of Adams and Clay had become the target of domestic political opposition, this reading of the 1823 message would also not go unchallenged.

3

A Declaration, a Doctrine, and a Disavowal

F ew would have predicted in 1840 that Monroe's 1823 message would become a cornerstone of American foreign policy. References to the message had become few and far between in the 1830s. The issues addressed by the Monroe cabinet in 1823 seemed irrelevant to an increasingly secure American union. Monroe's message appeared destined to be remembered as an important, but isolated, episode in the nation's diplomatic history. That this did not occur resulted not from the message itself, but from the sectional and partisan politics of the 1840s.

Much had changed since the mid-1820s when the message—now christened "Monroe's declaration" or "Monroe's doctrine"—reentered American politics and diplomacy. Powerful economic, demographic, and geopolitical forces pushed Americans farther westward. Many statesmen in Washington set their sights on the acquisition of ports on the once distant Pacific coast. This expansionist impulse triggered diplomatic conflict with foreign nations. It also deepened sectional and political divisions at home. Increased anxiety among Southern slaveholders, combined with the conversion of the British to the antislavery cause in 1833, made it impossible for those who invoked the 1823 message to dodge the slavery issue. Far from sidestepping the issue, John C. Calhoun interpreted the 1823 message as the foundation of a proslavery foreign policy. Just as the hardening of positions on slavery led to sectionally divisive interpretations of Monroe's message, so, too, did the establishment of the second party system lead to its entanglement in the partisan disputes between Whigs and Democrats. The 1840s thus gave birth to multiple, competing interpretations of Monroe's message.

A Proslavery Declaration

Ardent nationalism marked the early political career of John C. Calhoun. The South Carolinian first appeared on the national stage as a "war hawk" in the run-up to the War of 1812; he supported the nationalist economic legislation of the Madison years; as Secretary of War under Monroe he sought to reform the War Department to better deal with the "Indian problem" and to prepare the union for future conflict with the powers of the Old World; he supported the Missouri Compromise; he played a key role in the drafting of Monroe's 1823 message. But as the years ticked by, the tune in the background, as well as Calhoun's dance, changed. The political radicalization of his home state of South Carolina, where paranoia about slave rebellions and anger at Yankee tariffs ran amok, prodded Calhoun into assuming a harder line on sectional issues, a position he willingly assumed.

Yet Calhoun was not the simple "father of secession" that Americans after the Civil War would remember. His goal was not to destroy the union, but to preserve it by securing the interests of the slaveholding states. Calhoun envisaged a federal government committed to the institution of slavery. He devoted his considerable talents and energies to constructing political and constitutional safeguards for the slaveholding South: he embraced nullification; he formulated the doctrine of the concurrent majority; he attempted to organize Southerners into a political coalition; and he tenaciously opposed abolitionists at every turn.

Calhoun sought to protect the slaveholding South from its external as well as internal enemies. Two and a half decades after helping draft the 1823 message, this South Carolinian would reinterpret it as a call for a proslavery foreign policy. Calhoun long had recognized that international winds blew against the South's peculiar institution. He opposed participation in the Panama Congress back in 1825–26, despite being vice president to John Quincy Adams. Calhoun feared that the conference would somehow extend legitimacy to the black republic of Haiti, an issue that involved "the peace and perhaps the union of the nation."[1] In the following years, more than just Haiti loomed in Calhoun's nightmares. When the South Carolinian consulted a map of the Western Hemisphere, he became alarmed. The peculiar institution was on the retreat. The Northern states of the union had gradually abolished slavery in the late eighteenth and early nineteenth centuries; it was possible that the slave states of the upper South, such as Delaware and Missouri, might follow suit. The picture was similar in Latin America, where the rebellions against Spain destabilized the slave system. The new republics were in the process of abolishing slavery. Some, such as Mexico in 1829, had already achieved this end.

Most terrifying of all to Calhoun and his allies was the conversion of Britain to the antislavery cause. Once the engine behind the slave trade and its entrenchment in North America, the world's most powerful nation now committed itself to ending slavery. It is hard to overstate the significance to the United States of the United Kingdom's Slavery Abolition Act of 1833, which began the process of emancipation in British possessions in the Caribbean. British abolition further radicalized both sides of the slavery debate in the United States. It was a boon to opponents of the peculiar institution, encouraging radical abolitionists and African Americans to demand an immediate end to slavery.

At the other end of the spectrum, British emancipation heightened Southern anxiety, prompting theorists to formulate an unapologetic proslavery ideology.[2]

Antislavery ideology united the foreign and domestic enemies of the slaveholding South. The toxic combination of internal and external threats long feared by American statesmen became reality to Southerners in the 1830s: a newly assertive abolitionist movement emerged within the union just as Britain threw her immense power behind the antislavery cause. These circumstances prompted Calhoun and like-minded Southerners to formulate new policies aimed at the preservation and, in certain circumstances, the extension of the peculiar institution.

Calhoun sought to contain the cancer of abolition. He concluded that the South could not allow the contagion to spread to the remaining strongholds of slavery in North America: Cuba and Texas. Most pressing was the situation in Texas. American immigrants had poured into this province of Mexico in the 1820s and '30s at the invitation of Mexican officials. Many of these American settlers disregarded Mexican laws, including a prohibition on slavery. When Mexican officials moved to tighten their grip on the renegade province, the Anglo population responded by declaring its independence in 1836, which it de facto achieved after a series of military victories. The Jackson administration wasted little time in extending recognition to the Republic of Texas, as it called itself, but stopped short of immediate annexation on the grounds that it would provoke Mexico and trigger domestic political conflict. Thus began Texas's brief and insecure period of independence. With the revival of conflict with Mexico looming, Texans looked for foreign support. Given that annexation to the United States was not in the immediate cards, some Texans, led by Sam Houston, tested the waters with the British. The ensuing Anglo-Texan flirtation was the result of mutual attraction. For Texas, Britain offered security against Mexico, a source of racially "pure" immigrants, and, perhaps most important, a trump card that might prompt the United States to finally agree on annexation. From the British perspective, Texas provided an alternative trading partner and source of cotton, a bulwark to American expansionism, and an opportunity to extend emancipation into the heart of the North American continent.

The prospect of an independent Texas allied with antislavery Britain terrified American slaveholders. To Calhoun and like-minded Southerners, an independent Texas that might go down the abolition path owing to British pressure was an unacceptable threat. If emancipation occurred in Texas, the argument went, slavery within the United States itself would be doomed. It would continue the spread of abolition, this time in a territory geographically and climatically suited to the peculiar institution that bordered the South itself. A free Texas would block the future westward expansion of slavery. Geographically contained, slavery in the American South would wither away and die, just as it had on the islands of the British West Indies. An antislavery Texas also would be a magnet for runaways from Arkansas and Louisiana, thus destabilizing slavery on the southwestern periphery. A similar process was already occurring in the upper South states such as Missouri and Kentucky that bordered the free states of the North. With their investments insecure, slaveholders in these outer regions of the South might be seduced by schemes of compensated emancipation. Slavery would then be confined to the states of the Deep South. The political power of slaveholders within the union would be greatly diminished. American slavery would be destroyed.

This doomsday scenario prompted proslavery statesmen to orchestrate the annexation of Texas. It is no coincidence that the three masterminds behind annexation—President John Tyler and his two secretaries of state, Abel Upshur and John C. Calhoun—were Southerners determined to protect the peculiar institution. British interest in "the emancipation of slaves in Texas," Tyler wrote to Calhoun, "decided me on the question as

it did . . . Mr. Upshur."[3] Dispatches from informants outside the
United States reinforced the fears of these proslavery statesmen.
From Kingston, Jamaica, U.S. consul Robert Monroe Harrison
reported that British emancipation had been an economic disaster. Harrison believed that the British were intent upon weakening their commercial rivals by destroying the profitable system of
slavery. He informed Washington of an alleged British plot that
would spread abolition to Texas, if not to the United States itself,
by the horrifying means of exporting a Haitian-style slave insurrection. From across the Atlantic in London, the Tyler administration received equally alarming dispatches from its envoy Duff
Green (the "American Ambassador of Slavery," as John Quincy
Adams called this Calhounite). Green caught wind of a rumor
that Britain would extend financial support to independent Texas
in exchange for abolition. Predisposed to see threats to slavery,
the Tyler administration latched onto the reports of Harrison and
Green, disregarding the dispatches of the U.S. minister to London, Edward Everett of Massachusetts, which downplayed the
threat of British intervention in Texas.[4]

There is little question but that the proslavery statesmen of
the Tyler administration exaggerated the British threat in Texas.
Britain was not "using all her diplomatick [*sic*] arts and influence
to abolish slavery" in Texas, as Calhoun feared.[5] To be sure,
Britain aimed to contain American slavery: British statesmen
openly desired an independent, antislavery Texas; they deployed
the power of the mighty Royal Navy against the international
slave trade; diplomats on the periphery liberally interpreted their
instructions from London; British abolitionist societies propa-
gated antislavery literature, as well as helping to mobilize and
fund the abolitionist movement in the United States. Foreign
Secretary Lord Aberdeen even attempted to maneuver the
French into joining him in supporting Texan independence and
pursuing resolution of the infant republic's ongoing troubles with
Mexico. But Aberdeen proceeded with great caution on the

Texas question, stopping short of policies that would antagonize the United States. For all their interest in an independent, antislavery Texas, British statesmen never were prepared to risk provoking the United States through an interventionist policy aimed at that end. When the United States made its final move toward annexation in 1844–45, the British rolled over.[6]

To the proslavery advocates of the annexation of Texas, the distinction between British ambitions and actions was beside the point: slavery was on fragile ground in the Lone Star Republic, and circumstances might force Texans into Britain's antislavery orbit. Even if the British government was disinclined to intervene, it had little control over private abolitionist societies, which would continue their assault on slavery unabated. Moreover, they argued, the British would back down only if the United States made its position crystal clear. Proslavery statesmen concluded that the annexation of Texas was the only way to prevent the doomsday scenario from unfolding. They argued that the circumstances demanded preemptive action on the grounds of national security. A proslavery reading of Monroe's 1823 message provided the appearance of precedent for such a course: after all, they argued, the Monroe administration clearly had its eye on Texas when it rejected Canning's proposal. "Mr. Monroe's message," one South Carolinian suggested, "furnished a precedent & a noble model" for stopping the abolitionist intrigues of the British.[7]

The annexation of Texas involved both the external threat of antislavery Britain and the internal politics of the union. Calhoun hoped that annexation would kill two birds with one stone: it would provide strategic advantage in the international rivalry between his slaveholding republic and antislavery Britain, and it would enhance the political power of the slave states by increasing their number and unity. Calhoun went to great lengths to make his intentions explicit. He considered annexation paramount to Southern security; but he also thought it important to exploit the issue to unify Southerners into a single political coalition. "I only ask the south to stand by me," Calhoun asserted. "Now is the time to vindicate our institutions." He could have packaged annexation as a national program of "Manifest Destiny." Other proponents of the move did just this in order to broaden its appeal to the nonslaveholding electorate of the North. Instead, Calhoun (now operating as Secretary of State after the death of Upshur) presented annexation as a measure to protect slavery. In his infamous 1844 "Pakenham letter," Calhoun publicly lambasted the British for daring to express their anti-slavery principles. The South Carolinian went further, defending slavery as beneficial to whites and blacks alike and presenting annexation as a necessary act of self-preservation for slaveholders. Calhoun next contended that the pact between the states consummated in the 1787 Constitution pledged the federal government to protect each state from "whatever might endanger their safety, whether from without or within." Calhoun's call for a federal government committed to protecting slavery anticipated the demands of Southerners a decade later for a federal slave code for the territories and rigid fugitive slave laws.[8]

With slavery so prominent a rationale for acquiring Texas, the annexation process proved rancorous and sectionally divisive. Some Northern Democrats joined Whigs from both sections in decisively voting down the treaty of annexation (35 to 16) in June 1844. Annexation was achieved early in 1845 only by the new method of a joint congressional resolution (which, unlike a treaty, required only a simple majority). Important to the Senate's narrow passage of the Texas annexation joint resolution (27 to 25) were the promises of President-elect James K. Polk to negotiate the disputed Mexico-Texas border, which he later disregarded.

The annexation of Texas, John Quincy Adams wrote in his diary, treated the Constitution like "a menstrous rag" and portended the establishment of "a military monarchy" in the United States. Adams's use of "monarchy" is revealing, for it was probably the most offensive name he could think of for the republic that he previously viewed as marching toward millennial perfection. The proslavery and constitutionally questionable dimensions of annexation led Adams to completely reverse the position he took on Texas in the cabinet debates of 1823, when he had held out hope for future acquisition of the territory (as well as Cuba). Adams became so despondent about the increasingly proslavery slant of his beloved union that he came to see Britain as the last hope for maintaining freedom in the New World. "The freedom of this country and all of mankind," Adams privately confessed, "depend upon the direct, formal, open and avowed interference of Great Britain to accomplish the abolition of slavery in Texas." In this remarkable passage, the statesman most important to the formulation of the message of 1823, the statesman who had passionately argued against accepting Canning's offer, now called for his nation's greatest rival to intervene in a territory he had long coveted.[9]

In the case of Texas, protecting slavery required the annexation of territory. But Calhoun's proslavery foreign policy was not uniformly expansionist. Calhoun understood that external threats and opportunities needed to be balanced with internal politics. The South Carolinian opposed the Mexican War on the grounds that it would mobilize antislavery forces by seizing territory where slavery had yet to take root. Mexican territory was also undesirable owing to the presence of the allegedly racially inferior and Catholic Mexican population. "Mexico is to us the forbidden fruit," Calhoun wrote; "the penalty for eating it would be to subject our institutions to political death." The introduction of the Wilmot Proviso in 1846, which sought to prohibit the introduction of slavery into any territories taken from Mexico, confirmed his worst fears that precipitate Southern expansion would play into the hands of the opponents of slavery.[10]

Calhoun most fully articulated his vision for a proslavery reading of the 1823 message in an 1848 speech. The occasion for

Calhoun's address was provided by Polk's final invocation of the
1823 message as President (we shall examine his earlier usages of
it shortly). This time the prize was the Yucatán Peninsula, where
Creole elites, embroiled in a conflict with indigenous Indians,
seceded from Mexico and appealed to the United States for support. The Yucatecans masterfully played their hand by shrewdly
exploiting the Polk administration's fears of British intervention.
While Yucatecan officials fired off requests to Spain and Britain
for assistance, their representative in Washington, Justo Sierra,
appealed to the "doctrines of Presidents Monroe and Polk."
Sierra pushed at an open door. His well-crafted requests for support found a receptive audience in an administration always on
the lookout for expansionist opportunities and always fearful of
European action in the New World. Though outright annexation
was not at this point publicly suggested by either the Yucatecans
or the Polk administration, opponents of the administration sur-
mised that the episode could well move in that direction. Indeed,
inside Polk's cabinet, Secretary of the Treasury Robert J. Walker
called for annexation as part of his strategy for the conquest of
"All Mexico."[11]

Polk's message to Congress, delivered in April 1848, first
argued for intervention in Yucatán on humanitarian grounds:
"savage" Indians, he reported, "were waging a war of extermina-
tion against the white race," something that should "excite the
sympathies of all civilized nations." But though the matter concerned all civilized nations, the 1823 message meant that only
the United States could do anything about it. Polk referred to
"authentic information" that if the United States did not accept
the offer to assume "dominion and sovereignty" in Yucatán,
"such aid will probably be obtained from some European
Power." He cited Monroe's 1823 message, as well as his own 1845
message, to provide intervention in Yucatán with the cover of
diplomatic tradition. "According to our established policy," Polk
declared, "we could not consent to a transfer of this 'dominion

and sovereignty' either to Spain, Great Britain, or any other European power."[12]

Polk's message foreshadowed the logic of the Roosevelt Corollary to the Monroe Doctrine a half century before its articulation: "civilization" needed to be imposed upon Latin Americans unable to maintain their own stability, but the 1823 message meant that only the United States could shoulder this burden. But the President had cried wolf too many times. Though the Yucatecans had sought British and Spanish support, there was no evidence to suggest that foreign intervention was imminent. Indeed, the first draft of the message authored by Secretary of State James Buchanan made no reference to foreign intervention, an omission that the President himself changed. Apart from a few hardcore expansionists, few in Congress took the "authentic information" of imminent European intervention seriously.[13]

Though Polk's Yucatán project went nowhere, the episode provided Calhoun the opportunity to articulate a proslavery reading of Monroe's 1823 message. In a speech delivered to the Senate, Calhoun objected to intervention in Yucatán. To make his case, he referred not to "Monroe's doctrine," as Polk had previously, but to "Monroe's declaration." This choice of words illustrated Calhoun's central point: Monroe's message dealt with specific circumstances in 1823 and was never intended as a binding "doctrine" to be followed by subsequent administrations. Indeed, to blindly uphold such a doctrine would lead to perpetual entanglement in wars peripheral to national interests and security. "Every case must speak for itself," Calhoun stated; "every case must be decided on its own merits." Having been present at the creation in 1823, Calhoun's exposition on "Monroe's declaration" carried a stamp of authority.[14]

Calhoun feared that Polk's reading of the 1823 message would commit the United States to a never-ending series of interventions in the unstable politics of Latin America. But this great proslavery theorist had no problem with a binding foreign

policy doctrine, so long as it suited the interests of the slaveholding states. Back in 1823, Calhoun argued, Monroe had identified
threats and then acted accordingly (in this case, by delivering the
message to Congress). Statesmen should do the same in the
future. Calhoun did not regard the situation in Yucatán as necessitating action. But he made clear what would constitute a threat
to national security. The South Carolinian gave two examples of
where "Monroe's declaration" should be invoked and enforced:
Texas and Cuba (ironically, the two territories that he had been
prepared to abstain from annexing when he urged acceptance of
Canning's offer back in 1823). In contrast to Yucatán, where
emancipation triumphed in 1829, both places permitted slavery.
In Calhoun's eyes, the 1823 message aimed to protect the interests of Southern slaveholders by containing the spread of emancipation in places of strategic importance in the New World.
Calhoun went further, making it clear that the nation's foreign
policy should be premised not only on securing slavery but also
on protecting the "white race" from alleged racial inferiors,
including slaves. "I think that this Government, upon all occasions," he averred, "ought to give encouragement and counte-
nance, as far as it can with safety, to the ascendancy of the white
race."

Thanks in part to Calhoun's efforts as Secretary of State, the
foreign (or abolitionist) threat to Texas had been countered. In
the case of Cuba, Calhoun was content to allow Spain to continue
to govern the island so long as slavery remained intact. But if
Spain ever lost its grip on the island or flirted with abolition, the
United States would have to take preemptive action. The South
could not allow a British-controlled antislavery Cuba, let alone an
autonomous, multiracial republic of the Haitian model, to exist
just ninety miles from the slave state of Florida. This thinking
would shape the 1854 Ostend Manifesto, in which Democratic
statesmen of the Pierce administration called for acquisition of
the island on the grounds of "self-preservation" lest Cuba "be

Africanized and become a second St. Domingo [Haiti], with all its attendant horrors to the white race, and suffer the flames to extend to our own neighboring shores, seriously to endanger or actually to consume the fair fabric of our Union." Had the Civil War not broken the political power of Southern slaveholders, this proslavery reading of Monroe's message might well have led to the annexation of the slave state of Cuba.[15]

As he expounded the doctrines of nullification and the concurrent majority, Calhoun similarly interpreted "Monroe's declaration" as an instrument to shelter slavery from those who sought its demise. He tightly defined the scope and purpose of the 1823 message, believing that it would be a valuable addition to the proslavery instruments he would bequeath to his Southern successors.

An Imperialist Doctrine

President James K. Polk certainly was a friend of the South. A Tennessean who owned a cotton plantation in Mississippi, Polk purchased slaves while in the White House "like a speculator in a bullish stock market," in the words of the historian William Dusinberre. The farther south Polk looked on a map of North America, the more excited he became about expansionist opportunities. Indeed, at the very moment Calhoun gave his speech on "Monroe's declaration," the President unsuccessfully attempted to purchase Cuba from Spain, a move that would have safeguarded slavery on the island and increased the political power of the South.[16]

It would be a mistake, however, to view Polk purely as a proslavery Southerner. As much as his presidency advanced Southern interests (or, indeed, hurt them by setting in motion a chain of events that would lead to the Civil War), he also was a nationalist from the school of Andrew Jackson. Polk's nickname of "Young Hickory" reflected the influence of "Old Hickory" on his political worldview. Like other expansionist Democrats, Polk contended that territorial acquisitions would benefit all states and regions of the union. Polk sincerely believed that the expansion of the republic into a transcontinental empire would unite the sections of the union in nationalist fervor, thus pulling the rug out from under the radicals on either side of the slavery question. After his narrow victory over Henry Clay in the 1844 election, Polk set his sights on territorial expansion. He wanted as much of the Oregon Territory as Britain would let him have, a Texas reaching at least to the Rio Grande, the New Mexico territory, and, most of all, California.

Polk's nationalism embraced an imperial destiny for the United States. Yet he and other expansionists confronted the problem of squaring their imperial objectives with the perceived tradition of anti-imperialism. One did not need a crystal ball to predict that it would require unsavory means to acquire coveted territories such as California. The expansionist ideology of Manifest Destiny, which proclaimed the divine right of the nation and its superior Anglo-Saxon constituents to expand across the North American continent, was one way of squaring this circle. Manifest Destiny also presented territorial expansion as a national or racial issue, rather than as one that might benefit certain sections and interests of the union more than others. The Manifest Destiny trope became a favorite of Democrats, particularly those in Northern states who sought to insulate themselves from anti-slavery critics.[17]

Polk certainly subscribed to the core tenets of Manifest Destiny. But he appears never to have used the phrase publicly, and he shied away from framing his foreign policy in ideological terms. The Tennessean was concerned less with the fate of republicanism outside the United States than he was with the promotion of his nation's strategic, economic, and territorial interests.[18] Polk differed in this regard from the "Young America" ideologues within his party, such as John O'Sullivan, the journalist promoter of "Manifest Destiny," who sought ideological as much as territorial expansion. While O'Sullivan beat the Manifest Destiny drum, Polk made the case for an imperialist foreign policy on the hardheaded grounds of preemptive expansion justified by national security. The President enlisted what he called "Monroe's doctrine" to achieve his expansionist objectives. Polk's reading of the 1823 message shaped the way and the urgency with which he went about achieving his expansionist agenda. "Monroe's doctrine" also became the centerpiece of the administration's public relations campaign to garner domestic support for his expansionist agenda.

The underlying assumption of the 1823 message—that Old World powers sought to expand their interests in the New World—reinforced Polk's conception of British and European foreign policy. It requires much historical imagination to understand how deeply Polk, as well as many of his contemporaries, internalized this notion. In part, Polk took European intervention in the Western Hemisphere as a given because it was what he had always been told. The state papers of Jefferson and Jackson—the intellectual and political founders of Polk's Democratic Party—were laden with Anglophobic statements that presumed the incompatibility of monarchical and republican governments. So, too, did a hostile Britain and Europe comport with Democrats' own experiences. Many of the formative events for Polk's generation of politicians involved conflict, both real and imagined, between the United States and Old World powers: the War of 1812, the Holy Alliance crisis of 1823, Indian uprisings that were blamed on the British, the abolition of slavery in the British West Indies, and alleged British meddling in Texas. Furthermore, the threat from the Old World was not just diplomatic and strategic. The early and mid-1840s were years of economic depression, which witnessed nine states of the union default on their debts held largely by British capitalists. Presiding over a nation deeply indebted to the very foreigners who had burned Washington, D.C., to the ground in his own lifetime, Polk never saw reason to question his assumption that Britain and other European powers were hostile to the United States.

When the President looked at a map of North America, he believed it self-evident that California, then part of Mexico, would be a valuable addition to the union. It would make the United States a transcontinental empire; it possessed deep harbors that opened the continent to the markets of East Asia; it had fertile valleys for yeoman farmers; it would fortify national security by eliminating a possible British or European stronghold on the nation's vulnerable western frontier. The importance of California was so obvious, and Mexico's grip on it so weak, that Polk convinced himself that statesmen in Britain and Europe were also plotting to acquire it. The reports of American agents on the ground in California reinforced the Polk administration's tendency to see hostile Britons and Europeans behind every tree. Just as Duff Green's dispatches had fueled Southern fears of British antislavery activity in Texas, the reports of Thomas Larkin, the U.S. consul in Monterey, increased the anxiety of statesmen in Washington. Larkin's dispatches were long on rumor but short on fact. Though some British adventurers hatched half-baked schemes to augment their interests in California, the British government made no moves to detach California from Mexico (indeed, Foreign Secretary Aberdeen turned down a Mexican offer that would have given Britain parts of California in exchange for support against U.S. expansionism). In an ironic reversal of the 1820s, it was Old World powers, particularly Britain, that were reacting to the aggressive policies of the United States.[19]

The Polk administration's heightened perception of threat stemmed from the fact that it had already determined its foreign policy goals. Instead of perceptions of threat shaping the formulation of policy, the Polk administration reversed the process:

fixed policy objectives dictated its threat perception. Or, to put it more concretely, Polk's determination to seize California led him to see the possible ways in which foreign powers might stand in the way. Secretary of the Navy George Bancroft later recalled that the administration did not fear outright "conflict with any European power" over California. Rather, alarm arose from potential actions of European powers in California—increasing a consular or naval presence there, for example—that would complicate (or, as Bancroft put it, "inconvenience") the Polk administration's quest for annexation, most likely by supporting Mexico's hold on what was, after all, her territory.[20]

The problem the Polk administration faced was that not all Americans shared its objectives and therefore did not share its heightened perception of threat. Even within the President's own party there lurked a growing number of opponents of immediate territorial expansion (revealingly, from both the North, such as Martin Van Buren, and from the South, such as John C. Calhoun). These intraparty divisions would prove greatly problematic for the administration in the future. But in 1845, Polk feared the Whig opposition more. Whigs did not uniformly oppose the annexation of a port on the Pacific at some point in the future, but they did not sign up for Polk's aggressive expansionism. Indeed, during the election of 1844, Henry Clay opposed the annexation of Texas on the grounds that it would inflame sectional tensions, provoke Mexico, and divert resources from the more important goal of internal improvement. "Our augmentation is by growth, not by acquisition," the Whig leader Daniel Webster declared; "by internal development, not by external accession." The anti-expansionism of the Whigs led some in the party to advocate the establishment of independent republics in Texas, California, and, one day, Canada. A coalition of like-minded republics in North America, Clay maintained, "would emulate each other in improvements, in free institutions, and in the science of self-government." This thinking was a striking contrast to the Jeffersonian vision of a harmonious and eternally expanding federal union.[21]

Polk wanted none of this. The President feared that independent republics would invite European meddling in North America. But he and his advisers well knew that their domestic opponents could foil their expansionist plans. The great lesson the Polk administration took from the annexation of Texas was that Whigs and renegade antislavery Northerners were more able to stop territorial expansion than was Mexico and more willing to do so than was Britain. George Bancroft, Polk's closest confidant, put it best when he privately wrote, "I fear nothing but divisions at home."[22] If the administration did not achieve its expansionist goals quickly, all might be lost if Whigs were to triumph in the next election. Polk had clear goals, and, crucially, he had a clear deadline for achieving them.

It was in this context that Polk invented "Monroe's doctrine" in late 1845. The creation of this new "doctrine" owed as much to domestic politics as it did to foreign threats; it was equal parts domestic salesmanship and international statesmanship. The President invoked this new "doctrine" not only to send a message to the statesmen of the Old World, but also to disarm his political opponents at home. He presented his partisan foreign policy as the outgrowth of an imagined era of prepartisan nationalism. The possessive he used—"Monroe's doctrine"—ascribed divisive foreign policies to a popular president of the past. The Polk administration transformed the 1823 message from a cautious and reactive statement of national security requirements into a proactive call for territorial expansion.

Polk considered invoking the 1823 message in his inaugural address, but opted to save his ammunition for the most important address he would deliver as President: his first annual message to Congress in December 1845, the same forum Monroe had used twenty-two years earlier. President Polk took this message very seriously, instructing members of his cabinet to compose drafts of the section on foreign affairs. Of most interest is George Bancroft's draft, which viewed Monroe's 1823 message as inaugurating the spread of an "American system"—appropriating here for different purposes the old phrase of Adams and Clay—at the expense of "European monarchies" stuck in "past ages." Bancroft, America's answer to the great English historian Thomas Macaulay, was not one to understate his case. It is said that every page of Bancroft's *History of the United States of America* voted for Andrew Jackson. So, too, did his *History* vote for the territorial expansion that Polk hoped to accelerate (emblazoned on the book's cover was the phrase "Westward the star of empire takes its way"). Yet Bancroft was no simpleminded imperialist, even if his draft version of the 1845 message included some chest-thumping jingoism. He alone in the Polk cabinet in May 1846 would argue that there were insufficient grounds for a declaration of war against Mexico (though he would quickly fall into line once news of the Mexican "attack" on Taylor's troops reached Washington).[23]

In his draft version of Polk's 1845 message, the Secretary of the Navy asserted what might be called "Bancroft's doctrine": "Our country can never extend its territory by conquest." Instead of waging a war of conquest, Bancroft outlined a policy more in tune with the ideology of Manifest Destiny, which presumed the inevitable expansion of the United States across the American continent. The United States would reissue the warning of 1823, and, free from the threat of European intervention, American migration—the American population, Bancroft stated in his draft, had "at least doubled since Mr. Monroe gave his message to the world"—would take care of the rest. After all, if it was the nation's "manifest destiny" to stretch across the continent, there was no need to pursue an aggressive foreign policy.[24]

The changes Polk made to Bancroft's draft reveal how much he feared that his foreign and domestic opponents would preclude the fulfillment of his nation's manifest destiny. Despite the pleas of Secretary of State Buchanan to temper his language, Polk's 1845 message brashly laid the groundwork for an expansionist foreign policy.[25] In the final version of his message, Polk changed the future pledge of "Bancroft's doctrine" to a past-tense statement: "We have not sought to extend our territorial possessions by conquest." This was a remarkable alteration (not to mention a flawed reading of his nation's history—just how would Polk characterize Indian removal?). Polk's change of tense from the Bancroft draft candidly portended the President's policy. A war of conquest could not be ruled out. Indeed, the 1845 message asserted the right of "the nations of America . . . to make war [and] to conclude peace" free from outside intervention (a line that had not appeared in Bancroft's draft).

Polk, however, had not yet determined his course of action when he invoked Monroe's doctrine in December 1845. The war of conquest against Mexico to which he would soon commit the nation had not yet been decided upon. The President did take a harder line, however, dispatching John Slidell to Mexico City in a last-ditch attempt to purchase the territory he desired. To further turn the screw on Mexico, the administration informed Larkin that it would support a Texas-style rebellion in California that would pave the way to annexation. On the Oregon side of affairs, Polk rattled the saber in public but moved in the direction of a compromise agreement with the British in private.

The beauty of Monroe's message to Polk was its negative framing. The 1823 message stated only what European powers could not do; it did not prescribe policy for the United States. Polk exploited fears of foreign intervention in order to build up domestic support for active policies in the future, but he did not publicly commit himself to any particular diplomatic approach, nor, it should be said, to any particular objective. "In reasserting Mr. Monroe's doctrine," Polk confided in his diary, "I had California and the fine bay of San Francisco as much in view as Oregon."[26] Yet no one would know this from his 1845 message, which carefully avoided identifying the acquisition of California as the chief objective of the administration's foreign policy. It was a masterful move, for few would dispute the reassertion of the prohibition on European colonization (even John Quincy Adams—a great opponent of Polk—applauded the 1845 message on these grounds[27]).

Though the 1845 message did not articulate specific policy aims, a careful reading of it reveals the administration's expansionist intentions. Important here were the ways in which Polk's message departed from that of Monroe in 1823. Whereas Monroe's 1823 message warned European powers not to intervene in or colonize parts of "the American continents" and "any portion of this hemisphere," Polk referred only to "this continent" and "the North American continent." In this smaller geographic area, Polk made it clear that Monroe's doctrine "will apply with greatly increased force should any European power attempt to establish any new colony in North America." This was quite the contrast from the noncommittal message of 1823, which dodged William Wirt's question about its enforcement. Drawing on Bancroft's draft, the President went further, emphasizing the power of the United States. Polk declared that "the reassertion of this principle [noncolonization], especially in reference to North America, is at this day but the promulgation of a policy which no European power should cherish the disposition to resist." The certitude underlying Polk's message was not just ideological, as it had been in 1823, but was rooted in the increased power of the United States.[28]

Like his hero Andrew Jackson, Polk cared little about Latin America (excepting, of course, the Mexican territories he hoped to acquire). When the Peruvian government revived the idea of a hemispheric conference in 1847, the Polk administration declined the offer with little debate. The U.S. consul in Lima, Stanhope Prevost, begged the administration to send even an unofficial representative to the proceedings on the grounds that such a gesture would help mitigate growing Yankeephobia in Latin America.[29] This appeal fell upon deaf ears in Washington. After revisiting the arguments he gave against attending the Congress of Panama back in 1826, Polk was more certain than ever that participating in a hemispheric conference ran counter to American interests and traditions. "I have carefully read over my speeches on that occasion, and would now re-affirm all the doctrines which they contain," the President confided in his diary.[30] Polk so explicitly constricted the geographic scope of the 1823 prohibition on foreign intervention that it is possible he intended to send a dog-whistle message to European powers that so long as they acknowledged U.S. supremacy in North America, they could help themselves to South America. Indeed, when the British and French intervened in a dispute between Argentina and Uruguay in 1845, going so far as to blockade Buenos Aires and seize the island of Martín García, Polk, like Andrew Jackson during the British seizure of the Malvinas/Falklands in the early 1830s, looked the other way.

Polk's 1845 message also differed from Monroe's of 1823 in the European actions it identified as a threat to national security. Polk thrice referred to the attempt "of the powers of Europe" to implant their "doctrine" of "the balance of power" on the North American continent. The source of this alleged scare was a speech given by the French statesman François Guizot in June 1845. Guizot stated that it was in France's interests for no single power to dominate North America. Expansionists and the Democratic press in the United States exploited Guizot's statement for all it was worth. Conjuring up images of corrupt Old World leaders divvying up territory in smoke-filled rooms, Democrats depicted "the balance of power" as an instrument of a monarchical international order hostile to the republican United States. "We all know that this balance of power in Europe," the Democrat Lewis Cass declared in the Senate, "is nothing more or less than a balance to maintain monarchical institutions under the guise of supporting a necessary equality."[31] The vague threat to the United States that Polk conjured up with the "balance of power" differed from Monroe's specific identification of colonization and the extension of the Holy Alliance's "political system" to the New World. What exactly "the balance of power" was and how it might threaten the United States was not explained. Polk sought to preserve for himself the right to decide what European actions threatened the United States, as well as what actions were required to counter the threat.

It is significant that Polk referred to the "balance of power" as a "doctrine," for here might lie the origins of that peculiar second word of the subject of this book. Polk's purpose appears to have been to contrast European statecraft with that of the United States. Noah Webster's 1828 *American Dictionary* defined "doctrine" as "whatever is laid down as true by an instructor or master." Important, however, was Webster's qualification that "a doctrine may be true or false."[32] Nineteenth-century doctrines, in other words, were not accepted by all, but competed with other doctrines. South Carolina's "doctrine of nullification" opposed the "doctrines of Andrew Jackson" during the showdown of the early 1830s; Abraham Lincoln's advocacy of the "doctrine of no more slave states" challenged Stephen Douglas's "Nebraska doctrine" and "Freeport doctrine" during the famous 1858 debates. Polk and other expansionists—for other Democrats began using the phrase "Monroe's doctrine" at roughly the same time as did Polk[33]—sought to draw a line between the United States and Europe. It was a shrewd move designed to present an either-or proposition to the administration's domestic critics: either they were in favor of "Monroe's doctrine," or they were in favor of the European "doctrine of the balance of power." This theme would appear time and again in the nineteenth century. "The Monroe Doctrine is to America," wrote one of its first historians in 1885, "what the Balance of Power is to Europe."[34]

Polk's purpose in invoking Monroe's doctrine was to promote

American domination of the continent. But he flexibly pursued this goal. Ever the diplomatic realist, Polk carefully calibrated ambitions with capabilities. In the Oregon dispute with Britain, he accepted a compromise agreement, though this entailed selling members of his own party down the river. The 1845 message overreached on this issue: it heightened expectations among Midwestern expansionists that the administration would support their calls for "fifty-four forty or fight" (a reference to the northernmost latitude of the Oregon Territory). But Polk had no stomach for fighting the powerful British over Oregon. He eventually cut a deal that divided the territory at the 49th parallel, much to the consternation of Midwestern Democrats betrayed by an administration that had talked tough but soon proved willing to compromise with the hated British.

Mexican weakness allowed Polk to take a harder line on the issues of California and the Texas border. When the Mexicans refused to sell their northern territories to the United States, Polk aggressively dispatched troops to the disputed Texan-Mexican border. A military confrontation in the disputed area provided the administration the pretext for sending a war message to Congress, which both houses of Congress passed overwhelmingly in May 1846. By September of the following year, American forces occupied California, New Mexico, and Mexico City itself.

The military triumphs of the war against Mexico raised troublesome questions at home. What would become of the occupied territories? If they were annexed, would slavery be allowed? The Wilmot Proviso of 1846, introduced in the House by Pennsylvania Democrat David Wilmot, heightened sectional tensions by introducing the possibility of prohibiting slavery from territories seized from Mexico. Just as Clay had predicted back in 1844, the acquisition of new territories threatened the union by inflaming sectional passions. Clay continued to preach the "no territory" principle in 1847 (that is, taking no territory from Mexico). He was joined by other Whigs, some of whom advocated the creation of a "Pacific Republic" that would be allied with, but independent of, the United States. The "no territory" principle took aim at Polk's central objective in the war against Mexico: the acquisition of California. The President once again turned to Monroe's doctrine to counter his domestic opponents. In his third annual message to Congress in 1847, Polk invoked Monroe again—curiously, citing his 1824 message this time—to discredit what he called "the doctrine of no territory." This doctrine, the President asserted, would embolden "some foreign power" to seize California by conquest. Having initially used Monroe's doctrine to whip up support for an active foreign policy, Polk now employed it as justification for keeping hold of the territory that had been conquered.[35]

Though Polk eventually settled for less territory than he wanted, the Senate's ratification of the 1848 Treaty of Guadalupe Hidalgo with Mexico gave him the prizes he had sought: California, New Mexico, and a Texas that stretched to the Rio Grande. The treaty placed Whigs in the uncomfortable position of having to choose between their desire to end the war against Mexico and their "no territory" doctrine. Fourteen of the twenty-one Whigs in the Senate held their noses and voted to ratify the treaty, fearful of the political repercussions of opposing a favorable treaty that had the extra benefit of ending a war they opposed. Some found solace in the lip service the treaty paid to traditional anticolonialism: it presented the conquest of northern Mexico as a financial transaction (the United States compensated Mexico $15 million for the territories it took) and enabled Mexican citizens living in the conquered territories to become citizens of the United States (an estimated ninety thousand Mexicans plus a larger number of Indians). But these were hollow deeds. This bargain sale of territory came at the barrel of a gun. And, despite their U.S. citizenship, many of the Mexican inhabitants of these new territories of the United States would find their rights infringed in the coming decades by predatory speculators and biased law enforcement. The treaty, a Whig publication asserted, was "a Peace which everyone will be glad of, but no one will be proud of."[36]

Polk entered the White House in 1845 with clear objectives and left having achieved them four years later. The war against Mexico demonstrated the newfound power of the United States. "One of the most important results of the war into which we were recently forced with a neighboring nation," Polk declared in his last annual message to Congress, "is the demonstration it has afforded of the military strength of our country."[37] Yet if he achieved his expansionist goals and displayed American power, Polk failed to advance the long-term interests sought by the Monroe administration. Back in 1823, Monroe and his cabinet had balanced international objectives, foreign threats, and the internal dynamics of their union. They moved cautiously, careful not to overreach diplomatically lest they endanger their union at home. Polk, in contrast, formulated a bold plan of foreign conquest. His assumption that imperial nationalism would trump sectional and partisan divisions proved greatly mistaken. The war of conquest against Mexico opened deep fissures at home: Southerners feared for the future stability of their peculiar institution in light of the Wilmot Proviso; antislavery activists objected to the potential expansion of slave territory; Northern expansionists cried foul when Polk compromised with the British on the Oregon boundary but went to war against Mexico for southern territory; Whigs feared that Polk had fatally undermined the principles and political practices of their republic. The war against Mexico set in motion a chain of events that resulted in the American Civil War.[38]

Polk's invocation of "Monroe's doctrine" undermined another objective sought back in 1823: the strengthening of republican government and economic liberalism in Latin America. The war against Mexico discredited the very political and economic system that Americans hoped to export to Latin America by associating it with foreign conquest. Rather than strengthen the independence of Mexico, Polk exploited its weakness. Polk hoped that the $15 million indemnity payment would help stabilize Mexico. But this sum could not restore Mexican finances, let alone resolve the internal political conflict there that the war exacerbated. These conditions in Mexico soon would lead to the very result Polk wanted to avoid: European intervention.

An Antiannexationist Disavowal

Polk's aggressive foreign policy presented the Whig Party with many dilemmas. It forced party leaders to prioritize maintaining peace with Britain (in Oregon) over relations with Mexico (in Texas). After their takeover of the House of Representatives in the midterm elections of 1846, Whig legislators had to walk the tightrope of opposing the administration's war against Mexico while still supporting the troops in the field (some of whom were the sons of prominent Whigs such as Henry Clay and Daniel Webster). The Wilmot Proviso exacerbated tensions between the party's growing antislavery Northern wing and its increasingly proslavery Southern constituency. And when Polk presented the Treaty of Guadalupe Hidalgo to the Senate, Whigs had little choice but to accept the territorial acquisitions that they long had opposed.[39]

Whig foreign policy is mostly remembered for its unsuccessful opposition to Polk's program of territorial conquest. But the Whigs' failure to stem the tide of aggressive expansion should not obscure the fact that they possessed a coherent conception of the nation's role in international affairs that was all their own. Far from just opposing Polk's agenda, Whigs conceived of and, when in power, implemented their own policies that constituted an internationalist and largely antiannexationist alternative to the Democrats' program of territorial expansion.

Though the Whig perception of threat differed greatly from that of the Democrats, they, too, voiced their opposition to European intervention in the Western Hemisphere and embraced the message of 1823. Daniel Webster, who served as the first secretary of state of the Harrison-Tyler administration, from 1841 to 1842, issued a hands-off warning of his own to the powers of the Old World. Webster informed Britain and France in 1842 that the Hawaiian Islands were not to be objects of European colonization. Dubbed by historians in the twentieth century as the "Tyler Doctrine" (after Webster's superior, President John Tyler), this statement effectively extended the 1823 message to Hawaii, a constellation of islands important to the growing East Asian trade trumpeted by Whig merchants. Webster was also interested in acquiring ports in California to promote the potentially lucrative East Asian trade. But in contrast to expansionist Democrats, Webster sought to obtain California through peaceful means, and he dropped the idea in 1842 when his diplomatic overtures found little traction in foreign capitals.

The means and style of diplomacy constituted a fundamental difference between Whig and Democratic statecraft. Whereas Polk's 1845 message warned Europeans that the United States would oppose violations of Monroe's dictum with "greatly increased force," the "Tyler Doctrine" warned only of diplomatic retribution (violations of Hawaiian sovereignty would be met with "a decided remonstrance" from the United States). Webster moved cautiously on the Hawaiian issue, sending a "commissioner" rather than a full-blown "minister" to the islands in 1843. Webster's reading of the message of 1823 differed from Polk's in another way: the Whigs invoked the principles of 1823 in order to support Hawaiian autonomy; Polk invoked Monroe's doctrine to justify taking territory from Mexico.[40]

Whigs joined Democrats in denouncing reactionary extremism in Europe, such as that which crushed the liberal 1848 revolutions in Europe. Even a conservative diplomat like Webster (who once again served as Secretary of State under President Millard Fillmore, from 1850 to 1852) publicly denounced the Austrian government for quashing an insurrection in Hungary in a widely reprinted diplomatic note written in 1850. Just as he had exploited the Greek issue as a young congressman back in 1824, Webster recognized in 1850 the domestic political benefits of condemning European monarchy. It is no coincidence that he composed this nationalist state paper in the context of the debates surrounding the Compromise of 1850, which provided temporary resolution of the question of slavery in the new territories taken from Mexico. Webster later wrote that he intended for his assertive note to the Austrian minister to "touch the national pride, and make a man feel sheepish and look silly who should speak of disunion."[41] Many Whigs also played upon the Anglophobia of the time. The New Yorker William H. Seward, for example, well understood the electoral utility of the occasional twist of the lion's tail in a state that was home to increasing numbers of Irish immigrants. Britain was "the greatest, the most grasping and the most rapacious" power on the globe, Seward once declared.[42]

Yet as aware as Whigs were of the political utility of opposing the Old World, they could not conceal their admiration of Britain. Here they differed from their political opponents in the Democratic Party. In the eyes of many Whigs, England embodied the economic success and social order that they hoped to emulate. The formulation in this period of racist doctrines that heralded the superiority of the Anglo-Saxon race increased Whigs' admiration of their brethren across the Atlantic. "England was the home of my forefathers," one Whig diplomat stated in 1850, "and the blood of the Anglo-Saxon forms the basis of the population of this country."[43]

The Whigs' admiration of Britain also was rooted in the hardheaded calculation of their nation's material interests. Just as Clay's earlier "American system" referred both to domestic and foreign policies, Whig diplomacy aimed to advance the party's vision for economic development and internal improvement. Whig objections to territorial expansion during the Polk years stemmed less from identification with Mexico than from the view that priority should be given to internal development. Attracting investment capital from London banks was a key foreign policy objective of the Whigs, who sought British funds to finance the federal debt and to underwrite infrastructure projects such as the construction of canals and railroads. Throughout his political career, Webster served as an agent for Baring Brothers bank in London, the leading European firm in American finance. Even as he served as Secretary of State, Webster continued to advise the Barings on how best to keep capital flowing across the Atlantic. His British negotiating partner in the 1842 Treaty of Washington (which settled the disputed Canada-Maine border) was Lord Ashburton, who, remarkably, was a senior partner of Barings.[44]

Whigs' veneration of their former colonial master was not without its limits. They identified Britain as their greatest diplomatic and commercial rival, drawing here from the thinking of party grandees Adams and Clay. Most retained a distrust of their former colonial master. The Illinois Whig Abraham Lincoln relayed the story of the Indian chief who, when informed that the sun never set on the British Empire, responded with the quip, "I suppose it's because God wouldn't trust them in the dark."[45] When the British and French floated the idea of a tripartite agreement pledging all three parties not to annex Cuba in 1852, Webster rejected the offer, just as Adams had done in 1823 and 1825. But just as the enforcement of Monroe's message relied upon the Royal Navy, so, too, did the Whigs seek to harness British power for their own ends. This was particularly the case in matters of overseas commerce, where Whig statesmen sought to hitch a free ride on the Royal Navy. In East Asia, for instance, Whigs applauded Britain's forcible opening of the

China market in the Opium War of 1839–42, viewing the conflict as the introduction of "civilization" and commerce to the allegedly backward Chinese. The 1844 Treaty of Wangxia, which extended to the United States most-favored-nation status in China, was possible only because of British gunboat diplomacy.[46]

Whigs' preoccupation with overseas commercial expansion was rooted not only in economic self-interest but also in evangelical Protestantism. Whigs believed that commercial expansion and the spread of Christianity went hand in hand. Missionary activity constituted an important means through which the United States interacted with other peoples, particularly in East Asia. If Democrats can be viewed as imperialists in the traditional sense of conquering territory and ruling over the inhabitants thereof, Whig imperialism manifested itself in imposing upon others their commerce, culture, and religion.[47]

The Whigs, of course, did not have a monopoly on American Christianity. Providential ideas were also central to the Democrats' ideology of Manifest Destiny. Few Americans were more pious than James K. Polk, who rarely missed an opportunity to attend Sunday services at the First Presbyterian Church in Washington. But whereas expansionist Democrats typically summoned religion to illustrate America's exceptionalism, Whigs tended to be more internationalist in their Christian invocations. The pioneering scholarship of the Whig diplomat Henry Wheaton, for instance, sought to create a Christian basis of interstate conduct, which he called the "the law of nations" or "international law." Reformers such as William Ladd and Elihu Burritt, leaders of the evangelical American Peace Society, petitioned for arbitration clauses to be incorporated into future treaties and led American delegations at international peace conferences. Inspired by evangelical Christianity and his overseas connections in Britain, Ladd composed a pamphlet in 1840 that called for the creation of a permanent international body, a "Congress of Nations" that would formulate international law and arbitrate disputes among the "Christian and civilized nations." Ladd's precocious idea had wide appeal in Whig circles, leading John Quincy Adams to predict that it would be realized within two decades. Even John O'Sullivan, the radical Democrat and theorist of Manifest Destiny, embraced the proposed "Congress of Nations" in a resolution put before the New York State Assembly. As O'Sullivan's embrace of Ladd's idea suggests, Christian internationalism could appeal to even the most ardent of Democratic expansionists. But it was within the Whig Party that it had the most traction.[48]

All of these traits of Whig diplomacy—Christian internationalism, rapprochement with Britain, preoccupation with economics—shaped one of the most remarkable agreements in American diplomatic history: the Clayton-Bulwer Treaty of 1850. The treaty was a response to growing Anglo-American rivalry in Central America, where statesmen from both nations hoped to build an isthmian canal. American and British diplomats competed in the 1840s to secure right-of-passage treaties with Central American nations, if not the territory itself where such a canal might be dug. Reminiscent of the Ward-Poinsett duel in Mexico City in the 1820s, Frederick Chatfield (Britain's ranking diplomat in the region) and Ephraim Squier (of the United States) engaged in a diplomatic game of cat-and-mouse that threatened to embroil the two nations in outright conflict.

Soon after taking office in March 1849, Whig president Zachary Taylor acted to end the strategic jockeying in Central America. In his first annual message, Taylor declared that a canal open to the commerce of all nations on equal terms would "become a guarantee of peace instead of a subject of contention and strife." In this spirit he instructed Secretary of State John Clayton to commence negotiations with British envoy Henry Bulwer. The result of the negotiations was a pact that internationalized a future isthmian canal. In the Clayton-Bulwer Treaty of 1850, both nations agreed not to "occupy, or fortify, or colonize, or assume or exercise any dominion [in] any part of Central America." They further pledged to cooperate with each other in the construction of an isthmian canal and to open the future canal to the ships of other nations.[49]

Contingent circumstances help to explain this treaty that stood in such contrast to the unilateral and expansionist diplomacy of just a few years earlier. Embroiled in the domestic dispute over the extension of slavery resulting from the Mexican War that would not find settlement until the Compromise of 1850, the United States was in no position to pick a fight with the British over Central America. An equally important motive was the United States' need to attract British investment for the construction of a canal, a massive project that was certain to carry an unprecedented price tag. An Anglo-American treaty would establish the political stability in Central America that investors on both sides of the Atlantic viewed as a precondition to financing any isthmian enterprises.

Yet as much as the Clayton-Bulwer Treaty reflected these material interests and political circumstances, it also demonstrated the Whig's antiannexationist alternative to the territorially expansionist policies of the Democrats. "If there be any who would desire to seize and annex any portion of the territories of these weak sister republics," Taylor asserted in his endorsement of the treaty, "I do not concur in their policy."[50] The agreement sought to avoid the sectionally and politically divisive consequences of further territorial expansion. It aimed to advance American economic and security interests through international cooperation. It endeavored to draw the two Christian, English-speaking powers closer together and to advance their shared objective of commercial expansion. "It is our mission to extend commerce, the pioneer of civilization and child of peace to all parts of the world," the U.S. minister to London, Abbott Lawrence, informed Foreign Secretary Palmerston, "and to illustrate by our example the elevating effects of Christianity."[51]

Remarkably, Clayton appears to have disavowed "Monroe's doctrine" during negotiations with the British. "With regard to . . . Mr. Monroe's doctrine respecting the colonization of any part of the American continent by a European Power," the British minister to Washington reported back to London in 1849, "Mr. Clayton remarked that the present Administration of the United States in no way adopted that principle."[52] Bulwer later stated that successful negotiation of the treaty required that the diplomats "tacitly set aside the Munro [*sic*] doctrine."[53] One should not read too much into these statements, considering that the doctrine was at that point linked to Polk's expansionist program, something which would have been an obstacle in Clayton's negotiations with Bulwer.

Whigs disavowed Polk's reinterpretation of Monroe's 1823 message, not the message itself. When presenting the treaty to the Senate, President Taylor packaged the agreement as a means of advancing the principles of 1823 and forestalling future British colonial expansion in Central America. The President argued that he merely followed his predecessors by maintaining "the independence and sovereignty of all the Central American Republics." The treaty not only precluded future British expansion but also established the United States as an equal power in Central America when it had little such previous standing. Taylor went further, pledging to "dispose" of any "collision" between European powers and the republics of Latin America by "mediation and assistance." Diplomacy, not conquest, would provide the best means of advancing the principles of 1823.[54]

The question of whether the Clayton-Bulwer Treaty contradicted the Monroe Doctrine would reappear for the remainder of the nineteenth century. To Democrats at the time, there was little question but that the agreement repudiated the principles of 1823. "The Treaty altogether reverses the Monroe Doctrine," James Buchanan contended, "and establishes it against ourselves rather than European Governments."[55] In stark contrast to Polk's message of 1845 (as well as the ambiguous message of 1823), the Clayton-Bulwer pact explicitly forbade American territorial expansion. It is unique in nineteenth-century American statecraft for so doing. In this regard, the Clayton-Bulwer Treaty was more in the spirit of accepting Canning's 1823 offer to issue a joint declaration and renounce future territorial acquisitions than it was in tune with the noncommittal course ultimately pursued by the Monroe administration.

Though crystal clear on forbidding future American and British expansion in Central America, the treaty was ambiguous on the legitimacy of Britain's colonial arrangements established after 1823, the now sacred cutoff point for Old World colonization in the Western Hemisphere. Did Clayton-Bulwer, Democrats asked, legitimate Chatfield's hasty establishment of a British protectorate over the Mosquito Coast of Nicaragua in 1848? If so, they argued, the treaty itself violated the Monroe Doctrine. Clayton and Bulwer deliberately dodged such thorny questions on the grounds that an imperfect treaty was preferable to no treaty at all. "Words which cannot but be more or less offensive to us, which will be alarming to Capitalists [required to finance the building of the canal], and of which you can express the real value in other terms," Bulwer wrote Clayton during the drafting of the agreement, "cannot but be words that, on all accounts, had better be changed."[56]

The Clayton-Bulwer Treaty was not unique in provoking domestic debate. All of the major foreign policy initiatives of the 1840s proved divisive at home. Long gone was the brief consensus of 1823 in which statesmen from different sections and political persuasions came to agree on a general, if noncommittal, course of action. The more Americans discussed Monroe's message in the 1840s, in contrast, the more they disagreed with one another. This owed much to the enhanced security and international standing of the United States in the mid-nineteenth century. The European powers went out of their way to avoid direct conflict with the United States in this period (a courtesy reciprocated by even the belligerent Polk administration during the Oregon dispute). "Shall we expect some transatlantic military giant, to step the Ocean, and crush us at a blow?" a young Abraham Lincoln asked in 1838. "Never! All the armies of Europe, Asia and Africa combined, with all the treasure of the earth (our own excepted) in their military chest; with a Buonaparte for a commander, could not by force, take a drink from the Ohio, or make a track on the Blue Ridge, in a trial of a thousand years."[57] Americans certainly would have united had they faced a collective threat such as foreign invasion. The political mileage Polk milked out of the alleged Mexican "attack" on American forces testifies to this latent nationalism. Yet there was to be no foreign assault upon national integrity akin to those faced in the early nineteenth century.[58]

The importance of the foreign threat in this period lay in its symbiotic relationship with deepening domestic divisions. In the same 1838 address, Lincoln argued that the gravest threat "cannot come from abroad. If destruction be our lot, we must ourselves be its author and finisher." Americans viewed foreign affairs through the prism of the increasingly contentious politics within their union. The foreign threats of the mid-nineteenth century disproportionately confronted certain sections (such as the slaveholding states) or political persuasions (such as expansionist Democrats). The ensuing politicization and sectionalization of the foreign threat exacerbated domestic conflict. Whigs and Democrats feared that each other's policies would endanger the union by playing into the hands of the British: Democratic expansionists argued that antiannexationist Whigs collaborated with the British Empire; Whigs feared that free-trade Democrats were the unknowing stooges of British economic neocolonialism.

Most ominous was how both sides of the sectional debate

over slavery came to see each other in the light of foreign threats. Proslavery Southerners viewed the antislavery forces within and outside the union as interlinked; meanwhile, Northern anti-slavery activists interpreted slaveholding Southerners as an un-American elite, a "slave power" that found inspiration in the aristocracy of the Old World.[59] In the 1780s, external threats had helped bind the states together in a collective security pact. By the mid-nineteenth century, however, security considerations led some Americans to a different conclusion. Most notable in this regard were an increasingly radical and vocal group of slavehold-ing Southerners who contended that the union that had pro-tected and expanded their interests now threatened their "peculiar institution." Traditional party loyalty could trump this sectionalized politics for only so long. The departure of many Northerners to the Free-Soil Party in 1848 portended the col-lapse of the second party system that had tied the sections of the union together in the preceding decades.

Yet even in the fog of this political and sectional rancor, hints of future consensus on foreign affairs are dimly visible. If Whigs and Democrats employed different means, they both sought to limit British and European expansion in areas deemed vital to national interests. Neither took much note of the views of the other inhabitants of the Americas: Polk attempted to erase Mex-icans from the territories he coveted (the lands seized from Mexico, Polk informed Congress, were "almost unoccupied"[60]); Clayton and Bulwer barely consulted the governments of Central America, despite the fact that they negotiated a treaty pertaining to their territory. Both Whigs and Democrats hoped to expand overseas commerce; both sought to harness British power for their own ends; both agreed that the United States should call the shots in the Western Hemisphere. If Americans could set-tle the slavery issue, a national Monroe Doctrine might emerge.

4

Civil Wars

The two dangers long feared by American statesmen simultaneously materialized in the mid-nineteenth century: a group of states withdrew from the union and sought to ally themselves with foreign powers, and a European power intervened in the Western Hemisphere to establish a puppet monarchy in a Spanish American state. That Americans had long dreaded these contingencies made them all the more menacing when they appeared. The Republican statesman William H. Seward feared that the dissolution of the union imperiled the independence Americans had worked for nearly a century to establish. "Our country, after having expelled all European powers from the continent," Seward lamented, "would relapse into an aggravated form of its colonial experience, and, like Italy, Turkey, India, and China, become the theatre of transatlantic intervention and rapacity."[1]

Americans constructed a new Monroe Doctrine as they acted to counter this doomsday scenario. What had been a routine presidential message, then a contested and partisan symbol, attained the status of national dogma in the mid-nineteenth century. The phrase "Monroe Doctrine" became entrenched in the American vocabulary, appearing for the first time without the possessive and often as a proper noun with both words capitalized. A prominent pamphlet labeled the Doctrine "an axiomatic truth in political science"; *Harper's Weekly* declared "the Monroe doctrine is unquestionably a fixed principle of American political faith"; the House of Representatives unanimously passed a resolution modeled after the principles of 1823; and President Ulysses S. Grant projected this consensus backward in 1870 when he stated that "the doctrine promulgated by President Monroe has been adhered to by all political parties."[2] Such talk transformed the Doctrine into a powerful nationalist symbol that politicians from across the spectrum raced to claim as their own.

The Monroe Doctrine that emerged in the turmoil of the mid-nineteenth century was new in substance as well as style. Nationalist statesmen formulated newly assertive policies to confront their enemies, both internal and external. As the federal government used force against the Southern states to preserve the union during the Civil War, statesmen in Washington contemplated active policies to promote their interests in the hemisphere, particularly in Mexico. Though the constraints of sectionalism and civil war limited foreign policy options in the immediate term, this new Monroe Doctrine laid the foundations for the American imperialism of the late nineteenth century.

"The Dignified Appellation"

In January 1853, the Michigan Democrat Lewis Cass introduced a Senate resolution modeled after Monroe's 1823 and Polk's 1845 messages. It included the noncolonization clause of the 1823 message but applied it, as Polk had before, only to North America. Cass's resolution also covered new ground in referencing Cuba, an island that many Democrats openly coveted. The resolution warned that the United States would view the transfer of Cuba from Spain to any other power as an "unfriendly act" to its "southern coast" that would "be resisted by all means."[3]

An experienced diplomat and longtime stalwart of the Democratic Party, Cass had several motives for introducing his resolution. He sought to undermine the Clayton-Bulwer Treaty of 1850, an agreement many Democrats continued to view as an "anti-American alliance" that enabled British aggression in Central America.[4] In contrast to the high hopes of internationalist Whigs, the treaty's vision of Anglo-American cooperation in Central America proved elusive. Both nations continued to jockey for supremacy in the region, despite the treaty's prohibition on colonization. Britain maintained a protectorate over Nicaragua's Mosquito Coast (the likely eastern terminus of an isthmian canal), as well as tightening its grip over the Bay Islands and Belize. The United States assumed an even more aggressive stance in the region. The U.S. Navy sloop *Cyane* bombarded the Nicaraguan port of San Juan del Norte following a commercial dispute in 1854. Democratic president Franklin Pierce openly advocated further territorial expansion. In 1856 the Pierce administration extended recognition to the illegitimate Nicaraguan government of William Walker, an American adventurer who led a private army of "filibusters" that conquered the nation. The United States and Britain, in short, continued to stumble toward conflict in Central America. Cass's resolution aimed to rally support for an assertive policy in the region, as well as to send a message to the British that the United States was in Central America to stay. The resolution, the London *Times* scoffed, "represents with great fidelity the ignorance, the intemperance, and the bad feelings of the lowest class of the populace [in the United States] toward foreign countries."[5]

Yet Cass had more on his mind than rivalry with the British. Though his resolution would be debated throughout the 1850s, he never pressed for a vote on it, preferring instead to keep debate open on the Central American issue in order to use the Monroe Doctrine to the Democrats' domestic political advantage. With Northern and Southern Democrats increasingly at odds over the question of the extension of slavery, Cass seized the opportunity to unite the party by stirring up the Anglophobia that connected members from both sections. Cass recognized that the Monroe Doctrine could be used as a club to attack the Whigs and their increasingly unpopular Clayton-Bulwer Treaty. It was a shrewd move from a veteran of the era's partisan politics. But it was not without irony: Cass chose the very symbol to unite the Democratic Party that had helped tear it apart during the Polk years.

Though an old hand introduced the resolution, the debate on the Monroe Doctrine came to be dominated by a new generation of statesmen. There remained important politicians from the generation that came of age in the nationalist era of the War of 1812, such as Cass and James Buchanan. But most of the statesmen who had formulated and first argued over the Monroe Doctrine—John Quincy Adams, John C. Calhoun, Henry Clay, Daniel Webster, and James K. Polk—were now gone. In their place stood a new generation of politicians whose formative experiences came from the partisan and sectionally divisive era of the 1830s and '40s. They tended to be less willing to compromise on issues relating to the debate over slavery (though, as we shall see, there were important exceptions on this score). On foreign affairs, they embraced assertive and active policies, confident that the time had arrived for the United States to join the ranks of the world's powers. They were less inhibited by the insecurities and heightened perception of threat that had preoccupied their forebears. The British minister to Washington, John Crampton, noticed not only their assertive views on foreign policy, but also their appearance: they "let their hair grow long—don't brush their coats—look sallow and sour . . . a more uncommonly common and unprepossessing set of fellows I seldom saw."[6]

Stephen Douglas quickly upstaged Cass to emerge as the Democrats' most ardent promoter of the Monroe Doctrine. An Illinoisan whose diminutive stature belied his political power, the "Little Giant" embodied the imperialist nationalism of the mid-nineteenth-century Democratic Party. Douglas had supported the conquests of the Polk years with great enthusiasm. His only complaint was that Polk had not seized more territory. He expressed little concern for the peoples who stood in the way of the United States' manifest destiny, whether they were Mexican, Native American, or British. Similarly, Douglas held no firm moral views on slavery. "Whenever it becomes necessary, in our growth and progress to acquire more territory," he asserted in his famous debates with Abraham Lincoln, "I am in favor of it, without reference to the question of slavery."[7] The Little Giant maintained that the settlement and exploitation of the nation's vast territory—objectives that he was well placed to oversee as chair of the Senate Committee on Territories—were of greater importance than the slavery question, which only delayed the consolidation of the emerging American empire.

The Monroe Doctrine appealed to this archetypal antebellum imperialist. Indeed, Douglas played the final role in its christening, noting that the principles of 1823 had "assumed the dignified appellation of the 'Monroe doctrine.'" The Doctrine became shorthand for Douglas's vision for the United States. The Little Giant hoped to create a giant nation that would dominate the whole of North America. This American colossus would enable white men to elevate their social position, to enrich themselves by the economic exploitation of the continent's vast resources, and to enjoy their freedom through the exercise of popular sovereignty, another of Douglas's favorite concepts. He saw no need to share desirable territories with others. Just as he had no compunction about seizing land from Mexicans or Native Americans, Douglas lambasted Whigs for committing the nation to an "entangling alliance" (the Clayton-Bulwer Treaty) that was a "negation and repudiation" of the Monroe Doctrine. Why share the strategically vital region of Central America with the British when the United States could have it all to itself, he asked. Douglas's signature speech on the Monroe Doctrine culminated

in order to demonstrate his patriotism and as a sign of respect for its primary author (Seward's hero was John Quincy Adams, whose biography he wrote in 1849). Even at this early point in his career, Seward viewed the Monroe Doctrine more in relation to domestic politics than foreign policy.

Seward's international vision called for the expansion of the nation's commerce. He foresaw great power competition, not just in the Western Hemisphere, but in the "seas of the East where . . . the prize is to be found." Just as Douglas's speeches on the Monroe Doctrine climaxed with his expansionist vision, Seward concluded his discussion of the Doctrine with what lay closest to his heart: "the commerce of the world, which is the empire of the world." Seward's Monroe Doctrine called for internal development in order to compete more effectively against the European powers in the battle for global commercial supremacy, particularly in East Asia. "Open up a highway through your country from New York to San Francisco," Seward declared. "Put your domain under cultivation, and your ten thousand wheels of manufacture in motion. Multiply your ships, and send them forth to the East. The nation that draws most materials and provisions from the earth, and fabricates the most, and sells the most of productions and fabrics to foreign nations, must be, and will be, the great Power of the earth."[14]

Douglas and Seward articulated different Monroe Doctrines. One sought territorial expansion and unilateral domination of North America and the Caribbean; the other embraced internationalism to advance American interests and principles, even as it anticipated a global struggle for commercial preeminence. Yet these two Doctrines were not incompatible on all points. Douglas also called for commercial expansion, and Seward left the door open to territorial acquisitions, though differences over slavery clearly divided the two on this last issue. Careful observers also noted that as the Senate debates on the Monroe Doctrine progressed, they became less about distinctive foreign policy visions and more about seizing the patriotic high ground. "A great deal of this language is held for home political purposes," the British minister John Crampton wrote in 1853, "each party out-bidding the other in its offer of 'Americanism.' "[15]

The Senate debates associated the Monroe Doctrine not with a political party, nor with specific individuals, but with a broader "Americanism." Lord Napier, who in 1857 succeeded Crampton as British minister in Washington, found that the Central American issue was a subject on which "Democrats and Republicans agree here when they agree on nothing else."[16] The party realignment of this period contributed to this convergence of views. When many Northern Democrats bolted their party to join the upstart Republicans, they brought with them their views on foreign policy. As the two parties began to inch toward one another, competition to claim the Monroe Doctrine intensified. Democratic newspapers ran stories lambasting their opponents for betraying the Doctrine. At their 1856 convention in Cincinnati, the Democrats placed a Monroe Doctrine plank in their party platform—the first time the phrase appeared in a political platform. Republicans were slow to counter these moves, largely because Democrats successfully merged the Doctrine with territorial expansion, which the new party opposed so long as the slavery issue remained unresolved. Yet some Republicans recognized the political benefit in claiming the Doctrine as their own. When rumors circulated that Seward opposed the Monroe Doctrine, he wrote private letters to set the record straight: "I came out flat-footed for his [Cass's] resolutions and gave conclusive arguments from the Monroe Doctrine," Seward informed a correspondent who had questioned his position.[17]

The deepest fault line that the Monroe Doctrine debates exposed was not between parties, but between sections. Despite Douglas's efforts to use the Doctrine to bridge the gap between North and South, many saw the debate for what it was: an attempt to divert attention from the sectional divide over the expansion of slavery. Those from both sides of the Mason-Dixon Line frustrated Douglas's attempt to use the Doctrine as a unifying symbol. The South Carolina senator Andrew Pickens Butler, drawing from Calhoun's old view of "Monroe's declaration," argued against a broad invocation of the Doctrine. Butler feared that an expansive Doctrine might endanger the South's peculiar institution by mobilizing the opponents of slavery both in and out of the United States. Other Southerners used the occasion to argue that the security interests of the slaveholding states required an expansionist foreign policy, particularly in Cuba. These proslavery expansionists took a page from the 1854 Ostend Manifesto in arguing for preemptive annexation: rather than allow emancipation to occur in Cuba, the United States should act first and seize the island, preserving slavery there and increasing the political power of the South in the process.

Northerners countered with sectional arguments of their own. "The northern States are content now," Seward maintained, "and do not want Cuba."[18] John P. Hale of New Hampshire responded to Cass's resolution on Cuba by introducing one of his own: if the United States must warn the European powers away from Cuba out of concern for the Southern states, it should do the same regarding Canada on behalf of the North. Other antislavery Northerners followed the example of John Quincy Adams in hoping for British antislavery intervention in the New World. Charles Sumner, the Massachusetts statesman whom the South Carolinian Preston Brooks caned on the floor of the Senate in 1856, urged his friends in England to use their influence to promote abolition in Cuba.[19]

The Democrats' use of the Monroe Doctrine thus backfired. Similar to Douglas's unsuccessful attempts to diffuse the combustible issue of slavery in the territories through popular sovereignty, the Little Giant's advocacy of the Monroe Doctrine only increased tensions between the two sections. Not even the genius of the Monroe Doctrine—its negative framing in terms of what foreign powers could not do, rather than calling for specific action on the part of the United States—could find consensus among American politicians, particularly those from the South who demanded ever more guarantees that the federal government would protect their peculiar institution.

The Democrats' use of the Monroe Doctrine in diplomatic exchanges with the British concerning Central America was also counterproductive. When James Buchanan, the U.S. minister to Britain, invoked Monroe's message in 1856, the foreign secretary, Lord Clarendon, responded that "Her Majesty's government cannot admit that doctrine as an international axiom which ought to regulate the conduct of European states." This first invocation of the Doctrine in formal diplomacy was a flop, stiffening British resolve to stand firm against American demands. "In dealing with Vulgar minded Bullies, and such unfortunately the people of the United States are," Lord Palmerston wrote, "nothing is gained by submission to Insult & wrong."[20]

When resolution to the Central American issue came in 1860, it was in spite of, not because of, American invocations of the Monroe Doctrine. Having faced recent diplomatic crises in the Near East and India, British statesmen feared that there was little domestic support for an active policy in distant Central America. Many concluded that the economic benefits of cordial relations with the United States, Britain's largest trading partner and greatest source of cotton, were of greater value than Central America. Though Palmerston loathed Yankee saber-rattling, he acknowledged that American ascendancy in Central America might have its advantages. "Commercially," he wrote, "no doubt we should gain by having the whole American continent occupied by an active enterprising race like the Anglo-Saxons instead of sleepy Spaniards."[21] In 1860 Britain ceded the Bay Islands to Honduras, withdrew from the Mosquito Coast, and granted Greytown status as a free port. Meanwhile, the domestic crisis in the United States thwarted the Democrats' schemes of territorial conquest in the region. Thanks to internal divisions over slavery, the expansionist Democratic administrations of the 1850s acquired only a sliver of territory in what is now southern Arizona and New Mexico (the so-called Gadsden Purchase of 1853, named after the U.S. minister to Mexico, James Gadsden). By 1860, the two English-speaking nations reached a tentative, if temporary, truce in Central America.

Unlike the Clayton-Bulwer pact of 1850, this de facto Anglo-American accord was not premised on equality. There was no hiding the fact that the United States' reach in Central America already eclipsed that of Britain, even if it did not seize territory as it had in the previous decade. The case of Panama reveals the new ways in which the United States exerted influence in Central America. The annexation of California rapidly brought this isthmian province of Colombia into the orbit of the United States. For American migrants seeking to make their fortune in the gold mines of California, it was quicker to reach their destination via the Panamanian isthmus than by traversing the rugged trails across the American West. Indeed, it appears that more migrants from New York in the 1850s reached California through Panama than by making the covered wagon journey of American folklore. The Panamanian leg of the trip became even easier in 1855 with the opening of the American-owned Panama Railroad, the world's first transcontinental railway. The railroad's Caribbean terminus of Colón (or Aspinwall, as Americans called it in honor of the financier behind the railroad, William Aspinwall) became an American enclave that portended those established in the Caribbean by the United Fruit Company and other American business interests in the early twentieth century.

The presence of American migrants and commercial interests soon left its mark on Panama. The opening of the railroad exacerbated social and political tensions by putting out of business the local boatmen and muleteers who previously had operated the isthmian passage. Tensions reached a boiling point in 1856 when a minor dispute between an American and a local watermelon seller triggered a riot that left seventeen dead. Incidents such as the "watermelon war" led American officials to use the powers granted to them in the 1846 Bidlack-Mallarino Treaty (with Colombia) to intervene to restore order in the isthmian passageway. Though the interventions were aimed at upholding Colombian sovereignty in Panama, they revealed the increased power of the United States in the region. Between 1856 and 1903, the United States would intervene in Panama no less than thirteen times.[22]

The United States' policy toward Mexico in the late 1850s also hinted at a transition from the land-grabbing policies of earlier times to the neocolonialism of the late nineteenth century. Though many Democrats continued to call for the outright conquest of Mexican territory, domestic political opposition precluded such a move. But the goals of limiting European influence in Mexico, as well as promoting American interests there, remained. The Buchanan administration (1857–61) reluctantly considered other policies to achieve these objectives. The result was the McLane-Ocampo Treaty of 1859, in which the United States received transit rights across Mexico's Tehuantepec Isthmus, as well as favorable tariff and trading concessions, for the bargain price of $4 million. The treaty included a further provision that allowed the American military to intervene within Mexican territory to secure the isthmian passageway. The Mexican government of Benito Juárez accepted the treaty on the grounds that it would avoid outright American conquest and might spur economic growth at home.[23]

The McLane-Ocampo Treaty aimed to make Mexico and its isthmian passageway a protectorate of the United States. Though it was the brainchild of a Democratic administration, many Republicans initially welcomed the agreement on the neocolonialist grounds that it conferred "all the advantages of ownership of the soil without the burdens of governing," as the *Chicago Press and*

Tribune put it. The Senate, however, soon rejected the treaty, with not one Republican voting in favor. This change of heart was motivated partly by concerns that the provisions of the agreement might commit the United States to free trade and partly by fears held among Northerners that Southern expansionists were behind the agreement. In 1860 the McLane-Ocampo Treaty was dropped, but not forgotten—even among the Northern Republicans who voted against it.[24]

The increased power and assertiveness of the United States did not yet lead to a revival of the idea of a hemispheric conference or political association. Unlike the enthusiasts of economic expansion in the early and late nineteenth century, the Democrats of the 1850s saw no need to improve diplomatic relations with the republics of Latin America. Like Polk before him, James Buchanan had opposed the Panama Congress back in 1825–26. Rather than engage with the Peruvians (who took the lead on hemispheric collaboration in this period), the Buchanan administration recalled its minister in Lima over a claims dispute. Buchanan had no interest in bridging the widening divide between Latin and Anglo Americans. His 1858 annual message urged Congress to authorize special powers to the President to militarily intervene in Central America and Mexico in order to protect isthmian passageways. The message also contained a litany of complaints against Latin American nations. Buchanan criticized Nicaragua, Mexico, New Granada, Brazil, and Costa Rica for failing to repay claims owed to U.S. citizens. He also threatened Paraguay with gunboat diplomacy—a threat that did not prove hollow when a naval expedition arrived in Asunción the following month to demand an apology for an incident back in 1855.

Not surprisingly, Latin Americans increasingly viewed the United States as a menace and threat. The term "Latin America," which first came into use in Spanish in the 1850s (and would soon be picked up by English speakers), differentiated the peoples of the American hemisphere. When the 1856 Congress of Santiago convened, Latin American representatives sought not to engage with the United States, but to join together to guard against future aggressions from their northern neighbor, such as those perpetrated in Nicaragua by the filibuster William Walker. To those in the United States who had dreamed of establishing a hemispheric American system back in the 1820s, this was a sad state of affairs indeed. "We have lost the confidence of the South American republics," Bell of Tennessee stated, "and it may be doubted, whether, at this day if there should be a war between the United States and Great Britain, the sympathies of most of these republics would not be with Great Britain."[25]

The Dual Crises of the 1860s

The American Civil War was not the only civil war in North America in the mid-nineteenth century. While Americans killed one another, so, too, did Mexicans in a series of conflicts waged in the 1850s and '60s. The issue at stake in Mexico was not slavery (which had been abolished back in 1829), but how best to bring order and stability to a nation that had verged on collapse for much of its brief existence. Liberals, led by Benito Juárez, sought to wrest power from the Catholic Church and the military, as well as initiate liberal political and economic reforms known as La Reforma. Conservatives looked to the very institutions that liberals opposed to bring order to their crumbling nation: the Church, the military, and a strong central government modeled after the monarchies of the Old World.

The policies pursued by the European powers are a major difference between the two civil wars. Americans settled their differences without outside intervention; Mexicans did not. This was not because the American Civil War lacked an international dimension. Indeed, Southern secession itself reflected the potential power of new international political and economic arrangements. Despite their suspicion of antislavery Britain, the slaveholders of the Deep South concluded that their interests would best be advanced through an independent confederation allied not to the Northern states, but to their largest consumer of cotton, the British. Throughout the conflict, Confederate emissaries sought the support of Britain, as well as governments in Europe.

That Confederate leaders rejected the old logic of union and independence testifies both to their perception that slavery would be endangered in a union increasingly under the control of Northern Republicans and to their certitude that cotton could serve as the foundation for a new set of beneficial political and economic arrangements with the British. In order to secure the independence of their slaveholding republic, Confederate statesmen repudiated American diplomatic traditions: they called for British intervention in North America, they embraced "entangling alliances" with Old World powers, and they attempted to exploit the "balance of power" that their Southern forebears had long denounced. Southerners such as George Bagby even argued that after secession, "the Monroe doctrine is very dead for all time to come," a development that would play into the hands of the upstart Confederacy. "We of the South strengthen ourselves by multiplying rival nations, and thus preventing the undue preponderance of any one of them," the proslavery spokesman George Fitzhugh wrote in an 1861 article arguing that a French reconquest of Haiti would advance Confederate interests. The contrast with the geopolitical thinking of Southerners earlier in the century, who called for the elimination of all Old World powers within the union's neighborhood, could not have been starker.[26]

Confederate diplomats employed a variety of arguments to procure British and European assistance: they argued that secession was an act of self-determination, a principle that had much traction in liberal quarters of Europe; they dangled the possibility of a free-trade agreement with any government that would extend recognition; they dramatized and exaggerated Northern aggression; they downplayed slavery and instead drew attention to the racial superiority of white peoples the world over. Most of all, Confederates appealed to the economic self-interest of the British and French, whose large textile industries relied upon their cotton. Confederates initiated an unofficial cotton embargo to prompt the British to act in favor of their independence movement. "King Cotton" diplomacy, as it became known, failed to secure foreign support for the Confederacy. The economic blackmail of the cotton embargo antagonized British statesmen. Southerners also miscalculated the power of cotton, which was counterbalanced both by antislavery sentiment and by British commercial and investment interests in the Northern states. Though the division and weakening of the increasingly powerful United States appealed to British statesmen, few in London were eager to endorse independence movements with discontent running high in their own colonial possessions of Ireland and India.[27]

Union diplomacy also deterred Old World governments from extending support to the Confederacy. The Lincoln administration never invoked the Monroe Doctrine in its dealings with the British or French. It nonetheless made clear that any move in favor of the Confederacy would be interpreted as an act hostile to the United States. Seward, who was now Lincoln's secretary of state, exploited his reputation across the Atlantic as a wild Anglophobe, convincing the British that he might be crazy enough to wage a destructive Anglo-American war that would be far costlier to Britain than temporarily living without Southern cotton. The Secretary of State repeatedly informed the British that recognition of the independence of the Confederacy would be tantamount to a declaration of war. No British statesman wanted a costly war with the United States, which would be unpopular at home and might well result in the loss of Canada. Even a friendly offer of mediation, Seward asserted, would be interpreted as a hostile act, for it would make real the traditional fear of American statesmen: the wedding of the Union's internal and external enemies. "The conditions of society here, the character of our government, the exigencies of the country," Seward informed the British, "forbid that any dispute arising among us should ever be referred to foreign arbitration." Congress reinforced this idea with its Monrovian "Resolutions Against Foreign Mediation" passed in March 1863. The British prime minister, Palmerston, got the message. "We are adopting your Monroe Doctrine in our non-intervention," he told a Confederate envoy in 1862.[28]

The Lincoln administration complemented this hard-line approach with timely diplomatic compromises. Lincoln toned down some of Seward's more bellicose dispatches to London, thus avoiding unnecessary provocation of the British. When war loomed during the 1861 *Trent* crisis, the result of a Union naval commander's illegal seizure on the high seas of a British steamer that carried Confederate diplomats en route to Europe, Lincoln tactfully bowed to British demands. The Union's flexible and pragmatic diplomacy helped to prevent the Civil War from becoming an international conflict.

Matters were much different in Mexico, where European governments concluded that the economic and strategic rationale for intervention outweighed the potential costs. When the beleaguered Juárez government suspended payment on its foreign loans in 1861, it quickly found warships from Britain, Spain, and France demanding payment at its main port of Veracruz. The British and Spanish soon left; the French remained with the intent of establishing a puppet monarchy on the ashes of the Mexican republic. French emperor Napoleon III hoped that this action would pave the way to an expansive French New World empire that would tilt the European balance of power in his favor. Just as Robert E. Lee's army invaded the North in the run-up to the battle of Gettysburg in the summer of 1863, French forces entered Mexico City. Allied with local conservatives, Napoleon installed the Austrian archduke Maximilian on the newly created throne of Mexico in early 1864. This move intensified liberal opposition, fueling a bloody war of resistance (the Mexican holiday of Cinco de Mayo celebrates an early victory in this struggle against the French).

The French intervention in Mexico constituted an ideological and geopolitical challenge to the United States and its Monroe Doctrine. After decades of shadowboxing, American statesmen actually confronted what they long had feared: a European power invading a New World republic and bringing with it a puppet monarch. To be sure, the monarchical French intervention posed an ideological threat to the republican vision of the United States, as Americans pointed out with great frequency at the time. Yet it was the geopolitical dimension of the affair that gave it such importance. American statesmen long had considered Mexico vital to national security. It was a nation whose political system, as well as its territorial borders and economic practices, the United States itself sought to direct. From Joel Poinsett's meddling in the factional politics of the 1820s to the support extended to Juárez's liberal government in the 1850s and '60s, the United States—in ways not entirely unlike the French—cultivated relations with political groupings within Mexico that were responsive to its objectives. The year 1863 was not the only time in the mid-nineteenth century that foreign troops occupied Mexico City.

Many Northerners viewed the French intervention in Mexico and the secession of the slaveholding states of the South as interrelated. "The French invasion of Mexico," the Union general Phil Sheridan asserted, "was so closely related to the Rebellion as to be essentially part of it."[29] Many feared that the French intervention in Mexico portended a similar move in the American Civil War. After all, Confederate diplomats cheered Napoleon on in the hope that it would strengthen their quest for French recognition. Ulysses S. Grant viewed the French intervention in Mexico as nothing short of "a direct act of war against the United States."[30] Republicans used the common language of conspiracy to describe both occurrences: they attributed secession to a corrupt "slave power" and understood the intervention in Mexico as an extension of the "papal power" of Catholic France and the "money power" of European banking houses. Republicans argued that secession and the French intervention similarly aimed to undermine republican government by negating the truths of the Declaration of Independence. So, too, were Republicans aware that the Europeans violated the Monroe Doctrine only after the United States was preoccupied with an internal rebellion. "The final success of the whole programme," one Republican wrote of this alleged conspiracy against the Monroe Doctrine, "hinges upon the result of the first step, the breaking up of the American Union."[31]

These twin threats to the American union led Republican statesmen to consider new measures to achieve their goals. The breakthrough in this regard was the war against the Confederacy: with the federal government breaking the taboo of intervening (in this case, by force) in the states of its own union, why should it not actively respond to the similar threat posed by the French intervention in Mexico? This consideration of intervention in a foreign state was quite a development, considering the roots many Republicans had in the Whig Party. Yet many Republicans concluded that security interests demanded interventionist policies abroad as well as at home. As early as the spring of 1861, Seward predicted that the United States might have no choice but to adopt a "policy of protection and intervention" in Mexico. Francis Lieber, one of the leading Republican experts on international law, concluded that he could "not see but that we might be forced under certain circumstances to interfere in the Mexican chronic revolutionary disease." Lieber argued that "self-preservation" justified intervention, citing the actions of British foreign secretary Canning as precedent. Rather than promote nonintervention as a binding and immutable principle of international law, Americans now looked to the interventionist tactics of the hated Canning as a model.[32]

At the insistence of the British, the three European powers that intervened in Mexico in 1861 invited the United States, which also had outstanding claims in Mexico, to participate in the venture. On first glance, this would appear to be exactly the kind of action the Monroe Doctrine sought to avoid. It appears, however, that the Lincoln administration closely considered the proposal. In contrast to later interpretations of the Doctrine, the Lincoln cabinet acknowledged that foreign powers had a right to intervene in order to collect payment from a defaulting government in the New World. Nor did the administration object to the European proposal on anti-interventionist grounds. Led by Secretary of State Seward, the United States rejected the European offer to participate in a joint debt-collection action in Mexico, not because it violated Mexican sovereignty or the principle of nonintervention, but because American interests would best be served through unilateral action.[33]

The U.S. minister to Mexico, Thomas Corwin, cooked up an alternative to the European proposal. Corwin is an interesting figure who reveals much about the evolution of the Monroe Doctrine during the Civil War era. As a Whig senator from Ohio back in the 1840s, Corwin had denounced Polk's war against Mexico as unjust. Yet this did not mean that he would rule out active policies in the future. Corwin hoped to right the wrongs of the Polk years by strengthening republican government and economic liberalism in Mexico. To achieve these objectives, he believed that the United States needed to proactively direct Mexican development. "The United States are the only safe guardians of the independence and true civilization of this Continent," he wrote. "Let it be remembered that Mexico is our neighbour," Corwin informed Seward, "and enlightened self-interest requires that we should not be indifferent to the welfare of such."[34]

Corwin proposed the novel move of direct financial aid from the U.S. government to the Juárez regime in Mexico. A government loan of $11 million, Corwin argued, would achieve all of the United States' objectives. It would assist the Juárez government in its struggles against the enemies of republican government. Mexico could use the funds to repay foreign creditors, thus eliminating the pretext for European intervention. Or, to put it another way, the United States could pay European powers to respect the Monroe Doctrine. Furthermore, the proposed loan would promote American economic interests in Mexico. It would kick-start exports to Mexico, which still lagged behind those of Britain (Corwin calculated that the British controlled three-quarters of Mexico's trade). Corwin also drove a hard bargain in securing mineral-rich national lands and properties of the Catholic Church as collateral. The U.S. minister went further, hoping that his loan treaty would lay the foundations for future commercial agreements as well as transit concessions to American railroad developers. In short, Corwin sought to save Mexico by making it a satellite of the United States. As one American advocate of the Corwin-Doblado Treaty put it, "it will give a virtual control and protectorate over that country; and which control in its results will enable us to monopolize its commerce and prevent all invasion of its soil by any foreign power." Prime Minister Palmerston feared the worst, predicting that "a mortgage of Mexico to the United States . . . would certainly lead to foreclosing."[35]

The Corwin-Doblado Treaty represented a new conception of the Monroe Doctrine even as it synthesized the policies of the past. Its integration of political and economic objectives can be traced back to John Quincy Adams's diplomacy back in the 1820s. It also had much in common with the McLane-Ocampo Treaty. But it went further than previous policies in pledging federal funds to a foreign government, in its demands for collateral, and in its implicit long-term commitment to the internal affairs of another nation. By directly involving the U.S. government in this transaction, Corwin's scheme actually went further than many "dollar diplomacy" schemes of the early twentieth century. In Corwin's estimation, the threat posed by European intervention, as well as the possible economic benefits of the treaty, necessitated such departures. The treaty, however, met with ambivalence in Washington. Lincoln, it appears, shared the view of many in the Senate that the tenuous state of the North's already overstretched finances, as well as the possibility that the treaty would provoke the French into aggressive countermoves in Mexico, made it a risky proposition. The Senate never ratified the treaty. Interestingly, however, there was little outcry in the United States against the treaty on the grounds that it was interventionist or that it entangled the nation in the internal affairs of its neighbor. Republicans distanced themselves from the treaty in practice, not in principle.

That the Corwin-Doblado Treaty met with rejection in the United States rather than in Mexico reflects, in part, the plight of Mexican liberals in the 1860s. Besieged by domestic and foreign opponents, the Juárez government had little choice but to accept Corwin's terms. Yet many Mexican liberals welcomed an agreement that appears to the modern-day observer as legitimating economic imperialism. By promoting economic links with the United States, the treaty offered Mexican liberals an opportunity both to counter French power and to achieve the economic goals of La Reforma. The Mexican minister to the United States, Matías Romero, supported the treaty on these grounds. "Liberals propose to imitate the United States," he informed Abraham Lincoln in 1861, "in order to arrive by the same path of the important goal of fabulous prosperity and wealth which this country had already received."[36] To achieve that prosperity and wealth, Romero planned to use the capital and knowledge of the United States in much the same way that Americans had exploited the wherewithal of the British in the early nineteenth century.

Romero worked tirelessly to achieve these ends while in Washington. His enterprise and networking skills made up for his youth and inexperience (remarkably, Romero was only twenty-four years old when he arrived in Washington in 1861). He befriended figures from across the American political spectrum; he lobbied for support in the struggle against foreign monarchy; he provided intelligence to the State Department. Romero rightly recognized that American foreign policy had entered a period of transition. He hoped to seize the moment not only to achieve the short-term objective of obtaining American support in the struggle against the French, but also the long-term goal of harmonizing U.S.-Mexican relations. Romero argued that economic concessions to the United States would undermine the expansionist designs of the English-speaking republic. "The best means of impeding annexation," he wrote, "is to open the country to the United States, conceeding [*sic*] them all reasonable privileges, with the objective of making annexation unnecessary and even undesirable." Romero hoped that the United States would embrace a new Monroe Doctrine, in which "a powerful nation would declare its respect for foreign territory and for the rights of the weak."[37]

Romero was not the only Latin American statesman who made the case for closer relations with the United States in this period. Liberals in South American nations who prioritized economic development and political reform also turned to their northern neighbor for inspiration. No statesman embodied this spirit more than Argentina's Domingo Faustino Sarmiento. When a young Sarmiento read Benjamin Franklin's *Autobiography*, he "felt as though I were Franklin: and why not? I was very poor as he, studious as he." Just as Franklin's story of self-improvement provided a personal model for Sarmiento, so, too, did the United States' dramatic economic development provide a national example for Argentina. While serving as minister to the United States in the 1860s, Sarmiento founded the periodical *Ambas Américas* (*Both Americas*) to promote hemispheric links and wrote a biography of Lincoln in Spanish to spread the political and economic vision of this liberal statesman. Like liberals in Mexico, Sarmiento sought to emulate the example of the United States, not to place his nation in a subordinate neocolonial relationship. But he welcomed American conquest of South America in one regard: the spread of knowledge, technology, and innovation. "This is the only conquest worthy of a free people," he told an audience in Rhode Island in 1865; "this is the 'Monroe Doctrine' in practice."[38]

Sarmiento's embrace of the United States went further than that of most in Latin America. Many remained suspicious of the expansionist, English-speaking republic and continued to look to the Old World for inspiration, particularly those on the conservative end of the spectrum such as monarchists in Brazil. Nor was the cosmopolitanism of Sarmiento limited to the Western Hemisphere; he also hoped to cultivate relations with Europe. Nonetheless, the idea of hemispheric solidarity witnessed a revival in Latin America in the 1860s. In part, this testified to the increased traction of liberalism. Sarmiento's emphasis on economic development and political reform—much like La Reforma in Mexico—had appeal in a Latin America that entered a period of rapid change. Moreover, the American Civil War improved the Latin American image of the United States by removing from the picture the slaveholding expansionists who had been the architects of the land-grabbing foreign policies of the preceding decades. Costa Rican foreign minister Francisco Iglesias viewed Northern Republicans as "moderate, just and honest men" who might well give Latin Americans what they had long sought: a pledge not to annex further territories in the Western Hemisphere.[39] The security interests of states of the Western Hemisphere also converged in the 1860s. Many American nations confronted European intervention: the French invaded Mexico; the British and French contemplated intervention in the U.S. Civil War; Spain reasserted its claims on Santo Domingo and seized the guano-rich Chinchas Islands off Peru.

Plans for a renewal of an American system or congress, however, found little support in the United States. In 1862 the Lincoln administration rebuffed a proposal from a group of Latin American ministers in Washington to attend a hemispheric congress on the grounds that it might antagonize the powers of Europe. This rejection came despite the inclusion in the Latin American offer of a joint pledge not to recognize the Confederacy. Consequently, when invitations were sent out for the 1864 Congress of Lima, the United States was no longer on the guest list. Though Lincoln's worldview is notable for the absence of racialized thinking, the same cannot be said of that of others in his cabinet. "Torn by factions, down-trodden by a scheming and designing priesthood, ignorant and vicious," Secretary of the Navy Gideon Welles recorded in his diary, "the Mexicans are incapable of good government, and unable to enjoy rational freedom."[40]

The lack of support from the Lincoln administration disillusioned even the stalwart pro-American Romero, who supported the radical Republican John C. Frémont in the election of 1864. Remarkably, neither Lincoln nor Seward used the phrase "Monroe Doctrine" in public between 1861 and 1865. The avoidance of this loaded term fit with the administration's policy of consistent, yet cautious and nonconfrontational, opposition to the French intervention. Lincoln and Seward recognized that explicit invocation of the Monroe Doctrine might further provoke the French, a lesson learned from Buchanan's ill-fated invocations of the Doctrine during the isthmian diplomacy of the 1850s. The Lincoln administration saw no benefit in rattling the saber at the French when it already had its hands full in dealing with the rebellion at home. It was a striking contrast to Romero, who spoke of the Monroe Doctrine every chance he could in his campaign to garner support for the Juárez government in the United States.

Despite the Lincoln administration's refusal to invoke the Monroe Doctrine, it followed the course charted back in 1823 in a crucial regard: the co-option of British power. To be sure, tensions ran high in Anglo-American relations over possible British intervention in the Civil War. Yet this should not obscure a countervailing trend of the period. Similar to the Monroe administration in the 1820s, the Lincoln team sought to harness British power on behalf of their goals. Seward dropped not so subtle hints in diplomatic dispatches to London that the United States would appreciate British support in pressing the French to withdraw from Mexico. If Seward was disappointed that the Palmerston government did not promote the American position, he could take comfort in the fact that Britain withdrew from the Mexican venture and left the French to sink or swim on their own. Mexican policy was not the only occasion when the Lincoln administration sought to cooperate with the British. In 1862 the two English-speaking powers negotiated a treaty that pledged joint action against the international slave trade. Lincoln also hoped that free blacks in the United States might emigrate to British Honduras and Guiana. The Lincoln administration even sought to work with Britain in Central America. When political unrest threatened to destabilize the isthmian passageway in Panama in 1862, Seward invited Britain and France to join the United States in restoring order as allowed in the 1846 Bidlack-Mallarino Treaty (the British and French declined the offer).[41]

In part, these policies simply reflected the overstretch of the United States. With the resources of the Union being consumed on Civil War battlefields, it is not surprising that the Lincoln administration sought British assistance in its foreign policy. But these policies also reflected the willingness of Republicans to work alongside Old World powers, particularly Britain. When

Republicans looked across the Atlantic in the 1860s, they saw much that they liked. They identified racially with Europeans, particularly their fellow "Anglo-Saxons" of England. Political reforms such as the British Reform Act of 1867 convinced them that the old system in Europe was giving way to the political model of the United States. Even if the British retained their Queen, Francis Lieber argued, "there is far more liberty in monarchical England than in Republican South America." In terms of economics, the importance of the markets and capital of the Old World far exceeded the largely undeveloped economic connections between the United States and Latin America. The transatlantic telegraph of 1866 exemplified these links. News that previously took weeks to cross the Atlantic now did so in minutes, integrating the financial markets of New York and London as never before. Few such telegraphic links existed between the United States and Latin America until the 1880s. In short, despite the diplomatic complications arising from the civil wars of the period, the United States found itself more closely connected to the Old World, particularly its former colonial master. "We are one of the civilized nations," Lieber asserted in 1864, grouping the United States not with Latin American states but with the powers of Europe.[42]

These racial, political, and economic developments prompted many Americans to reconsider their international position and role. Even as they proclaimed their ideological affinity with the republics of the New World, American statesmen concluded that persistent instability in Mexico necessitated newly assertive policies. Though the United States did not intervene outright in Mexico in the 1860s, this was more a result of the constraints of the Civil War than a commitment to the principles of anti-imperialism and nonintervention. For all of the talk in Washington about resisting European colonialism and monarchy, American statesmen thought more and more like their counterparts in the Old World, particularly in Britain. "England and the

United States are natural allies," Grant wrote. "We together, or even either separately, are better qualified than any other people to establish commerce between all the nationalities of the world."[43] The dual crises of the French intervention in Mexico and the American Civil War demonstrated that the United States was not insulated from international rivalry. Cassius Clay, the U.S. minister to Russia, concluded that it was "useless to deceive ourselves with the idea that we can isolate ourselves from European interventions. We became in spite of ourselves—the Monroe Doctrine—Washington's farewell—and all that—a part of the 'balance of power.' "[44]

The Political Scramble

The more the United States acted like the imperial powers of the Old World, the more Americans spoke of anticolonialism and opposition to monarchy. The French intervention in Mexico largely accounts for this paradox, as it allowed Americans to understand their own increasingly active and interventionist policies as a continuation of anticolonial traditions. Indeed, it was the Monroe Doctrine's association with an imagined and mythic past of unalloyed anticolonialism that helps to explain its persistent appeal. Back in 1823, the Monroe cabinet feared that a European puppet monarchy in Spanish America would deepen political divisions at home. In the 1860s, however, this scenario triggered a scramble in which politicians from both parties raced to prove their fidelity to a popular and nationalistic Monroe Doctrine.

Just as Stephen Douglas had tried to use the Doctrine to paper over the sectional divide in the 1850s, so, too, did politicians from both sections invoke its principles as an instrument of reunion during the Civil War. Seward was the first to do so when he urged Lincoln in a confidential memo in April 1861 to "convene Congress and declare war" on Spain and France for their activities in the New World. Seward was convinced that such a move would "change the question before the public from one upon slavery . . . for a question upon union or disunion." Lincoln disagreed and tactfully rejected the advice.[45] Though Seward would pursue a more conciliatory diplomatic strategy in the future, other statesmen revived this use of the Monroe Doctrine during the Civil War. In the Confederate Congress, the Virginian D. C. DeJarnett hoped that Northerners could be coaxed into recognizing the independence of the South in exchange for Confederate support in kicking the French out of Mexico. The Monroe Doctrine also entered into the attempts to negotiate a peace between North and South. Most notable was the 1864–65 plan of Francis Preston Blair, an old Jacksonian Democrat whose son served in Lincoln's cabinet. Blair's scheme for reunification involved installing Jefferson Davis as the dictator of Mexico, a move that he hoped would pave the way for the annexation of Mexico to a newly restored union. Lincoln rejected the bizarre plan. Attempts to use the Monroe Doctrine as an instrument of reunification met with no more success during the Civil War than they had in the 1850s.

The Doctrine proved to be a more useful tool in the partisan politics of the Northern home front. Opposition to the Lincoln administration's conduct of the Civil War left critics open to charges of disloyalty, a dilemma that plagued Democrats throughout the war.[46] Patriotically challenging the administration's foreign policy, however, sidestepped this problem. With Seward and Lincoln careful to not use the phrase "Monroe Doctrine," they left themselves exposed to charges of weakness on national security. Indeed, during the 1860s, the words "Seward" and "Monroe Doctrine" were antonyms: to uphold the principles of 1823 meant to oppose the Secretary of State.

Both Democrats and radical Republicans used the Monroe Doctrine to attack the Lincoln administration. Led by the boisterous (and often intoxicated) California senator James

McDougall, Democrats attempted to introduce resolutions in the Senate calling for the strict enforcement of the Monroe Doctrine as early as 1863. Not to be outdone, the radical Republican from Maryland, Henry Winter Davis, drafted a similar resolution that condemned the French intervention. Davis, who also led the charge from the radical wing of the party against Lincoln's moderate reconstruction policy, had long denounced European monarchy. Back in 1852, he wrote a book that celebrated Monroe's 1823 message and predicted (with great accuracy, as it turned out) that Russia and the United States would wage a protracted ideological struggle in the future. In 1864, however, Davis's mind was preoccupied with more immediate objectives: to send a strong message to the French and to embarrass the Lincoln administration. Davis got his wish in April 1864 when the House unanimously passed his resolution, the first time Congress approved a resolution modeled after the 1823 message.[47]

The Monroe Doctrine also entered into the 1864 presidential contest. Lincoln's opponents—George McClellan, the Democrats' nominee, as well as intraparty rivals John C. Frémont and Salmon P. Chase—sought to claim the patriotic ground by stumping on the Doctrine. The case of Chase is revealing. As Secretary of the Treasury, Chase was involved in the cabinet discussions that formulated policy in response to the French intervention. In private correspondence he acknowledged the soundness of the administration's Mexican policy. Publicly, however, he sat idly by while his partisans attacked Lincoln and Seward for their alleged disregard of the Monroe Doctrine.[48]

All of this politicking fueled an unprecedented public discussion regarding the Monroe Doctrine. Though the phrase had gained popularity in the preceding decade, it became a nationalist symbol, a permanent feature of the political and diplomatic landscape, during the Civil War. Searchable collections of digitized nineteenth-century newspapers reveal that "Monroe Doctrine" appears twice as often in the 1860s as it does in the 1850s and 1870s. The Monroe Doctrine even entered into the complex and shifting politics at the state level, particularly in Louisiana during wartime reconstruction, where a group called Defenders of the Monroe Doctrine emerged, in part to ship arms to Mexican liberals, but also to challenge the pro-Lincoln elements in the state.[49]

It is a measure of the political adroitness of the Lincoln administration that it could blunt these criticisms without fundamentally altering its diplomatic strategy of nonconfrontational opposition to the French intervention. Seward published the diplomatic correspondence regarding Mexico at timely junctures to demonstrate to domestic critics that though the administration did not invoke the Monroe Doctrine, it was not acquiescent to French actions. Allies of the administration also played an instrumental role in countering criticisms. In the Senate, Charles Sumner proved an indispensable collaborator, using his power as chairman of the Foreign Relations Committee to silence debate on the Monroe Doctrine and prevent McDougall from taking the floor. Pro-Lincoln rallies during the 1864 campaign included testimonials to the administration's adherence to the Monroe Doctrine (even if the President himself continued to abstain from invoking it), and the vice-presidential nominee, Andrew Johnson of Tennessee, gave a widely reported speech that paid homage to Monroeism. The National Union Party platform of 1864 contained a carefully worded plank modeled after the Monroe Doctrine. Radical Republicans such as Henry Winter Davis had hoped for an across-the-board denunciation of monarchy in the Western Hemisphere. But administration loyalists succeeded in watering down the language of the resolution (including avoiding the phrase "Monroe Doctrine"), which Lincoln interpreted as an endorsement of his measured Mexico policy.[50]

After Lincoln's assassination in 1865, the onus of fending off demands for a more assertive Mexican policy fell to Seward. With the war at home now concluded, calls for demanding an immediate French withdrawal intensified. Ulysses S. Grant even urged President Johnson to invade Mexico and amassed U.S. troops on the border in preparation. The pressure to act was so great that one correspondent warned Seward that the Monroe Doctrine threatened the political position of the Republican Party: "The opposition party soon to be formed will take up the question of our governmental relations with Maximilian, and assume the assertion of the Monroe Doctrine as their great political principle; carrying it eloquently before the people, who undoubtedly have it warmly at heart; will they not gain a hold upon public favour not easily shaken off?"[51]

Seward limited the utility of the Monroe Doctrine to his political opponents. He tactfully co-opted their attacks, placating those demanding a more aggressive policy with symbolic gestures. Seward used stronger language in diplomatic dispatches to France and Austria (which contemplated intervention in Mexico to save native son Maximilian), though he continued to allow the French time for an orderly withdrawal; he reshuffled diplomatic appointments, appeasing his opponents through patronage without committing to follow their policy recommendations; he gave a prominent public speech predicting that "republican institutions, wherever they have been heretofore established throughout the American continents," would be "speedily vindicated, renewed and re-invigorated"; and he even began to talk of the Monroe Doctrine in meetings with congressional critics—though Secretary of the Navy Welles suspected that "Seward talks [of the Monroe Doctrine] but cares little about it."[52] Not only did Seward pacify his domestic critics, but he used their demands for the invasion of Mexico to his diplomatic advantage: if the French did not withdraw soon, he hinted that domestic pressure would give him no choice but to adopt more forceful tactics.[53] Seward's shrewd diplomacy soon paid off. The French conceded defeat to Mexican liberals early in 1867, leaving Maximilian to face his fate in front of a Mexican firing squad, before the political outcry for stronger action made Seward's position untenable. The domestic politicking over the Monroe Doctrine shaped how Americans came to understand their nation's role in international affairs. The jockeying between rival politicians and parties to become the most ardent defender of the principles of 1823 continued a process that began in the debates of the 1850s: American statesmen competed not only with other countries to establish hemispheric supremacy, but also with one another to win the confidence of voters that they could best achieve this objective. In their scramble to demonstrate their fidelity to the Monroe Doctrine, American politicians did not compete to become the most ardent allies of their sister republics in Latin America. They did not emphasize their ideological solidarity with their neighbors— a tactic that had blown up in the face of John Quincy Adams back in the 1820s. Rather, they competed to appear the strongest defender of national security and the most assertive promoter of national interests. They rationalized the need to uphold the Monroe Doctrine by emphasizing the alleged racial inferiorities of Latin Americans and their alleged subservience to the Catholic Church. Both racism and anti-Catholicism increasingly resonated with the voting public. "Scientific" racism reached its apogee in the second half of the nineteenth century, while anti-Catholicism, particularly after the increased immigration from Ireland in the 1840s and '50s, assumed an important role in the national identity espoused by the new Republican Party. Francis Lieber drew from both of these impulses when he interpreted the Mexican crisis as a case of "Catholic Latinism and absolutism . . . making a strong effort against Protestant Teutonic Freedom."[54]

It thus should come as little surprise that most Americans inflated their own role in ending the French intervention in Mexico. Never mind the blood and treasure expended by the Mexican resistance; never mind that the British and Spanish abandoned the intervention in Mexico; never mind the important role played by critics of Napoleon within France, who campaigned against the venture. Americans concluded that it was their Monroe Doctrine that prompted France's ignominious withdrawal from Mexico. In the coming decades, politicians would state this as truth, schoolbooks would teach it, and Americans would internalize it. "It was our use of the doctrine rather than internal problems in France or Mexico that ended Maximilian's adventure in the latter country," one late-nineteenth-century textbook stated.[55] As the newly restored United States entered the final decades of the nineteenth century, Americans convinced themselves that they had saved republicanism in Mexico and had forced a great European power to bow before the Monroe Doctrine.

All these themes can be found in the most important writing on the Doctrine of the era, Joshua Leavitt's 1863 pamphlet *The Monroe Doctrine*. Leavitt's pamphlet, which criticized the moderate foreign policy of the Lincoln administration, was on one level a political tract aimed at elevating the presidential hopes of fellow Ohioan Salmon Chase. Yet Leavitt also used the Monroe Doctrine to promote a new vision of the American nation and its role in international affairs. An evangelical who had authored one of the bestselling hymnals of the nineteenth century, Leavitt viewed the French intervention in Mexico as a papist plot to extend the control of the Catholic Church. He advocated a revival of the old Panama Congress of the 1820s to counter this scenario. But his idea of hemispheric solidarity was premised upon U.S. dominance, not the equality of the states of the New World. Leavitt's chief objective was the destruction of Catholicism in Latin America through the missionary activity of American evangelicals. With the United States purging slavery from its domain, Leavitt argued that the time was ripe to ensure that "the power of the Jesuits is broken in nearly every one of the Spanish American states." Ultimately, Leavitt aimed to "Americanize" not only Latin America, but also Europe.[56]

By the end of the Civil War, the Monroe Doctrine had

become a powerful nationalist symbol with appeal across the political spectrum. It also came to represent a newly active and assertive foreign policy. The line from the 1860s to the empire that the United States would establish in the coming decades was far from straightforward. But the Monroe Doctrine of the late nineteenth and early twentieth centuries owed more to the Civil War era than it did to the increasingly distant world of 1823.

5

Control

The Civil War transformed the United States. The old federal union of the early republic was forged into a new nation bound together by a powerful patriotic nationalism and governed by a stronger central state. The conflict reversed the nation's position on a central development of the nineteenth century: the abolition of slavery. The nation that had been the world's leading defender of slavery now joined Britain in the ranks of antislavery. This diminished the national political power of the former Southern slaveholding elite, as well as further isolating the remaining slave systems in the Western Hemisphere, the Spanish colonies of Cuba and Puerto Rico, and the independent and monarchical Brazil.

The Civil War ushered in fundamental changes in the American economy. The imperative of raising funds during the war transformed the nation's financial system. The Republican-led Congress instituted new taxes, raised tariffs, established a national currency, and organized the nation's largest banks. Just as important as these changes in political economy was the dramatic growth of the private sector. The war facilitated manufacturing and fostered financial independence from the Old World. Denied the funds from Europe that they had long relied upon, American financiers developed their own capital markets. The increase in financial transactions necessitated the construction of a new building on Wall Street in 1863, the New York Stock Exchange. Though the United States would continue to import capital from Britain in the late nineteenth century, the Civil War created a new class of American financiers and industrialists such as J. P. Morgan and Andrew Carnegie, who personified the nation's emerging economic power.

The removal of slavery from national politics and the development of the nation's economy accelerated the conquest of the American West. No longer paralyzed by the question of slavery in the territories, the Republican-dominated federal government lent support to private individuals and corporations that sought fortunes in the exploitation of the nation's vast Western territories. The nexus between individual citizens, a newly powerful central state, and an emergent Wall Street that had been instrumental in the Union's victory in the Civil War now turned its attention to the West. Legislation such as the Homestead Act and the Pacific Railroad Act (both passed in 1862), which encouraged westward migration and development, facilitated this process. Just as important was the federal government's policy toward Native Americans. Though they packaged their strategy as a "peace policy," the American effort to confine Native Americans to reservations relied upon military power.

One should keep the West in mind when approaching American foreign policy in the second half of the nineteenth century. Historians often ask why the United States did not establish a full-blown colonial empire until 1898. This question ignores the conquest of the West, the establishment of a colonial system to control Native Americans, and the colonization and economic exploitation of an extensive territory. Few Americans at the time, of course, viewed the "winning of the West" as an act of colonialism. Despite the need to structure and organize these vast areas, the United States never developed a European-style "colonial office," relying instead on an ad hoc administrative structure that combined military power, settler self-government, and powerful nonstate actors such as business and religious organizations. But if Americans continued to see themselves as different from the colonial powers of the Old World, their actions in the West drew them far closer to the practices of their old adversaries than they imagined. In time, American officials would recognize this, applying the lessons acquired from their dealings with Native Americans to their colonial projects in Cuba and the Philippines.[1]

In the decades immediately after the Civil War, the West consumed the resources and attention of the United States. But this did not mean that Americans were inward-looking or isolationist. Indeed, just the opposite. The decades after the Civil War witnessed the rise of a powerful cultural internationalism—a "global dawn," as the historian Frank Ninkovich recently put it[2]—in which Americans closely followed foreign affairs and increasingly viewed themselves as propagators of "civilization" from Europe to the wider world. This liberal internationalism drew from earlier traditions, particularly the Whiggery of the antebellum period. It also was the result of technological innovation, such as the laying of transnational telegraph lines, and of a sharp increase in the volume of international trade and investment. Such developments forged deep connections between the United States and the wider world in this early version of what we now call "globalization."[3]

The place of the Monroe Doctrine in this increasingly integrated world was much debated. With the slave power destroyed and a continental empire established, few viewed the Doctrine through the old prism of the combination of internal and external threats. There remained many Americans, however, who viewed the Doctrine in the traditional terms of an irreconcilable struggle between the Old World and the New World. These foreign policy conservatives came from both parties, though they were most often Democrats from the South and Midwest. They viewed the strict construction of the 1823 message as the best hope of recapturing an imagined past of isolationism, unilateralism, and unalloyed anticolonialism. The Monroe Doctrine, in this reading, was still necessary to insulate the United States from the dangerous machinations of the Old World.

To Americans of a more liberal stripe, however, the Monroe Doctrine needed to be updated to reflect the new internationalism of the era. The old division between the New World and the Old World, if it had ever existed, was now a dead letter thanks to the liberal reforms undertaken by many European governments, not to mention the connections that bound together nations around the globe. To the chagrin of traditional isolationists, internationalists increasingly emphasized the links between the United States and the "civilized" states of Europe, even taking foreign policy cues from the hated British. Americans of this ilk, the horrified *Southern Review* wrote, celebrated the opening of the transatlantic telegraph "as if it had been the outgrowth of the Monroe doctrine."[4] This wedding of the Monroe Doctrine with internationalism would reach its policy apogee in the statecraft of Hamilton Fish, the Secretary of State under President Ulysses S. Grant (1869–77). Fish fittingly operated from the new State Department building opened in 1875, the style of which mimicked the architecture of the French Second Empire.

In addition to the interpretations of liberal internationalists and conservative isolationists, a third broad reading of the Monroe Doctrine emerged in the postwar decades. Led by Republican secretary of state James Blaine, Americans of this stripe viewed the Doctrine as the symbol and instrument of an assertive and nationalist foreign policy. They sought to establish strategic and commercial control of the Western Hemisphere, which they increasingly referred to as "our hemisphere" or "our sphere of influence." The Monroe Doctrine, Iowa Republican John Kasson asserted in 1881, "is no longer for us a question of despotism extending its sphere of supremacy to America. It is a question now of commercial rivalry and commercial advantages."[5] These politicians invoked the Monroe Doctrine in support of active policies such as the annexation of islands in the Caribbean and Pacific, the unilateral construction of an isthmian canal in Central America, and the establishment of commercial supremacy in Latin America. Invocations of the dogma of 1823 presented these assertive measures as outgrowths of traditional anti-imperialism. The Doctrine also cloaked such policies in the guise of a distinctive American tradition, masking the influence of British imperialism on many of the foreign policies of the late nineteenth century.

The Monroe Doctrine thus remained a contested symbol that competing political groups used to promote divergent policies. If Americans increasingly agreed that they should call the shots in "their" hemisphere, they continued to part ways on how best to so do. By the 1890s, proponents of active, nationalist policies had gained ascendency. But this came only after a haphazard period of foreign policy disagreement and experimentation.

The Age of Gladstone

President Ulysses S. Grant's call to annex the Dominican Republic in 1870 made clear that the Monroe Doctrine would continue to provoke disagreement among Americans after the Civil War. Grant desired this strategically placed island in the Caribbean in order to guard the eastern approaches to a future isthmian canal, and he also held out hope that newly emancipated African Americans might choose to relocate there. His private secretary, Orville Babcock, negotiated a treaty of annexation with Dominican president Buenaventura Báez, who hoped that the move would secure his political position at home. Báez hastily arranged a plebiscite to demonstrate Dominican support for annexation, as well as to appeal to American sentiment by presenting it as an act of anticolonial self-determination.

An unusual group of bedfellows in the United States supported the scheme. The strategic rationale for the move found a receptive audience among naval officials and nationalist politicians such as the chair of the House Committee of Foreign Affairs, Nathaniel P. Banks. "I want to identify my name," Banks declared, "with the acquisition of the Gulf of Mexico as a Sea of the United States."[6] Grand strategy was not the only motivation for those in favor of the move. Many of the most vocal proponents of annexation, including Babcock himself, were landholders or investors in the Dominican Republic who stood to personally gain from the move. Others viewed annexation through the ideological lens of national mission. African American leaders such as Frederick Douglass and Mississippi senator Hiram Revels hoped that annexation would uplift the long-oppressed Dominicans. "It may, indeed, be important to know what Santo Domingo can do for us," Douglass asserted, "but it is vastly more important to know what we can do, and ought to do, for Santo Domingo."[7]

To critics of the administration, the whole venture reeked of imperialism and corruption. The annexation of territory in the Caribbean was too much for many Republicans, such as Charles Sumner, who had opposed similar moves back in the antebellum years. The Dominican plebiscite, which was marked by fraud and voter intimidation, did little to reassure skeptics. Nor was it lost on them that some annexationists sought personal advantage more than national interest. Many objected to the move on the racist grounds that Dominicans were unsuited for self-government and would contribute to the racial problems plaguing the postemancipation American South. The support given to annexation by black leaders might have undermined the project by highlighting the race issue.[8]

Sensing a lack of support for annexation at home, Grant

turned to the Monroe Doctrine. The Republican president took a page out of the playbook of antebellum expansionists. Like Polk before him, Grant trotted out the old formula of preemptive annexation: if the United States did not take the Dominican Republic, he warned, a European power would. The President exploited fears from the recent French incursion into Mexico, as well as Spain's ill-fated reannexation of the Dominican Republic in 1861. "The acquisition of San Domingo is an adherence to the 'Monroe doctrine,'" the President informed the Senate; "it is a measure of national protection."[9] By framing annexation as a reactive measure of national security, Grant hoped to mobilize anticolonial sentiment on behalf of an imperialist venture. But the Senate refused to take the bait, voting down the treaty in June 1870. Proponents of overseas expansion took note of this failed attempt to link the Monroe Doctrine with the annexation of island territories.

Secretary of State Hamilton Fish lost little sleep over the Senate's vote against Dominican annexation. A former conservative Whig from New York, Fish had never been an enthusiast of the Dominican project. He appears to have remained loyal to Grant during the episode in order to increase his influence within the administration on the foreign policy issues that were closer to his heart: improvement of relations with Britain and the avoidance of entanglement in a rebellion in Cuba. Though he did not get his way on Santo Domingo, Fish would shape the Monroe Doctrine more than any other American in the 1870s. A forgotten figure today, Fish was the longest-serving secretary of state in the nineteenth century (a fact he took great pride in pointing out in his diary). His foreign policy vision rested upon the pillars of rapprochement with Great Britain and "informal imperialism" in America's growing sphere of influence.

British liberals deeply influenced Fish's thinking. A cosmopolitan who thought that the ideological antagonism between the New World and the Old was a thing of the past, Fish believed that Gladstonian internationalism held the key to a new era in global politics. This approach to international affairs, associated with the British statesman William Gladstone, embraced open trade and international law. It sought to avoid costly and destructive wars through diplomatic engagement between the so-called civilized nations, such as Britian, the United States, and the powers of Europe. Prime Minister Gladstone also sought to replace the self-serving imperial rivalries of the past with international cooperation. Long an advocate of imperial devolution in Britain's settler colonies, such as Canada and New Zealand, Gladstone risked his political career by embracing the cause of home rule for Ireland. "The idea that the colonies add to the strength of the mother country," Gladstone asserted in words Fish held as gospel, "appears to me to be as dark a superstition as any that existed in the Middle Ages."[10] Gladstone, however, was not uniformly opposed to intervention or the use of force, particularly when disorder threatened British interests in regions of strategic importance. Such considerations led his ministry to intervene in Egypt in 1882 to secure the Suez Canal.

A longtime admirer of British liberalism, Fish formulated an American version of Gladstonian foreign policy. Rather than formally annex new territories, Fish advocated more cost-effective and ideologically attractive methods of projecting influence, such as establishing protectorates, acquiring new markets, and negotiating advantageous trade agreements. This "informal imperialism" would allow the United States to maximize economic and strategic benefits at minimal cost. Fish also aimed to bring the United States into the club of great European powers. Central to this objective was the improvement of relations with Britain, for which Fish laid the foundations in the 1871 Treaty of Washington. This agreement put to rest contentious issues arising from the Civil War. At the Geneva arbitration (established in the 1871 treaty), Britain agreed to compensate the United States for the damage inflicted by Confederate raiders that were built in British shipyards. Statesmen on both sides of the Atlantic heralded the agreement as an enlightened portent of a future in which "civilized" nations would avoid war through arbitration and diplomacy. "The treaty inaugurates a new era in the relations of the two governments," Fish boasted, "and possibly even beyond that in the mode of settlement of grave questions between great Powers." It also advanced the economic interests of the United States by spurring British investors to help refinance the nation's massive Civil War debt at a lower rate of interest.[11]

Fish's admiration of British liberalism did not preclude old-fashioned Anglo-American competition in Latin America, particularly when it came to the race for commercial supremacy. Fish was shocked when an 1870 State Department survey found that British exports to Latin America were more than double those of the United States. These statistics prompted Fish to reflect upon the history of the Monroe Doctrine in a circular drafted later that year.[12] Unlike many of his contemporaries, Fish did not blame the British for America's unfulfilled expectations in the hemisphere. After all, in taking advantage of the collapse of the Spanish Empire, the British only did what he himself sought to do. Rather, Fish pointed the finger at the United States itself. The problem had been the slave power, which had foiled the plans of John Quincy Adams and Henry Clay for hemispheric cooperation. "The necessity of that day of preserving the great interest of the Southern States in African slavery," Fish declared, "lost to the United States the opportunity of giving a permanent direction to the political and commercial connections of the newly enfranchised Spanish American states." But with the slave power now toppled, the time had come for the United States to "occupy of necessity a prominent position on this continent, which they neither can nor should abdicate, which entitles them to a leading voice, and which imposes upon them duties of right and of honor regarding American questions."

Fish premised his thinking on the assumption that Latin Americans were incapable of exercising responsible self-government. "The Spanish American colonies," he wrote, "had not the same preparation for independence that we had." With Latin American instability a given, Fish argued that the United States had to assume new responsibilities. But he disagreed with the policies of many of his predecessors. The Secretary of State explicitly repudiated interventionist applications of the Doctrine, noting that it was "not a policy of aggression . . . it does not contemplate forcible intervention in any legitimate contest." The United States, he privately informed the British minister, Edward Thornton, would "almost universally refuse to intervene" with force in Latin America.[13] In addition to bringing with it great financial and political costs, Fish argued, an interventionist foreign policy violated American traditions. The Secretary of State, however, also rejected isolation, going so far as to contend that a strict interpretation of Washington's Farewell Address would allow European powers to dictate international affairs.

Rather than engage in costly interventions or retreat into isolation, Fish argued that diplomatic and commercial engagement would best advance American interests. In the case of Hawaii, Fish negotiated a reciprocal trade agreement in 1875 that brought the strategically important islands into the economic and political orbit of the United States, but stopped short of formal annexation. The Secretary of State also used active diplomacy to advance American interests and to forestall European intervention in Latin America. Fish hoped to cultivate relations with Latin American liberals such as Sarmiento in Argentina and Aureliano Tavares-Bastos in Brazil. But he was not gun-shy when it came to asserting the interests of his nation. In the first of what would become many claims disputes with Venezuela, Fish bullied and threatened Venezuelan officials to meet their financial obligations, but he refused to intervene with force. When resolution to a war between Spain and several of her former colonies (Bolivia, Chile, Ecuador, and Peru) proved elusive, Fish invited the parties to the negotiating table in Washington, leading to an 1872 peace treaty. Nor, in Fish's estimation, did the Monroe Doctrine preclude the United States from diplomatically involving itself in European affairs. When war broke out between France and Prussia in the summer of 1870, Fish cabled Berlin and Paris with an offer of American mediation (a proposal that the Prussians quickly declined).

Fish's liberal internationalism shaped his diplomacy in what emerged as the two recurrent diplomatic issues in the decades following the Civil War: an isthmian canal in Central America and chronic instability in Cuba. In both cases, Fish persuaded a skeptical President Grant to follow his recommendations. In both cases, Fish prioritized cooperation with European powers over the interests of Latin Americans, whom he viewed with disdain. And in both cases, Fish's internationalist approach would only partially achieve his objectives.

In the years after the Civil War, the idea of establishing an isthmian canal under the exclusive control of the United States gained traction. Both William Seward and Ulysses S. Grant came to advocate this departure from the method of joint cooperation with the British as stipulated in the 1850 Clayton-Bulwer Treaty. They argued that unilateral control of a canal was essential to American naval and security interests. Continued instability in Panama, which necessitated brief U.S. interventions in 1865 and 1868, heightened fears that instability in Central America might provide the pretext for European intervention. The logistical triumphs of the Union effort during the Civil War, as well as the opening of the Suez Canal in 1869, imparted confidence that such a mammoth undertaking was now possible. "Now that the Suez canal has been opened for navigation," Secretary of the Navy George Robeson asserted in 1869, "we are doubly stimulated to such efforts as will lead to the success of our great enterprise."[14]

Fish, however, had little enthusiasm for unilateral action on the canal issue. He continued to advocate the old Clayton-Bulwer formula on the grounds that it drew the two English-speaking powers together, as well as paving the way for British financial support for the construction of the canal. When Grant's early efforts to proceed unilaterally yielded no result, Fish seized the initiative. In 1876 he persuaded the President to give him free rein to lay the diplomatic foundation for a privately constructed canal in Nicaragua (the then preferred route) under an international guarantee.

The way Fish went about achieving this objective reveals much about his diplomacy. He first discussed the matter with the British, with whom he planned to jointly construct and operate the canal under the terms of Clayton-Bulwer. Fish's draft treaty that laid out the principles of the future canal was a product of discussions he had with British minister Thornton, not negotiation with the Nicaraguan envoy, Adán Cárdenas. When Fish presented Cárdenas with the draft treaty, the Nicaraguan was shocked to find that its provisions violated his nation's sovereignty. Among other things, it gave the United States power to veto who would construct the canal, allowed foreign nations to build private docks with their own police forces on Nicaraguan territory, and set limits on Nicaraguan fiscal and immigration policies. Cárdenas objected, informing Fish that the draft treaty was "absolutely inadmissible, because restrictions are imposed upon Nicaragua . . . which cannot fail to affect her independence." Fish responded with great condescension. He lectured Cárdenas on why Americans and Europeans rather than Nicaraguans should control the canal and suggested that Nicaragua amend its constitution to comport with the draft treaty. When Cárdenas refused to accede to these demands, Fish dropped the canal scheme.[15]

Fish's canal diplomacy sought to achieve American objectives through cooperation with European powers, particularly the British. He cared little about the independence of Nicaraguans, who he believed required the oversight and tutelage of "civilized" powers. Fish responded similarly to the most important foreign policy issue of his tenure, the rebellion in Cuba known as the Ten Years' War (1868–78). Led by Carlos Manuel de Céspedes, Cubans rose up against their Spanish rulers in 1868. Though Céspedes was a member of the slaveholding elite, the rebellion quickly assumed a more radical form, with the rebels seeking the abolition of slavery, if not the construction of a new racial order. The protracted rebellion was a humanitarian disaster, marked by atrocities on both sides and an estimated death toll in excess of one hundred thousand.[16]

How to respond to this crisis became the central foreign policy issue of Grant's two-term presidency. Many argued that the instability in Cuba provided the pretext to finally annex the island that Jefferson and John Quincy Adams long ago had predicted would fall into American hands. As in the question of Dominican annexation, advocates of action in Cuba made the case in both material and ideological terms. Led by the Republican congressmen Nathaniel Banks and John Logan, proponents of an active Cuban policy blended traditional anticolonialism and Caribbean expansionism with the new antislavery mission of the United States. They reinterpreted the Monroe Doctrine as a call for intervention in the dispute to finally kick the Spanish out of the Western Hemisphere. Contingent events, such as Spain's heavy-handed seizure in 1873 of the *Virginius*, a ship flying the American flag, played into their hands. A headline in one newspaper declared ON TO CUBA! during a tense moment.[17] As in the Dominican episode, African American leaders also urged the Grant administration along. "The first gleam of the sword of freedom and independence in Cuba secured my sympathy with the revolutionary cause," declared Frederick Douglass.[18]

Fish opposed calls for an interventionist or annexationist foreign policy in Cuba. The Secretary of State recoiled at the prospect of annexing an island populated by what he viewed as racial inferiors. Cubans, he confided in his diary, "are of a different race and language, unaccustomed to our institutions or self government; we would not wish to incorporate them with us."[19] Fish also argued against action in Cuba on legal grounds, contending that the rebellion was an internal matter of the Spanish Empire and that the rebels did not yet merit belligerent status under international law. When Grant appeared to be on the verge of recognizing the belligerency of the Cuban rebels, Fish forestalled the move by threatening to resign from the cabinet.

The Secretary of State sought to avoid a costly intervention or occupation of Cuba, yet he still hoped to reap the strategic and economic benefits of controlling the island. Early in the rebellion, Fish formulated an alternative to annexation. He proposed that Spain grant Cuba both independence and emancipation in exchange for an indemnity payment guaranteed by the United States. Once freed from Spanish rule, Cuba would fall into the orbit of the United States as a result of its financial indebtedness to Washington and, as Fish hoped, the negotiation of a reciprocal trade agreement. It was an innovative and sophisticated approach for its time, portending the "dollar diplomacy" of the early twentieth century. But Spanish officials wanted none of it and rejected Fish's plan out of hand.[20]

The Cuban issue, however, refused to go away. Spain's iron-fisted response to the rebellion endangered American lives and property in Cuba, and the snail's pace of the abolition of slavery on the island caused further outrage in the United States (Spain did not fully abolish slavery in Cuba until 1886). When the Democrats assumed control of the House of Representatives after the midterm elections of 1874, Fish feared that the "blatant filibusters in a Democratic Congress" would embroil the United States in a conflict with Spain. With Congress threatening to act in Cuba, Fish restricted his goals. He jettisoned previous demands for full independence and abolition, calling upon the Spanish now only to restore stability to the island.[21]

To achieve this objective, the Secretary of State turned to the

British and Europeans for help. Fish invited six Old World powers to join the United States in demanding that Spain find a way to end the rebellion in Cuba and to restore stability to the island. "The time is at hand," Fish informed Britain, France, Russia, Germany, Austria, and Italy, "when it may be the duty of other Governments to intervene, solely with a view of bringing to an end a disastrous and destructive conflict, and of restoring peace in the island of Cuba."[22] Just as the British employed the "concert of Europe" to resolve problems in the Old World, Fish hoped to arrange a multilateral coalition to put an end to the intractable Cuban issue. It was a striking diplomatic approach for the United States to take in regard to an island that Americans had long hoped to control themselves. Fish's domestic opponents criticized the scheme, while observers across the Atlantic looked on with bemusement. "What has become of the Monroe Doctrine?" the London *Times* asked. "The right of the leading European Powers to interfere in the politics of the American Continent [has] been recognized, and in some sense invited, by the Department of State."[23]

Fish responded to his critics by launching a public relations campaign that presented the multilateral initiative as an outgrowth of the Monroe Doctrine. It was a sign of the Doctrine's newfound status that Fish found it necessary to justify his foreign policy in relation to the 1823 message. In an interview with *The World*, a sympathetic newspaper in New York City, Fish pointed as precedent to the diplomacy of John Quincy Adams and Henry Clay back in 1825 that similarly used multilateral means to maintain Spanish control of Cuba. Fish even ordered State Department clerks to compile a history of the Monroe Doctrine that emphasized the Cuban policy of Adams and Clay. To those critics who objected to his close relations with the British, Fish reminded them of Canning's flirtation with Rush, going so far as to attribute authorship of the 1823 message to the British statesman.[24]

The multilateral initiative of 1875 was a flop. Distracted by a crisis in the Balkans, European statesmen had little interest in lending a hand to the United States in the Caribbean. "I stand behind the players here and see the cards they are playing," a U.S. diplomat in Europe reported to Fish. "It is not our game."[25] But though it was a diplomatic failure, the scheme achieved its domestic objective of pulling the rug out from under proponents of intervention in Cuba. "So far as Home matters were concerned," Fish wrote of his Cuban policy, "it was intended . . . to stop the blatant filibusters in a Democratic Congress and to bring out the expression of what I never doubted existed, viz., the entire unwillingness of our people to wage a war for Cuba . . . The 'home-effect' has produced just what I expected."[26]

Fish's Monroe Doctrine both drew on and departed from nineteenth-century norms. Like so many other American statesmen, Fish most successfully used the Doctrine in the realm of domestic politics, in this case as a shield to protect himself from political opponents. So, too, was his ultimate diplomatic objective in harmony with that of his contemporaries: the pursuit of American interests in areas of strategic and economic importance. Yet the means Fish employed to achieve these objectives stand out. In contrast to most statesmen of the nineteenth century, Fish believed that cooperation with the powers of the Old World in affairs of the New carried more benefits than drawbacks. His desire to avoid the costs of unilateral intervention or annexation, along with his receptivity to Gladstonian tenets of international relations, led him to seek the assistance of the very European powers that the message of 1823 had targeted.

In both his canal and Cuban policies, Fish divided the globe in the opposite way than had the Monroe cabinet in 1823: between the Northern and Southern hemispheres, rather than Eastern and Western. Fish's racial assumptions regarding Latin Americans convinced him that they required the oversight of the United States, Britain, and Europe. Though few of Fish's successors would share his enthusiasm for cooperating with the powers of the Old World, they would agree that the United States had more in common with the powers of Europe than with the peoples of Latin America.

Toward the "New Imperialism"

Fish's internationalism looked across the Atlantic. He far preferred his meetings with the British minister, Thornton (often conducted after dinner over a glass of fine wine), to the rocky sessions he had with Cárdenas and other Latin Americans (often scheduled in the mornings). This was most directly a result of his racial views. But it also owed to the international context of the 1870s, which led Fish to the conclusion that old colonial rivalries were waning. However, the days of the ascendancy of Gladstonian aversion to formal imperialism were numbered, as the 1880s ushered in an era of "new imperialism." In the coming decades, the great powers devised programs of colonial expansion and economic nationalism. European imperial rivalry intensified, particularly in Africa, where an all-out scramble for territory began. As they raced to expand their empires, European powers (with the exception of the British) also constructed protective tariffs, which further fueled the race for overseas markets. To consolidate domestic support for costly imperial ventures, European leaders embedded imperialism into the political culture through dubbing heads of state "emperors" and establishing special "empire days" to celebrate overseas conquests. Indeed, the word "imperialism" itself was a product of this period, employed by Gladstone and other British liberals to denigrate the aggressive and self-serving policies of their political opponents.[27]

Latin America largely avoided the new imperialism of the late nineteenth century. To be sure, European powers, as well as the United States, turned their attention to the region, where they hoped to expand their economic interests. But there was little of the formal colonial expansion in Latin America that dominated Africa and Asia, in large part because Latin American states were strong enough to resist foreign invasion. The United States was once again blessed with favorable international circumstances. Yet very few American statesmen in this era considered themselves fortunate. They developed a newly heightened perception of threat, fearing that the scramble for Africa would spill over into Latin America and the Caribbean. American leaders also came to view the rising nations of Latin America as a potential threat to their objective of controlling the hemisphere. Much to the frustration of the United States, Mexico sought to define its disputed border with Guatemala without first clearing it with Washington. South American nations also challenged U.S. claims to hemispheric supremacy. Argentina, Brazil, and Chile entered a period of rapid economic growth in the late nineteenth century. They conceived their own foreign policy objectives, made their own claims for entry into the club of "civilized" powers, and directly competed with the United States to attract European investment and immigration. "Buenos Aires," the Cuban nationalist José Martí predicted in 1887, "will be a London and New York combined."[28]

James G. Blaine formulated a new foreign policy for the United States in this rapidly changing world. This Republican from Maine transformed the Monroe Doctrine into a symbol and instrument of an American version of the new imperialism of the late nineteenth century. Blaine saw himself as a disciple of American nationalists of the past such as John Quincy Adams, Henry Clay, and William Seward. Like his heroes, Blaine took a paradoxical view of Britain. Countering British power and commercial dominance in the Western Hemisphere was Blaine's central objective as Secretary of State in the 1880s. In contrast to Fish, Blaine had no interest in cooperating with his nation's former colonial master. Rather, he sought to employ a combination of firm diplomacy and nationalist economic measures such as high tariffs to counter, rather than co-opt, British power.

Yet Blaine's Anglophobia led him to study and admire the British Empire, as well as to embrace Anglo-Saxon racial superiority. Tutored as a boy by the uncle of the British minister to the Lincoln administration, Blaine literally learned at the knee of an Englishman. Blaine sought to reconfigure the successful tactics of the British to comport with his nation's traditional distaste of formal empire outside the contiguous United States. It was this desire to mimic the British Empire that led Democrats to charge this unimpeachable Anglophobe with being the architect of "the Republican party's British policy," as the 1884 Democratic platform put it. Blaine responded to such charges in kind, harnessing anti-British sentiments for his political ends. As one of his domestic critics put it, Blaine hated England "just enough to get the Irish vote, but not enough . . . to do her the smallest harm." Blaine's obsession with the British Empire was common for his time. But he differed from his contemporaries in one regard: having hired a substitute during the Civil War, Blaine was (in 1884) the only Republican presidential nominee up to Theodore Roosevelt in 1904 not to have worn a blue coat in the 1860s.[29]

A South American crisis confronted Blaine upon being named Secretary of State by President James Garfield in 1881. The War of the Pacific alarmed Blaine, for it merged the ambitions of a Latin American nation with the possibility of European intervention in the New World. The conflict grew out of a struggle between Chile and an alliance of Peru and Bolivia for control of a disputed region of the Atacama Desert that contained one of the world's greatest deposits of nitrates (a valuable resource in the nineteenth century for its use in fertilizers and gunpowder). When, in contravention of an 1874 agreement, Bolivia levied taxes on Chilean nitrate companies operating in the region, hostilities soon followed. Thanks to an earlier alliance, Peru joined Bolivia and became the primary opponent of Chile. The war soon became a one-sided affair, with Chile demolishing Peru's navy and seizing territory claimed by its enemies, thus giving Bolivia its current landlocked borders.

Blaine viewed the War of the Pacific through the lens of the Anglo-American struggle for supremacy in Latin America. "It is a perfect mistake to speak of this as a Chilian [*sic*] war on Peru," Blaine informed a congressional committee; "it is an English war on Peru, with Chili [*sic*] as the instrument, and I take the responsibility of that assertion."[30] Never mind the connections British investors had with both Chile and Peru; never mind that London offered to mediate the conflict in 1880 (a move the United States opposed). In Blaine's eyes, the conflict could be reduced to Britain's imperial ambitions in the Western Hemisphere. With the stakes so high, Blaine unprecedentedly involved the United States in a South American conflict. His efforts to mediate a peaceful resolution that restored the prewar status quo between Chile and Peru, however, staggered out of the gates thanks to an inadequate American diplomatic apparatus. The American representatives to the principal belligerents, Hugh Kilpatrick in Chile and Stephen Hurlbut in Peru, broke a cardinal rule of diplomacy when they openly sided with their host nation. In their zeal for their host governments, Kilpatrick and Hurlbut sent contradictory messages on the central issue of the United States' position on Chilean territorial expansion. With American diplomacy in disarray (and with the untimely deaths of both Kilpatrick and Hurlbut), Blaine dispatched William Trescot to the region to make clear American opposition to Chilean expansion. Trescot was to issue a veiled threat: if the Chilean government would not accept monetary reparations from Peru in lieu of territorial acquisitions, the United States would seek the support of other Latin American nations, including Chile's traditional rival, Argentina, in opposing Chilean expansion. The Chileans bristled at this hypocritical opposition to territorial expansion from a nation whose own borders had been dramatically extended at Mexico's cost only thirty years earlier.

Blaine went further, issuing invitations in late 1881 to all Latin American nations for a hemispheric conference in Washington to discuss under his leadership the War of the Pacific as well as broader political and commercial issues. The Chileans predictably opposed the scheme, but other Latin American governments were receptive to the idea. But the conference was not to be. Shortly after the assassination of President James Garfield, Blaine's tenure in the State Department ended when incoming president Chester Arthur, hoping to insulate himself from Blaine's unpopular policy, replaced him with Frederick T. Frelinghuysen. In an attempt to wash their hands of Blaine, Arthur and Frelinghuysen retracted the invitations for the hemispheric conference and ensured the failure of the Trescot mission. The result was a diplomatic disaster. "I think the outcome will be that we have offended everybody by our interference without securing a single advantage to either of them or ourselves," Trescot lamented.[31]

At the very moment when Blaine sought to contain Chilean expansionism, another challenge to American hemispheric dominance emerged: the construction of an isthmian canal by a French company. The United States was partly to blame for the development, for it had done little to advance the canal project after the failure of Fish's negotiations with Cárdenas. The Frenchman Ferdinand de Lesseps stepped into the void. A celebrity figure after his triumphant opening of the Suez Canal in 1869, de Lesseps attracted worldwide attention when he set his sights on the Central American isthmus. Operating under a contract obtained from Colombia in 1878, the ill-fated de Lesseps scheme bucked conventional wisdom when it started digging in 1880 in Panama rather than Nicaragua. If the old Frenchman underestimated the logistical obstacles to the project, he well understood the political ones. Aware that hypersensitive American nationalists would oppose his scheme because of his nationality, de Lesseps went out of his way to appease the United States. He repeatedly pointed out that his company was a private entity with no connections to the French government. He shrewdly pledged to put the headquarters of his company in New York if American investors took a majority of stock subscriptions (a contingency that predictably did not materialize). He offered ex-president Grant the presidency of the advisory board, a position that went to Secretary of the Navy Richard Thompson after Grant declined. De Lesseps even pledged his allegiance to the Monroe Doctrine, becoming the most prominent European up to that point to embrace in public the American shibboleth.[32]

De Lesseps's savvy public relations campaign presented problems for proponents of an American-controlled canal. But Republican nationalists were up to the challenge. They exploited memories of how economic interests had opened the door to French intervention in Mexico back in the 1860s. They stirred up Anglophobia, pointing to how the neutral Suez Canal had fallen under a British protectorate in 1882. Republican congressmen wheeled out the Monroe Doctrine, providing their relatively new demand for a canal under exclusive American control with the appearance of precedent and tradition. This was a bit tricky, given that the 1823 message, as de Lesseps pointed out, said not a word about the activities of private capitalists. But a creative rereading of the message provided a way around this problem. Not only did the 1823 message prohibit European colonization and political intervention, but the advocates of an American canal now found that it also placed "commercial interference" on the blacklist, despite the inconvenient fact that no such phrase appeared in the original document.[33]

The genius of the Republican offensive against the de Lesseps project was its blurring of the line between opposition to the Frenchman and advocacy of an American-controlled canal. Republicans well knew that the two were very different things, but they were not about to let pass this golden opportunity to transform the negative principles of the Monroe Doctrine into positive action. President Rutherford B. Hayes most prominently squared this circle. "The policy of this country," Hayes proclaimed in an 1880 message to the Senate, "is a canal under American control." Hayes contended that the United States' interest in the isthmus was "greater than that of all other countries" (including, apparently, Nicaragua and Colombia) because a canal would be "virtually a part of the coast line of the United States." The message concluded with a portentous twist: a canal controlled by the United States was in the interests of "commerce and civilization." It would not be the last time an American statesman sought to wed unilateral dominance with the broader interests of "civilization."[34]

Standing in Hayes's way was the Clayton-Bulwer Treaty. Though Hayes expressed reservations about the 1850 agreement in his message, close readers were disappointed to find that he stopped short of calling for its abrogation. James Blaine, however, was not one to waste a chance to twist the tail of the British lion. In his last weeks as Secretary of State in late 1881, Blaine ventured where Hayes had not. He drafted a series of belligerent notes to the British demanding modification of the old treaty so as to allow the United States to fortify and politically control a future canal. "This government," Blaine wrote, "will not consent to perpetuate any treaty that impeaches our rightful and long-established claim to priority on the American continent." After all, Blaine argued, the United States merely sought to do in its backyard what the British were doing in Egypt. Not to be outdone by his predecessor, Frelinghuysen went even further, invoking the Monroe Doctrine by name and pronouncing the Clayton-Bulwer Treaty void because of alleged British violations back in the 1850s.[35]

This truculence is best understood in relation to domestic politics. Given that Blaine hastily composed his dispatches to Britain in his last weeks in the State Department, it is not unreasonable to assume that part of his motivation was to shore up his future political prospects. Indeed, Blaine launched a public relations campaign shortly after leaving State to trumpet his foreign policy achievements, slim though they were, with the 1884 presidential election in mind (Blaine won the Republican nomination, but lost to Grover Cleveland in the general election). Upon replacing Blaine as Secretary of State, Frelinghuysen jumped at the chance to establish his anti-British credentials. The London *Economist* drove to the heart of the matter when it reassured its readers that American assertiveness on the canal issue "is intended to please Americans rather than to displease Englishmen."³⁶ The whole episode resembled the 1850s, as politicians invoked the Monroe Doctrine and played the Anglophobia card to advance their domestic political position; the only difference was that it was now Republicans who attempted to out-Monroe the Democrats (as well as each other). The diplomatic consequences of all this Monroe talk also resembled the 1850s in stiffening British resistance. Just as Clarendon had rebuffed Buchanan when he invoked the Doctrine back in 1854, Foreign Secretary Lord Granville demolished the arguments advanced by Blaine and Frelinghuysen. Granville refused to acknowledge the Monroe Doctrine or to consent to the demand to revise the Clayton-Bulwer Treaty.

For all their saber rattling, Blaine and Frelinghuysen's exchange with Britain had the ironic result of revealing the limits of American commitment to establishing a canal under its control. Proponents of an American canal raced ahead of congressional and public opinion. If fulminations against the Clayton-Bulwer Treaty paid political dividends, neither Blaine nor Frelinghuysen was able to assemble a congressional mandate for the logical next step: active policies in which the federal government lent support to the canal projects of private Americans or, alternatively, started digging itself. As the London *Times* put it, "The world is entitled to ask of the United States that they should make up their mind either to let M. de Lesseps do the thing himself by the resources at his command or to charge themselves with the task."³⁷ But this was not to happen. Throughout the 1880s, competing canal companies petitioned Congress for support. With the votes divided among those inclined to support canal projects, the Democrat-led opposition prevailed. Nor could Congress agree to part with the money for the ancillary investments required if a canal was to be built, such as subsidies to steamship and telegraph lines. With their government's policy in disarray, many American businessmen resigned themselves to the de Lesseps scheme on the grounds that it was the only show in town.[38]

In late 1884 the Arthur administration acted. It submitted to the Senate an agreement that gave the United States exclusive rights to construct a canal in Nicaragua. The Frelinghuysen-Zavala Treaty also made the canal route a virtual protectorate of the United States. The agreement said nothing of the Clayton-Bulwer Treaty, though it clearly violated that 1850 accord. Republican nationalists were elated. Yet it provoked fierce opposition, particularly on the grounds that it would entangle the United States in the unstable politics of Nicaragua, not to mention rousing the British by disregarding treaty obligations. These doubts narrowly prevented Senate ratification in 1885. When Grover Cleveland assumed the presidency later that year, he buried the treaty and reverted the nation's official canal policy to the idea of a private canal under an international guarantee, which in effect meant doing nothing.

The failed isthmian and South American diplomacy of the early 1880s further convinced James Blaine of the need for a more active and coherent foreign policy. His racial assumptions reinforced this conclusion. "I believe they need [arbitration] in a far greater degree than if they were dealing, as we are dealing, with an Anglo-Saxon population," Blaine stated, "because the Spanish population is hot-blooded, and when they are excited and get to fighting they do not know when to stop."[39] Blaine also took it as a given that Britain and other European powers would seek to capitalize on this instability, as they allegedly had done during the War of the Pacific. Even in his first stint at State, Blaine was already moving toward a more active diplomacy. Many of his ill-fated moves in 1881 anticipated future policies: abrogation of the Clayton-Bulwer Treaty, a hemispheric conference, a customs receivership in Venezuela. Shortly after leaving the State Department, Blaine explained that the "friendly intervention" of the United States would be required to "raise the standard of [Latin American] civilization."[40]

Blaine was not alone in recognizing the need for a new and more systematic diplomacy. Though Republicans and Democrats disagreed on issues such as the canal, they found common ground in calling for commercial expansion in Latin America. Reports of further decline in the United States' commerce in the region alarmed politicians from across the spectrum. By the mid-1880s, America's share of trade with the booming markets of Chile and Argentina was less than 10 percent. Its once proud merchant marine was almost nonexistent. "American steamers?" a Chilean asked. "I didn't know the Americans had any steamers. I never saw one." As American commerce faltered, the French and Germans moved in to challenge Britain's dominance. American statesmen became increasingly alarmed. They were losing the race for commercial supremacy in the hemisphere. The markets that they believed were rightfully theirs were controlled by Europeans. This was more than just a matter of national honor—though the significance of that abstraction should not be underestimated. The perceived problem of overproduction, as well as the rise of domestic agrarian and labor radicalism, transformed the markets of Latin America into a matter of preserving tranquillity at home. In a change from the thinking of the early nineteenth century, when American statesmen considered hemispheric trade in the 1880s, they thought more about preserving their own political system than about transforming those in Latin America.[41]

The commercial commission of 1884–85 constituted an early

step to combat this perceived "trade gap." Created by Congress and supported by the Arthur administration, the commission toured the United States and Latin America under instructions to find ways to increase America's share of hemispheric commerce. Headed by William Curtis, the commission reported that the federal government failed to support its men of commerce. When asked how the United States could augment its trade in Latin America, one Costa Rican responded, "Do exactly as the English, Germans, and French have done for the last two centuries."[42] The commission proposed that Washington adopt the measures used by Old World powers: subsidies to steamship lines, modernization of the consular service, and negotiation of more trade agreements. The commission went further, making the case that a hemispheric diplomatic conference would help advance the nation's commercial objectives. "We should not only have a larger share of that trade than any country but we should be able to control most of it," one commercial expansionist declared of Latin America in 1888. "But in order to meet with the fullest measure of success statesmanship must precede and open the way for the producers, tradesmen, and capitalists of the United States."[43]

The "First" Pan-American Conference

The United States' hemispheric commercial objectives led statesmen in Washington to involve themselves in Latin American affairs in new ways in the last decade of the nineteenth century. The Monroe Doctrine continued to represent a prohibition on European intervention, but it also became increasingly associated with new and proactive policies within the hemisphere. Such thinking led Congress to appropriate funds in 1888 for a hemispheric conference in Washington. The nation that traditionally had been cool, if not hostile, to hemispheric gatherings now took the lead. Just as striking was that the impetus for this move came from Congress, the very body that had been home to so many vitriolic opponents of hemispheric cooperation since the Panama debates of the 1820s. The legislation that called for the Washington Conference was a rare instance of bipartisan and bisectional cooperation—its sponsors were a Southern Democrat, James McCreary of Kentucky, and a Northern Republican, William Frye of Maine.

The United States assumed the lead in order to shape the agenda of the proposed conference. Objections to previous hemispheric gatherings had boiled down to the fact that they were organized by Latin Americans, whose interests often differed from those of the United States. The Washington Conference would differ from previous such congresses in this critical regard. This departure was evident in the conference's official name, "The First International Conference of the American States," which ignored previous gatherings organized by Latin Americans. The guest list also reflected American objectives. No European power received an invitation, despite the fact that many had an interest in the proceedings (most notably Spain and Britain). Canada was also snubbed because of its connections with Queen Victoria. Hawaii, in contrast, belatedly received an invitation.

The American wish list for the conference revealed the primacy of economic objectives. With the notable exception of arbitration, the principal items on the agenda aimed to promote hemispheric economic integration: a customs union, common coinage, hemispheric transportation and communication networks, and an agreed-upon system of weights and measurements. The ten American delegates at the conference, whose commercial credentials outweighed their nonexistent diplomatic ones (indeed, only one of the delegates was an experienced diplomat), further illustrated the centrality of economics. Latin American governments, in contrast, selected career diplomats and experts in international law to attend the gathering. "It seems that the intention," the Mexican diplomat Matías Romero said of the selection of American delegates, "was to select business men rather than diplomats."[44]

The United States' blueprint for the development of the hemispheric economy drew from the domestic legislation of the Civil War era. Americans aimed to apply at a hemispheric level the measures that had so successfully integrated and rationalized their own economy. A commercial bureau and inter-American bank would stabilize the hemispheric banking system much as the National Bank Act of 1863 had done at the national level; a common unit of exchange would regulate transactions as had the "greenbacks"; the hemispheric customs union would limit European commercial penetration as had the high tariffs of the 1860s; a pan-American railroad would bring the same benefits to the hemisphere that the Pacific Railroad Act of 1862 had brought the nation. Many Americans also pointed to the development of their own South and West as a model for how to bring Latin America within its economic orbit. American railroad financiers spoke about "Americanizing" Latin America and superimposed maps of Argentina on maps of the American West to demonstrate the viability of proposed rail lines.[45]

The American vision for hemispheric relations also drew from its greatest success in Latin America: Mexico. In the decades after the American Civil War, Mexico had fast become an economic satellite of the United States—"one magnificent but undeveloped mine—our India in commercial importance," as one American promoter put it. The neocolonial relationship that emerged in the late nineteenth century owed much to risk-taking American investors and financiers who poured money into Mexican railroads and mining projects. But it was also the result of the hospitable policies of the Mexican dictator Porfirio Díaz and his finance minister, Matías Romero, whose pursuit of foreign investment led them to draft laws and regulations favorable to American capitalists. Romero continued to hope that Mexico could exploit the economic power of his northern neighbor in a way similar to that by which the Yankees had harnessed Britain's wealth in the early nineteenth century. The policy proved successful in one sense: by 1902, American investment in Mexico totaled $503 million, making it by far the most important destination for American foreign investment. This figure would skyrocket in the first decade of the twentieth century. The neocolonial relationship that ensued, however, left Mexico vulnerable to vicissitudes in the American business cycle. More ominously, vast socioeconomic inequality, rural discontent, and political repression sowed the seeds of future troubles. The Mexican Revolution, however, lay in the distant future as American policymakers planned for the Washington Conference in 1889. What they saw in Mexico was an open economic system in which American entrepreneurs could profit from the exploitation of a developing economy without the need for costly interventions by the United States government. They hoped to extend this favorable system to the entire Western Hemisphere.[46]

The pan-American movement in the United States found further inspiration in the ideas and policies of the Old World. The very term "Pan-American" was itself one of many such conjunctions, such as Pan-Germanism and Pan-Slavism, that denoted the integration of peoples or economies in the nineteenth century. The plan for a hemispheric customs union drew from the German *Zollverein* of the mid-nineteenth century, which removed trade barriers between German states while maintaining them with foreign trade partners. As Prussian statesmen had used the *Zollverein* to establish their economic dominance over the other German states, so, too, would the United States employ a hemispheric customs union to establish its economic supremacy in the Americas. As always, Americans paid particular attention to the model of the British Empire. Proposals such as subsidies to steamship lines mimicked moves that had helped Britain establish commercial supremacy in Latin America. The proposal for a railroad and telegraph connecting Texas to Chile paralleled Cecil Rhodes's plans to establish a "Cape to Cairo" line in Africa under the British Union Jack. Many Americans went further, conceptualizing their relationship with Latin America as synonymous with European colonialism, even if they continued to prefer informal, economic imperialism over formal colonial expansion. "While the great powers of Europe are steadily enlarging their colonial domination in Asia and Africa," Blaine declared, "it is the especial province of this country to improve and expand its trade with the nations of America."[47]

Latin Americans were well aware of the United States' ambitions. Though all the governments save the Dominican Republic accepted the invitation to Washington, many feared that the United States sought to use the conference to entrench itself as the hemispheric hegemon.[48] " 'America for the Americans,' " the *Chileno* of Valparaiso informed its readers, "means simply 'South America diplomatically and commercially for the United States' . . . We Spanish-Americans have nothing in common with the people of the United States."[49] The reputation of the Monroe Doctrine in Latin America was so low that the British observer James Bryce commented that the "wisest among American Foreign Ministers . . . are those who have least frequently referred to the Monroe Doctrine."[50] The Cuban nationalist José Martí most eloquently articulated this growing Yankeephobia. Writing in the Argentine journal *La Nación*, Martí denounced the conference as the naked attempt of an expansionist power to bring Latin America into its orbit. The economic objectives of the conference gave Latin American nationalists such as Martí much to rail against. So too did a preconference train tour of the United States for the Latin American delegates. American conference organizers hoped that the forty-two-day, six-thousand-mile tour of the Northern states would convince Latin American delegates of the need to align their nations with the burgeoning American economy. The stops were designed with export opportunities in mind—the McCormick reaper facility in Illinois, steel mills in Ohio, textile mills and shipyards in the Northeast. The whole thing resembled the train journeys Native American leaders such as Red Cloud took to Washington before being bullied into signing away their tribal lands. The parallel was not lost on observers at the time.[51]

The two delegates from Argentina, Roque Sáenz Peña and Manuel Quintana, declined to take part in the train tour. Their refusal portended a central theme of the Washington Conference: persistent discord between the United States and Argentina. The source of this conflict, paradoxically, arose from the remarkable similarities between the two nations. By the 1880s, the resemblance was so evident that Americans, who usually boasted about their exceptionalism, even commented upon it. "The Argentine Republic," the 1885 commercial commission noted, "is the United States of South America." Like its northern counterpart, the Argentine economy rapidly grew as a result of booming trade and British investment in its infrastructure. Immigration from Europe increased Argentina's population and provided new pools of labor, just as it did in the United States. The development of the Argentine "frontier" and the conquest of outlying lands paralleled the American experience in the West. President Domingo Faustino Sarmiento even sent a delegation to Washington to get advice from the federal Indian Bureau on how best to deal with Argentina's native population. As in the United States, Argentine thinkers developed a racialized ideology to establish their claim to being the equals of "civilized" Europeans. As one prominent Argentinian put it in words that an American could have spoken of the United States, "The Argentine Republic now counts among the number of civilized nations."[52]

These similarities, however, did not lead to harmonious relations. An 1867 U.S. tariff on wool closed the American market to this major Argentine export, irritating relations in the process. The two nations competed in the wheat and meat export markets and vied to attract European capital. Nor had the two nations enjoyed close diplomatic relations. The Monroe Doctrine had provided no benefits to Argentina. Juan Bautista Alberdi was not alone when he credited Canning with protecting Buenos Aires back in 1823. Argentinians remembered Andrew Jackson's indifferent response when they had appealed to the United States to invoke the Doctrine when Britain seized the Malvinas/ Falkland Islands back in the 1830s. "The famous Monroe Doctrine will be enlarged," *Le Courrier* of Buenos Aires predicted of the Washington Conference; "it is not a question of the non-intervention of Europe in the affairs of the American continent, but of the preponderance . . . of the United States."[53]

The American objective of supplanting European influence in Latin America did not sit well with Argentine statesmen. The economic boom and cultural renaissance of late-nineteenth-century Argentina celebrated connections with the Old World. Argentinians saw hypocrisy in American denunciations of European influence in Latin America: having exploited British investment, transatlantic trade, and European technological and intellectual achievements for a century, Americans now sought to prevent Latin Americans from doing the same. Few in Argentina were willing to sacrifice their connections with the Old World in order to satisfy America's commercial objectives. "Taking the United States instead of Europe as the source of civilization," Alberdi wrote, "is getting European civilization second-hand." The Washington Conference provided Argentine politicians from the Europhilic ruling party, the Partido Autonomista Nacional, with an opportunity to proclaim on a world stage their cosmopolitan nationalism. "I do not lack affection or love for America," Sáenz Peña declared in what became one of the signature orations of the Washington Conference, "but I lack ingratitude or distrust toward Europe. I do not forget that Spain, our mother, is there, and that she watches with earnest rejoicing the development of her ancient domains . . . I do not forget that Italy, our friend, and France, our sister . . . are also there . . . Let America be for humanity."[54]

Sáenz Peña and Quintana opposed the U.S. agenda from the very beginning. They objected to the nomination of James Blaine to preside over the conference. Officially, the Argentinians opposed (unsuccessfully in the end) Blaine's nomination on the technical ground that he was not a delegate and therefore ineligible to hold such a post. Their real motive was to limit U.S. control of the proceedings. They next objected to the American ground rules for the conference, recommending instead the rules of order used at the recent Latin American convention in Montevideo in 1888. Not only were these conventions familiar, but they had the added attraction of placing stricter rules on parliamentary procedure, thus limiting the scope of the conference. The Argentinians won an early victory when the conference adopted the Montevideo practices.

The Argentinians shrewdly curried the favor of other Latin American delegates when they proposed the parity of Spanish and English during the conference. Remarkably, only one of the ten American delegates was fluent in Spanish, and many of the Latin Americans, including the Argentinians, spoke little English. The language divide, the Mexican delegate (and ad hoc translator) Matías Romero later wrote, "seemed even to threaten the success of the conference." When the Americans nominated William Curtis for the position of conference secretary, Quintana seized the moment. Curtis was an easy target: not only did he speak no Spanish, but he also was persona non grata thanks to a travel book he authored that presented the capital cities of Latin America in an unflattering light. The conference voted for a secretary for each language, though the language divide would plague the proceedings throughout. In this and other episodes, Argentina was joined by traditional rival Chile. The ambitions of the United States brought together historic adversaries.

The Argentine-led opposition caught the American delegates

by surprise. Unsubstantiated rumors circulated in the American press that Sáenz Peña and Quintana were the paid agents of Britain. Once again, Americans blamed the British for their problems in Latin America. If caught off guard, Blaine was quick to control the damage. Belying his nickname of "Jingo Jim," Blaine attempted to alleviate the concerns of Latin American delegates. He reassured them that the nations "shall meet together on terms of absolute equality" and promised "a conference in which there can be no attempt to coerce a single delegate."[55] Taking a page from Lincoln and Seward, Blaine appears never to have used during the conference the phrase "Monroe Doctrine," the paternalist connotations of which would have counterproductively antagonized Latin Americans. When proceedings reached an impasse, he invited delegates to his Washington home to discuss matters off the record. Blaine's attempts to find common ground received invaluable support from Romero, whose activities as unofficial translator symbolized the mediating role he assumed throughout the conference. Though border and trade disputes with the United States had qualified his admiration for his northern neighbor, Romero continued the role of advocate of hemispheric cooperation that he had first assumed as minister to Washington back in the 1860s. Midway through the conference, the United States also received the unexpected support of a new delegation from Brazil representing the provisional republican government that had overthrown that nation's long-standing monarchical regime.

This compromising spirit saved the conference from complete failure, an outcome that at points was a distinct possibility. But it limited the conference's achievements. This was particularly the case with one of the core American objectives, the mandatory arbitration of hemispheric disputes. Blaine hoped that arbitration would provide peaceful settlement to Latin American conflicts that had the potential to trigger European intervention, such as the War of the Pacific and the disputed Mexican-

Guatemalan border. But many Latin Americans, particularly the Chileans, Mexicans, and Argentinians, feared that a permanent arbitration tribunal in Washington would become an instrument of American foreign policy. After protracted and heated debate, the conference opted only for a watered-down recommendation of a nonbinding form of arbitration.

Latin American opposition merged with American indecision to undermine the key commercial proposals of the conference. Given the combustible nature of the currency issue in the United States, the proposal for a common silver coin was destined to go nowhere. Bemused Latin American delegates watched their U.S. counterparts argue with one another over the respective merits of gold and silver. "How can a single delegation advance two opinions, two ideas, two plans so entirely distinct that they contradict each other openly?" Quintana could not resist asking.[56] The idea of a hemispheric customs union also found little support. Latin Americans objected on the grounds that the scheme was unworkable and would deprive national treasuries of customs revenue, the central source of funds for many governments. Nor did the idea have much traction in the United States. Remarkably, at the very moment that the Washington Conference was considering ways of promoting hemispheric trade, the Republican Congress drafted the highly protectionist McKinley Tariff of 1890. The tariff, Blaine wrote McKinley, was "a slap in the face of the South Americans, with whom we are trying to enlarge our trade."[57] It undermined Blaine's attempt to cultivate commercial relations with the new republican government in Brazil. In one of his last political triumphs, Blaine persuaded McKinley to include a provision in the tariff bill that authorized executive negotiation of bilateral reciprocity deals with Latin American governments. But this last-minute victory fell far short of the utopian dream of establishing a *Zollverein*. The end product with respect to trade at the Washington Conference, which passed over the no votes of Argentina, Chile, and Bolivia, was the mere endorsement of future reciprocity deals.

To be sure, the conference was not a complete failure. Though it ended with few concrete achievements, it set a precedent for future pan-American meetings (next held in Mexico City in 1901–1902). It established a new institution in Washington charged with promoting hemispheric trade, the Commercial Bureau of the American Republics. In the twentieth century, the Commercial Bureau would evolve into the Pan American Union and, later, into today's Organization of American States. Blaine's willingness to compromise during the conference assisted Latin American advocates of hemispheric integration. "Almost all of the Latin American nations came to Washington with a fear that the United States intended to impose upon them its material superiority," Romero reported, "and they went back satisfied that, far from being so, this country had only sentiments of respect and consideration for its sister-republics, and that the United States simply intended to accomplish what was of mutual advantage to all."[58]

The United States, however, had set the bar much higher than just improving its image in Latin America (and even on this score Romero's view was not shared by all). It sought to promote its exports and establish economic ascendancy in the hemisphere; it sought to find ways of establishing regional stability; and it sought to curb European influence. The conference failed on all of these counts. Blaine's claim that the watered-down agreement on arbitration constituted a "new Magna Carta" proved laughable when not one government ratified the conference's recommendation. Indeed, many of the recommendations from the conference remained only recommendations. Hopes that the conference would jump-start plans for an inter-American bank, a railroad connecting Texas to Chile, and a new transportation network of steamships were soon disappointed.

Though the conference laid the foundation for future pan-American meetings, it failed to win converts to the idea in the United States. The two most tangible accomplishments of the conference—the endorsement of reciprocity and the Commercial

Bureau—were undermined not by Argentine or Chilean resistance, but by domestic opposition within the United States. Soon after the conference, the Harrison administration bullied eight Latin American governments into signing reciprocity agreements by threatening to impose duties on their food and raw material exports. The agreements barely had a chance to go into effect. A Democrat-controlled Congress that favored lowering duties across the board repealed the reciprocity deals in the Wilson-Gorman Tariff of 1894. The Democrats also targeted the Commercial Bureau, which they viewed as a power base for their political opponents. Democratic resentment of the Bureau increased after eight Latin American governments defaulted on their maintenance costs. Though in the end Congress reduced, rather than ended, the Bureau's funding, it sent a clear message that it would view future pan-American projects with suspicion. Time would soon reveal the full nature of the Democrats' conception of the United States' role in the hemisphere.[59]

The Republican administration of Benjamin Harrison—the very administration that had presided over the conference—also proved unwilling to stand by the pan-American principles it espoused in 1889–90. In a diplomatic crisis soon after the conference, Harrison showed the limits of his administration's commitment to that new Magna Carta, the principle of arbitration. A dispute between Chile and the United States provided the perfect opportunity to implement this enlightened principle. The conflict grew out of domestic political turmoil in Chile in 1891, which saw the congressional opposition rebel against the government of José Manuel Balmaceda. Once again, the United States interpreted a Latin American crisis through the lens of Anglophobia, remaining sympathetic to Balmaceda because of his earlier attempts to curb Britain's economic influence within his nation. Balmaceda obtained the support of Patrick Egan, the U.S. minister to Santiago and a naturalized Irishman with a visceral hatred of the English, by shrewdly exploiting his fears of Britain. The constitutional crisis ended with Balmaceda on the losing side and with the Congressionalists enraged by the one-sided neutrality of Egan and the United States. Relations between the two nations reached a crisis point when a crowd in Valparaiso attacked a group of American sailors on shore leave from the USS *Baltimore*, killing two and injuring another seventeen.

Requiring disinterested examination of the circumstances of the incident, the *Baltimore* affair was a crisis tailor-made for arbitration. Yet President Harrison, who managed most of the crisis owing to Blaine's illness, had little patience in the matter. In the eyes of this old Civil War veteran, the matter was a simple one of national honor and pride. Harrison interpreted the rowdy bar brawl in Valparaiso as a deliberate insult to the armed forces of the United States. The President rejected arbitration in favor of issuing an old-fashioned ultimatum: if Chile did not apologize for its role in the affair and provide reparations for the dead American sailors, Harrison would sever diplomatic relations and advise Congress to take "such action as may be deemed appropriate."[60] This aggressive diplomatic approach achieved American objectives. The Chilean government backed down, issuing the required apology and agreeing to an indemnity payment for the families of the slain sailors.

The Chilean crisis of 1891–92 revealed the weakness of pan-Americanism in the United States. Having attempted only a couple of years earlier to establish a permanent mechanism for the arbitration of hemispheric disputes, the United States now rejected the idea, seeking instead to impose its will upon a fellow American nation. The crisis led the Republican senator William Chandler to the conclusion that the United States "cannot maintain the Monroe doctrine and our position as the leading and dominant power in the western hemisphere by mere negotiations."[61] "Arbitrage would be an excellent thing," José Martí prophetically wrote in 1889, "if [the United States] would yield its own appetites."[62] Revealing, too, was the combustible state of public opinion in the United States, where jingoism, or bellicose patriotism, had become a powerful impulse. Many politicians and newspapers turned the diplomatic issue into a matter of national honor and patriotism, portraying the Chileans as infantile inferiors in the process.

Among the jingoes was Theodore Roosevelt, an ambitious Republican from New York. Roosevelt applauded Harrison's assertive policy. His only complaint was that the President appeared reluctant to declare war on "a tenth rate country like Chili [*sic*]." An observer recorded Roosevelt boasting that "for two nickels he would declare war himself." The ultimate lesson that Roosevelt took from the Chilean crisis, however, was not that Latin Americans needed the occasional chastisement, nor that the British could not be trusted (he was already convinced on both of these points). Rather, in Roosevelt's eyes, the crisis revealed that the greatest threat to the goal of American hemispheric supremacy resided at home, particularly among unmanly Democrats and Northeasterners. "They showed no hesitation in playing into the hands of our open enemies, the Chilean aggressors, and of their abettors, the English residents in Chile," Roosevelt wrote. In the coming years, Roosevelt would use the Monroe Doctrine not only to curb the ambitions of European rivals, but also to attack domestic opponents who opposed his interventionist foreign policy.[63]

6

Intervention

A n uneasy relationship existed between the Monroe Doctrine and interventionist foreign policies in the nineteenth century. The framers of the 1823 message sought to prevent the Holy Allies from intervening in the new states of Spanish America and thus proclaimed the principle of nonintervention. In the coming decades, the idea that the Monroe Doctrine constituted an enlightened and anti-imperial alternative to the interventionist policies of European colonial powers became dogma in the United States. Yet the Monroe Doctrine was never purely noninterventionist. American statesmen viewed it as a call to establish their regional supremacy, an objective that often necessitated interventionist tactics.

American interventionism in the nineteenth century assumed a number of forms. At one end of the spectrum lay ministerial meddling in the internal politics of host nations, such as that of Joel Poinsett in Mexico City in the 1820s and Patrick Egan in Santiago in 1891. Private individuals, such as the military adventurer William Walker in Nicaragua in the 1850s, intervened more forcefully in the affairs of Central American states, though the U.S. government did not always sanction such acts. The United States at times enshrined the right of intervention in treaties with Latin American states, such as the Bidlack-Mallarino Treaty of 1846 with Colombia, which authorized the frequent landing of U.S. troops in Panama to secure the isthmian passageway. In the case of the war against Mexico, American interventionism took the form of outright military invasion.

Nonetheless, many nineteenth-century Americans were uncomfortable with the idea of an openly interventionist Monroe Doctrine. The State Department recalled to Washington meddlesome ministers such as Poinsett with surprising regularity. It is significant that the United States intervened in Panama; but it is also significant that those interventions were limited in scope and short-lived. And if Americans had no desire to reverse the annexations of the 1840s, they could salve their consciences by condemning Polk's policy after the fact and attributing the war against Mexico to the discredited slave power. That war of aggression, Ulysses S. Grant wrote in his 1885 memoirs, was "one of the most unjust ever waged by a stronger against a weaker nation."[1]

This all changed at the dawn of the twentieth century. American intervention, particularly in the Caribbean, became more frequent and systematic, broader in its scope and objectives, and more fully rationalized and justified. In 1895 the conservative administration of Democratic president Grover Cleveland diplomatically intervened in an obscure border dispute between Venezuela and British Guiana. Three years later, the United States declared war on Spain, whose Caribbean and Pacific colonies it gobbled up after a decisive military victory. And in 1904, President Theodore Roosevelt explicitly transformed the Monroe Doctrine into an instrument of intervention.

The goal in all of these episodes was to establish the hemispheric supremacy of the United States. But Americans continued to disagree on what forms that supremacy should take, as well as on the best means of achieving it. The story of the Monroe Doctrine at the turn of the century is one of policy debates followed by a series of compromises, culminating in the 1904 Roosevelt Corollary to the Monroe Doctrine.

Isolationist Intervention

Grover Cleveland stands apart from the other presidents of his era. Until Woodrow Wilson won the election of 1912, he was the lone Democrat to occupy the White House after the Civil War. Cleveland remains the only president in American history to serve two nonconsecutive terms (1885–89 and 1893–97). His political philosophy and views on foreign affairs also set him apart from his contemporaries. At a time when many American politicians came to accept a more active role for the federal government, Cleveland looked backward, insisting upon the strict construction of the Constitution and the delegation of power to states and local communities. When Congress passed a bill providing relief to drought-ridden farmers in 1887, Cleveland vetoed it, preferring that private charities do the work. "Though the people support the Government," Cleveland asserted in his veto message, "the Government should not support the people."[2] The only thing Cleveland feared more than an active federal government was the increased traction of radical ideas, such as socialism, trade unionism, and agrarian populism. When workers at the Pullman Car Company in Illinois went on strike in 1894, Cleveland and his then attorney general Richard Olney deployed federal forces to break it up. This aggressive use of federal power sat uneasily beside Cleveland's vision of a passive central government. It would soon have a foreign policy parallel.

Cleveland's vision of foreign affairs was similarly backward-looking. He formulated his diplomatic thinking in opposition to his Republican rival in the election of 1884, James Blaine. While Blaine trumpeted pan-Americanism and a robust Monroe Doctrine, Cleveland ran on a platform that resolved "in regard to for-

eign nations, so long as they do not act detrimental to the interests of the country or hurtful to our citizens, to let them alone."[3]
Blaine's heroes were the formulators of active foreign policies:
John Quincy Adams, Henry Clay, and William Henry Seward.
Cleveland, in contrast, turned toward the alleged stalwarts of
nonentanglement: Washington, Jefferson, and Jackson. Before
the Venezuela crisis, Cleveland avoided public use of the phrase
"Monroe Doctrine," which he "knew to be troublesome."[4] The
central objective of his foreign policy was retrenchment: he
scotched the Republicans' attempt to unilaterally construct an
isthmian canal; he quickly withdrew U.S. forces from Panama,
despite calls at home to stay, after a brief intervention in 1885; he
repudiated reciprocal trade agreements with Latin American
states; he backpedaled from commitments in Samoa; he withdrew from the Senate's consideration a treaty that would have
annexed Hawaii in 1893.

It comes as a great irony that this apostle of nonentanglement
would pursue an aggressive and interventionist policy at the end
of his second term in office. The very man who knew the Monroe
Doctrine "to be troublesome" would invoke it more assertively
than any of his predecessors. The great opponent of the interventionist policies of the Republicans now changed course by
provocatively intervening in a long-simmering boundary dispute
between Venezuela and Britain (whose colony of British Guiana
bordered the South American republic). Cleveland's predecessors
had steered clear of entangling themselves in the affair. They
extended mild support to the Venezuelan call to refer the dispute
to international arbitration, but hoped that the matter somehow
would resolve itself.

This all changed in the summer of 1895, when Cleveland
instructed his new secretary of state, Richard Olney, to invoke
the Monroe Doctrine and demand that Britain submit the matter
to arbitration. Olney drafted a formal dispatch to British foreign
secretary Lord Salisbury that aggressively asserted the right of

the United States to intervene in the dispute under the unilateral Monroe Doctrine. Like Jefferson and Monroe before him, Olney framed hemispheric relations in ideological terms. "Europe as a whole is monarchical," Olney declared, glossing over the profound political changes the Old World had undergone since 1823. "America, on the other hand, is devoted to the exactly opposite principle—to the idea that every people has an inalienable right of self-government." Olney contended that these persisting political antagonisms made British activities in the Western Hemisphere a threat to national security. To the traditional arguments of ideology and national security, Olney added a new one to justify American intervention in the Venezuelan dispute: the power of the United States. "Today the United States is practically sovereign on this continent and its fiat is law," Olney boasted.[5]

Cleveland called Olney's dispatch a "twenty-inch gun," something more powerful than the twelve-inch guns on the battleships of the day. "It's the best thing of the kind I have ever read," Cleveland informed his secretary of state, "and it leads to a conclusion that one cannot escape if he tries—that is if there is anything of the Monroe Doctrine at all."[6] The diplomatic note, Olney later admitted, was "undoubtedly of the bumptious order."[7] But it was so intentionally. Olney fired the twenty-inch gun at two targets. The first and most obvious was the British. Well aware that Britain's long-standing policy was to exclude key portions of the disputed territory from arbitration, Olney knew that a mere suggestion that the whole area, including that populated by British settlers, be submitted to arbitration would be insufficient. He ratcheted up the rhetoric to ensure that the British listened. Invoking the Monroe Doctrine by name was the diplomatic equivalent of thumping his chest and jumping up and down.

Olney's twenty-inch gun also targeted the domestic opponents of the Cleveland administration. Within the Democratic

Party lurked populists and Anglophobes, such as the Southern expansionist John T. Morgan and the presidential aspirant William Jennings Bryan, who threatened to break the party line of retrenchment in foreign affairs. More ominous was the threat from across the aisle. An economic collapse in 1893 resulted in a Republican landslide in the midterm elections of 1894, extending much leverage to these proponents of an active foreign policy. A pamphlet authored by William Scruggs, an American adventurer on the payroll of the Venezuelan government, brought the obscure border dispute to the attention of the newly elected Republicans. The title of Scruggs's 1894 pamphlet said it all: *British Aggressions in Venezuela, or the Monroe Doctrine on Trial.* Republican nationalists soon sang from Scruggs's hymnbook, exploiting the Venezuela issue to make demands for an expansionist foreign policy and continued naval buildup. The Massachusetts senator Henry Cabot Lodge penned an article in the *North American Review* warning the administration that if it did not act on the Venezuela matter, the Republican-dominated Congress would.

Cleveland and Olney championed the Monroe Doctrine in order to counter their domestic and foreign opponents. Not to embrace the Monroe Doctrine would expose the administration to charges of being soft on national security. But Olney's twenty-inch gun cannot be entirely explained as an act of political posturing. While composing the dispatch, Olney immersed himself in the history of the Monroe Doctrine. He came to see parallels between the 1820s and the circumstances he faced in the 1890s. The Venezuela issue itself did not concern Olney as much as did the larger geopolitical context in which it emerged. The Secretary of State feared that the European powers were on the offensive in the Western Hemisphere, a situation similar to that faced by the Monroe cabinet back in 1823. Cleveland and Olney looked upon British and German actions in Central America with much anxiety; they worried that instability in Brazil might lead to

European intervention; they predicted that European immigration to South America might adversely influence American interests. Most alarming was the prospect that continued instability in Cuba, where another rebellion broke out in 1895, might tempt newly assertive European powers to intervene in this island that was paramount to U.S. national security.

The twenty-inch gun expressed these anxieties. If the United States allowed Britain free rein in Venezuela, Olney wrote, an all-out imperial scramble might ensue: "what one power was permitted to do could not be denied to another, and it is not inconceivable that the struggle now going on for the acquisition of Africa might be transferred to South America." Cleveland and Olney harked back to the fear of 1823: imperial rivalry at the United States' doorstep would force dramatic changes at home. If such a struggle was allowed to take place, "the ideal conditions we have thus far enjoyed can not be expected to continue." The United States would have no choice but to engage in the arms race gripping Europe, which would "convert the flower of our male population into soldiers and sailors." Americans would have to alter their political system, adopting a more powerful and centralized government to mobilize the resources required for protracted imperial rivalry.

The Cleveland administration thus viewed the Monroe Doctrine as a means of maintaining the principles it held dear: limited and decentralized government at home and nonentanglement overseas. By sending a strong message to the British and placating domestic opponents at home, the Monroe Doctrine could achieve these objectives. Intervention in Venezuela paradoxically would eliminate the need for future entanglement in Latin America. Europeans would know not to test American resolve in the future, and Republicans at home would be denied their rationale for an expansionist foreign policy. Only by dominating the hemisphere could the United States take little concern with what happened within it.[8]

But here the Cleveland administration encountered a number of obstacles. How could they appease an increasingly excitable public at home without further inflaming the situation? How could they satisfy Republican jingoes—those bellicose nationalists who called for an assertive foreign policy—without antagonizing the British so much that they refused arbitration? And, most fundamental, how could they invoke the Monroe Doctrine in a matter peripheral to their conception of the national interest without transforming it in the process into the very call for an active, interventionist, and entangling foreign policy that they sought to avoid?

The twenty-inch gun attempted to square these circles. To justify intervention in the Venezuela issue, Olney invoked international law, republican ideology, and the Monroe Doctrine. But he very carefully qualified the Doctrine in order to limit its utility in the future to jingoes like Lodge and Roosevelt. His boasts of American power notwithstanding, Olney emphasized "the precise scope and limitations" of the Doctrine. "It does not establish any general protectorate by the United States over other American states," he carefully wrote. "It does not relieve any American states from its obligations as fixed by international law nor prevent any European power directly interested from enforcing such obligation . . . It does not contemplate any interference in the internal affairs of any American state or in the relations between it and other American states. It does not justify any attempt on our part to change the established form of government of any American state."[9] When Monroe had stated that the Western Hemisphere was off-limits to European colonization and political intervention, Olney continued, he meant just that, and only that. Just as Cleveland and Olney strictly interpreted the Constitution, the twenty-inch gun narrowly viewed the Monroe Doctrine as a negatively framed diplomatic principle, which the United States was free to invoke whenever it wanted. "It is sometimes asserted that this administration . . . enlarged the Monroe Doctrine,"

Olney wrote a year later. "Nothing could be farther from the truth. It, in reality, defined it and confined its application within narrower limits than had ever been fixed by previous administrations or public men."[10]

Olney's note did not have the immediate diplomatic impact that he intended. The louder the Americans screamed about the Monroe Doctrine, the less the British seemed to hear. Lord Salisbury did not even respond to the July note until late November. When the response finally came, it resembled those of Clarendon (in 1854) and Granville (in 1882), who had refused to be browbeaten by saber-rattling Americans. "The Americans are not people to run away from," the British statesman Joseph Chamberlain wrote; "it is essential that the reply should emphatically repudiate this attempt to apply the Monroe Doctrine."[11] Salisbury's response denied the validity of the Doctrine in international law as well as its applicability to the Venezuela border dispute. He left the door open to arbitration but firmly expressed his government's refusal to include territories inhabited by "large numbers of British subjects" from any such tribunal.

Up until this point, the exchange resembled the ill-fated American invocations of the Doctrine in the 1850s and '80s. The United States appeared on the verge of retreating once again when Olney advised excluding the counterproductive Doctrine from further talks with the British. But Cleveland refused to let the matter drop. He continued to fear the Republican Congress. And his anger at the British reached a boiling point when he read Salisbury's reply. "It would have been exceedingly gratifying and a very handsome thing for Great Britain to do," he informed his ambassador in London, "if, in the midst of all this Administration has had to do in attempts to stem the tide of 'jingoism,' she had yielded or rather conceded something (if she called it so, which I do not) for our sake."[12] Cleveland hastily drafted a special message to Congress, delivered on December 17, that was a twenty-incher in its own right. In it, Cleveland reassured Americans that the Monroe Doctrine remained "strong and sound" and unilaterally pronounced it a principle of international law. He then stated that, given Britain's refusal to arbitrate the matter, the United States would have no choice but to determine the Venezuela–British Guiana boundary itself.[13]

Cleveland's message triggered a brief war scare. On both sides of the Atlantic, religious organizations, financial interests, and others opposed to a third Anglo-American war campaigned for a peaceful resolution. In reality, there was little chance that the imbroglio would lead to hostilities. Despite its bombast, Cleveland's message tactfully stopped short of setting a deadline for British acceptance of arbitration. For their part, British statesmen had little desire to fight over disputed territory in South America when they had more pressing concerns in Africa and Europe. So long as Britain's commercial position in Latin America was not compromised and the rights of its settlers in Guiana were respected, statesmen in London were prepared to give ground to the United States if pressed. The Yankee doctrine was a bitter pill to swallow, to be sure, but it came with a sugar coating for the overstretched British. The whole affair might become a way to coax the United States into shouldering some of the burden of policing Latin America. "She assumes under the 'Monroe Doctrine' a kind of protectorate over both the American continents," the London *Economist* pointed out, "yet she does not enforce any order among the States she protects."[14] The British went so far as to float the idea of holding an international conference charged with defining the Doctrine. Olney quickly rejected the proposal out of suspicion that it might lead the United States to assume the very active role in the hemisphere that he sought to avoid. The British reluctantly acceded to a unilateral Monroe Doctrine and accepted arbitration of the disputed border.

An important American concession, however, came in return. Olney agreed to exclude from arbitration any territories settled by British subjects for more than fifty years. News of this compromise triggered riots in Caracas. Venezuela had repeatedly opposed British attempts to make such an exemption in previous negotiations between the two nations. But now the United States, despite all its tough talk, had sold Venezuelan interests down the river. The Venezuelan government had played their hand well by employing Scruggs to exploit the Monroe Doctrine on its behalf. But the matter was taken out of their hands once Cleveland and Olney took up the issue. In fact, Olney never even discussed U.S. policy with the Venezuelans during the key months of the crisis, despite the fact that the affair involved their territory. Such "entanglements" with Latin Americans were exactly what the Cleveland administration hoped to avoid by endorsing a robust, yet limited, Monroe Doctrine. Nor did the United States object in 1899 when the arbitration commission upheld most of the British territorial claims, with the notable exception of the southern portion of the Orinoco River delta, which went to Venezuela.

The Cleveland administration's diplomacy during the Venezuela crisis verged on the schizophrenic. Olney's dispatch and Cleveland's message articulated the right of the United States to intervene in a faraway border dispute in which it had no stake. By excluding the Venezuelans from the negotiations with the British, Olney coldly rejected the spirit of hemispheric cooperation that even an assertive nationalist like James Blaine had embraced just a few years earlier. "In an application of the Monroe doctrine," Cleveland explained, "though another country may give the occasion, we are I suppose not looking after its interest but our own."[15] In declaring the United States "practically sovereign" over the entire hemisphere, Olney's interpretation of the Monroe Doctrine went further than any of his predecessors'. And in ultimately getting the British to acquiesce to the Doctrine, he succeeded where previous secretaries of state had failed. Yet the objective of the Cleveland administration was not merely to strengthen the Monroe Doctrine. Fortifying the

Doctrine was actually a means to the larger end of establishing conditions that would eliminate the need for the United States to pursue interventionist policies. Even as they expanded the Doctrine by using it as justification for meddling in the Venezuela border dispute, Cleveland and Olney sought to limit its scope by explicitly disassociating it from protectorates and intervention in Latin America. "The truth is," Olney stated, "that the Monroe Doctrine was never so carefully defined and so narrowly restricted as in the second Cleveland administration."[16]

Cleveland and Olney were unable to maintain control of the Monroe Doctrine. Proponents of the very interventionist policies that they sought to undermine picked up the newly assertive Monroe Doctrine and high-stepped into the endzone. Theodore Roosevelt's letter to Olney during the crisis is revealing: "I must write you just a line to say how heartily I rejoiced at the Venezuela message. I only wish you would take the same line as regards Cuba."[17] Roosevelt composed a bumptious essay of his own on the Monroe Doctrine during the crisis. In contrast to the backward-looking Cleveland and Olney, Roosevelt aimed to reconfigure the principles of 1823 into a newly assertive and activist foreign policy. It was not just tradition that justified the Doctrine, but the duties and obligations of the newly powerful American nation. "If the Monroe Doctrine did not already exist," Roosevelt wrote, "it would be necessary forthwith to create it."

Roosevelt could not understand why the Cleveland administration worried so much about the legal dimensions of the Venezuela issue, nor about precisely defining the Doctrine. In his eyes, the whole matter could be reduced to a simple test of patriotism and national honor: Would the American people uphold the "essentially moral and essentially manly" Monroe Doctrine, or would the "anti-American side . . . whose Americanism is of the timid and flabby type" prevail and bow once again before the British? Roosevelt recognized that public support for the administration's actions would lead the overstretched British to back down. As the crisis progressed, he thought less about the British and more about those at home who hoped to find a peaceful settlement to the crisis—indeed, he directed his strongest criticism not at the English, but at his domestic opponents. His fellow nationalist Henry Cabot Lodge sang from the same hymnbook. When Lodge wrote about the persistence of "colonialism in the United States," the greatest threat he identified came not from British expansionism, but from those Americans of the "leisure class" who aped the customs of the Old World. "The antics of the bankers, brokers and anglomaniacs generally are humiliating," Roosevelt informed Lodge at the height of the Venezuela crisis. "I rather hope the fight will come soon. The clamor of the peace faction has convinced me that this country needs a war."[18]

The Debate of 1898 and Its Aftermath

Roosevelt would have to wait almost three years for his war, and to settle for fighting the Spanish instead of the British. The cause would be the recurrent instability in Cuba. Once again, the United States became entangled in the dissolution of the Spanish Empire. As in earlier anticolonial rebellions, politicians from across the spectrum viewed Spain's heavy-handed response to the Cuban rebellion as a threat to the United States' interests and ideals. But in contrast to earlier rebellions on the island, when Cubans rose up against the Spanish this time, jingoistic sentiments predominated in the United States. This highly charged public atmosphere not only contributed to the United States' declaration of war against Spain in April 1898, but also played a key role in the decision to annex many of Spain's former colonial possessions at the conclusion of what one American diplomat dubbed "a splendid little war."[19]

Though the rebellion in Cuba paralleled the circumstances of previous invocations of the principles of 1823, the Monroe

Doctrine is most notable for its absence in the debates in the run-up to the United States' declaration of war in April 1898. A few exceptions notwithstanding, the Doctrine was the dog that did not bark. The so-called large policy men—those such as Roosevelt, Lodge, and the naval theorist Alfred Thayer Mahan, who advocated declaring war with Spain and using the conflict to pursue expansionist policies thereafter—generally steered clear of the Monroe Doctrine in 1898. In part this was because of the Doctrine's recent association with conservative Democrats like Grover Cleveland who hoped to avoid entanglement in the Cuban rebellion, not to mention the annexation of Spain's overseas possessions.[20]

The "large policy men" also avoided the Monroe Doctrine because the national exceptionalism it embodied contradicted their rationale for colonial expansion. When arguing for the acquisition of the Philippines, Guam, Puerto Rico, and possibly Cuba, the expansionists made their case in cosmopolitan terms. Colonial expansion was not just the duty of the United States, but it was the obligation of racial superiors the world over, the "white man's burden." Expansion enthusiasts pushed aside traditional suspicion of the British Empire and marveled at the colonial triumphs and administrative efficiency of their "Anglo-Saxon" brethren. "If England can govern foreign lands, so can America," the arch-expansionist Albert Beveridge declared at the height of the expansionist fervor in 1898. Just as Britain and the European powers assumed colonial responsibilities in Africa and Asia, so, too, did the imperialists of 1898 argue that the United States was obliged to uplift the "uncivilized" in Spain's former colonies. Colonial expansion would have the added benefit of strengthening the moral fiber of the imperialist. "India has done an incalculable amount for the English character," Roosevelt wrote. "If we do our work well in the Philippines and the West Indies, it will do a great deal for our character." Such considerations led Roosevelt to form a volunteer regiment, the "Rough

Riders," that arrived in Cuba in time to help take San Juan Hill from the Spanish in 1898.[21]

With its connotations of American exceptionalism and anti-colonialism, the Monroe Doctrine hindered more than helped the proponents of colonial expansion. When the "large policy men" looked back on their nation's history, they emphasized not the Monroe Doctrine, but that other concept with the same capitalized initials—Manifest Destiny. Albert Beveridge's classic imperialist call to arms, "The March of the Flag," chronicled American territorial expansion but neglected to mention the Monroe Doctrine. "We have a record of conquest, colonization, and territorial expansion unequalled by any people in the nineteenth century," Henry Cabot Lodge boasted.[22] Roosevelt similarly trumpeted the conquest of North America and the subjugation of Native Americans in his multivolume *The Winning of the West*. In the 1900 edition of the work, Roosevelt presented 1898 as the culmination of centuries of Indian wars and westward expansion. The expansionists of 1898 drew deeply from the colonialist experience with Native Americans: there was a close correlation in Senate voting patterns on colonialist legislation targeted at Indians and Filipinos; the army applied tactics learned on the Great Plains to the Filipino rebellion; and American courts drew from earlier rulings on Indians as precedent for denying constitutional rights to the new subject peoples in the Philippines.[23]

Those who invoked the Monroe Doctrine in 1898 were not the "large policy men," but rather those who opposed the annexation of Spain's former colonies. Many of these so-called anti-imperialists were old-fashioned liberals of the Hamilton Fish mold (indeed, the president of the American Anti-Imperialist League was an old ally of Fish's from back in the Grant cabinet, George Boutwell). The Anti-Imperialist League boasted powerful supporters, including former presidents from both parties (Benjamin Harrison and Grover Cleveland), a leading business tycoon (Andrew Carnegie), a labor leader (Samuel Gompers), a social reformer (Jane Addams), and an author (Mark Twain). But if the anti-imperialists spanned the political and professional spectrum, they tended to be similar in one regard: age. A study of twelve leading anti-imperialists found their average age to be sixty-nine, a remarkable statistic given the short life spans of the era.[24] Anti-imperialists were often political veterans who looked upon the annexation of Spain's former colonies as a great policy departure. Many had track records of opposing expansionist designs in the Caribbean, such as those promoted by proslavery Democrats or post–Civil War Republicans such as Ulysses S. Grant and James Blaine. Even the younger members of this loose coalition, such as the rising Democrat William Jennings Bryan, looked to past foreign policy traditions for guidance on future policy.

In the hands of these old-timers, the Monroe Doctrine symbolized an imagined tradition of nonentanglement and unalloyed anticolonialism. "Philippine annexation," one anti-imperialist wrote, "is so diametrically opposed to the principles embodied in the Monroe Doctrine that the people of the United States should make a careful study of the subject before abandoning a Doctrine that thus far has been a rudder to the ship of state and a guarantee of good faith to the whole world."[25] Such interpretations required airbrushing out of American history episodes such as Indian removal and the war of conquest against Mexico. Some anti-imperialists argued that the policy and moral failings of these episodes provided reason not to embark upon overseas colonialism. But most simply ignored these past episodes or explained them away by attributing them to the repudiated slave power.

Rather than provide objective history, the anti-imperialists focused on the debate at hand. They aimed to separate the causes of the war with Spain, which many of them had supported on anticolonial grounds, from its far from inevitable consequence of assuming colonial rule of Spain's former possessions. They depicted the program of colonial expansion as the adoption of the very Old World system that the Founding Fathers had repudiated in 1776. Annexation of overseas colonies, William Graham Sumner argued in 1899, constituted the "conquest of the United States by Spain."[26] The anti-imperialists also feared that participation in the game of Old World colonial rivalry would invite European countermoves in the Western Hemisphere. "The Monroe Doctrine is gone," Massachusetts Republican George Frisbie Hoar lamented. "Every European nation, every European alliance, has the right to acquire dominion in this hemisphere when we acquire it in the other."[27] Just as alarming was the prospect of a formal political arrangement with peoples, such as Filipinos and Cubans, whom many anti-imperialists deemed racially inferior and unfit for inclusion into the United States. Anticolonial traditions, geopolitical realism, racism—all these and more were grounds for avoiding a new overseas empire in the eyes of the anti-imperialists.

The anti-imperialists lost the political battle following the War of 1898, in part because of disunity in their own ranks. William Jennings Bryan reluctantly endorsed the Treaty of Paris, which ended the war and ceded Spanish territories to the United States, hoping to take the fight over colonial possessions directly to the American people in the forthcoming election of 1900. Bryan persuaded just enough Democratic senators to vote for the agreement's ratification. With a single vote to spare, the United States annexed the Philippines, Guam, and Puerto Rico as well as securing Spain's withdrawal from Cuba, which was now occupied by American troops. When these events are combined with the annexation of Hawaii earlier that year, 1898 witnessed rapid and dramatic overseas colonial expansion.

Yet the anti-imperialists did not suddenly disappear in 1899. Barely had the ink on the Treaty of Paris dried before they began a campaign promoting withdrawal from the Philippines. An anticolonial rebellion in the Philippines—waged now against, rather than alongside, Americans—played into their hands. The annexationists' promises that colonialism would uplift Filipinos and strengthen Americans alike were undermined by the appalling humanitarian and financial costs required to suppress the Filipino rebels. The anti-imperialists continued to oppose the formal annexation of Cuba. They pointed to the Teller Amendment, passed by Congress in the run-up to the war against Spain back in April 1898, which prohibited the United States from annexing the island. It is a sign of the continued traction of anti-imperialism that the proponents of an interventionist foreign policy appropriated the language and symbols of their opponents. Such would be the case with the Monroe Doctrine, which reemerged in the years after 1898 as the nation's chief foreign policy symbol. The Monroe Doctrine at the turn of the century, however, carried with it new meanings and applications, for it reflected a convergence of thinking between those on either side of the debates of 1898.

One dimension of this convergence was conceptual: the fusion of a unilateral, realist tradition with the newer language that emphasized the imperial responsibilities and duties that a "civilized" nation must shoulder. As the historian Frank Ninkovich has made clear, Roosevelt presented the Monroe Doctrine as an instrument that advanced both the specific interests of the United States and the larger interests of "civilization" itself. The Doctrine, Roosevelt wrote, "is to be justified not by precedent merely, but by the needs of the nation and the true interests of Western civilization." The benefits to the United States were self-evident: the Monroe Doctrine secured American strategic and economic interests in the Western Hemisphere. But Roosevelt went to great lengths to emphasize the advantages it yielded to the broader constituency of civilization. These were twofold. First, the Monroe Doctrine carried with it imperial responsibilities to spread "civilization." It compelled the United States, despite its tradition of nonentanglement, to promote its values and political practices to putatively less civilized peoples.

Second, by establishing U.S. control of the Western Hemisphere, the Monroe Doctrine could eliminate great-power rivalry in areas of strategic importance, such as Cuba and the isthmian passageway in Central America. American hegemony, in this formulation, benefited everyone because it preempted potential wars between civilized powers. Indeed, Roosevelt lamented that no power was strong enough to implement a Monroe Doctrine in China, where imperial competition threatened international stability.[28]

The wedding of nationalism and internationalism broadened the appeal of the Monroe Doctrine. Just as significant to the reemergence of the Doctrine at the turn of the century was a policy convergence between the two sides of the 1898 debate. The "large policy men" distanced themselves from further colonial annexations, while the "anti-imperialists" proved to be the opponents of "colonialism" but not a more general "imperialism." This convergence helped to create a new Monroe Doctrine that was more explicitly interventionist and proactive than its earlier incarnations, but reflected traditional qualms about the formal annexation of peoples of different races in noncontiguous territories. Two important episodes at the beginning of the twentieth century illustrate this emerging synthesis. Both prepared the way for the new conception of the Monroe Doctrine that Theodore Roosevelt would announce in 1904.

The first was Cuba, whose uncertain political status concerned American statesmen in the years following 1898. Though the island remained under the control of an American occupation force led by the military governor Leonard Wood, the 1898 Teller Amendment closed the door to formal annexation. The prospect of full Cuban independence, however, terrified American statesmen. Wood and Secretary of War Elihu Root feared that withdrawal would cede control to what Wood called the "radical elements" of Cuba. Both preferred Cuba to be run by the "business and conservative elements" that would respond to the needs of the United States. "People ask me what we mean by a stable government in Cuba," Wood wrote. "I tell them that when money can be borrowed at a reasonable rate of interest and when capital is willing to invest in the Island, a condition of stability will have been reached."[29]

Wood and Root searched for a way to achieve their objectives in Cuba in early 1901. Reflecting a growing consensus about the high price of the acquisition of the Philippines, both men wanted to avoid the formal annexation of Cuba—and the anticolonial rebellion that any such move might trigger. "We should not commit ourselves to actions which, like some of those of '98, will give us cause for regret and annoyance," Wood wrote.[30] With annexation out of the picture, Root looked to Britain's relationship with Egypt as a model. The Secretary of War marveled at how the British had withdrawn from Egypt but retained the "right of intervention . . . and still maintain[ed] her moral control" over the strategically vital territory. Britain's Egypt policy inspired Root to formulate a plan to establish a U.S. protectorate in Cuba. This move aimed to maximize the strategic and economic benefits of controlling the island while minimizing the risks of triggering a revolt by Cuban nationalists and reopening the divisions at home over annexing new territories.[31]

The Platt Amendment instituted Root's vision. The brain-child of the Secretary of War, this rider to an army appropriations bill placed conditions upon Cuba's independence. It limited Cuba's ability to pursue an independent foreign policy, restricted its ability to borrow money from foreign lenders, and ceded Guantánamo Bay to the United States. Article 3 of the amendment explicitly granted the United States the right to intervene in Cuban affairs. In Root's eyes, this article was the key to the new strategy. The right of intervention would protect American interests and prevent the ascendancy of Cuban radicals. It would signal to European rivals that though the United States was not annexing Cuba, it retained control over the island. And, if agreed to by Cuban leaders, it would provide legal cover for future actions of the United States—something that Root, a former lawyer, was keen to establish. Root and his allies carefully avoided presenting the Platt Amendment as the imperialist arrangement that it was. Rather, they packaged it as the only viable means of Cuban independence. Wood and Root reassured themselves that Platt was the logical extension of the anticolonial Monroe Doctrine, even though no European threatened at the time to intervene in Cuba. It merely "amplifies the Monroe Doctrine," Wood informed Root. Yes, Root responded, "it is the Doctrine itself as international principle."[32]

This argument helped many in the Senate reconcile anticolonialism with calculations of the strategic and economic benefits of controlling Cuba. Old anti-imperial stalwart George Frisbie Hoar bought into the legerdemain. The Platt Amendment, Hoar conceded in the Senate, was "a proper and necessary stipulation for the application of the Monroe Doctrine to the nearest outlying country in America, except Mexico."[33] "Even Hoar, by a path so bewilderingly devious that I am really unable to follow the windings," a jubilant Roosevelt crowed, "has come around to the support of the treaty."[34] Fourteen senators who had supported the Teller Amendment back in 1898 voted for Platt, which passed by the wide margin of 43–20. The Platt Amendment was a tougher sell in Cuba, but Root and Wood gave Cubans little choice. A combination of tough talk and timely reassurances that intervention would be a measure of last resort led Cuban political leaders to accept the Platt arrangement in a 1903 treaty with the United States. Though nominally independent, Cuba would remain a protectorate of the United States until 1934. "There is, of course," Wood wrote to Roosevelt in 1901, "little or no independence left to Cuba under the Platt Amendment."[35]

At the same time American statesmen implemented the Platt Amendment, they developed an interventionist policy in another issue of long-standing importance, an isthmian canal in Central

America. Calls for acting unilaterally on the canal issue intensified in the 1890s. Leading the charge was the naval theorist
Alfred Thayer Mahan, whose research mined Britain's naval history for lessons on how to establish control of the seas (it was perhaps no coincidence that the British also had captured Havana,
Cuba, and Manila, in the Philippines, during a war against Spain
back in the eighteenth century). The 1898 war with Spain was
grist for Mahan's mill. The protracted voyage of the battleship
Oregon, which took more than two months to steam from her base
in San Francisco to the action in the Caribbean, made clear the
strategic benefit of an American-controlled canal. The economic
case for constructing the canal also grew as a result of the increasing lure of the China market, which the United States hoped to
exploit through an "open door" policy that would provide it with
commercial access equal to that enjoyed by European powers.
The failure of the old policy of leaving the construction of a canal
to private companies (several of which had gone bankrupt by this
point) further underscored the need for government action. Even
many Democrats who had previously opposed governmental
action on the canal issue reconsidered their position.

But the 1850 Clayton-Bulwer Treaty still stood in the way.
Secretary of State John Hay had little trouble in getting the
British ambassador, Julian Pauncefote, who well understood the
shift in the balance of power in Central America since 1850, to
revise the old agreement so as to allow the United States to unilaterally construct the canal. This long-sought concession, however, was not enough for the U.S. Senate. Politicians from both
parties railed against the first Hay-Pauncefote Treaty, labeling its
provisions for the neutrality and demilitarization of the future
canal "a deadly blow to the Monroe Doctrine."[36] The Senate now
demanded the right not only to unilaterally construct the canal
but to fortify it as well. Such views of the old 1850 treaty were
not limited to politicians. One historian of the era declared that
Clayton-Bulwer "marks the most serious mistake in our diplo-

matic history, and is the single instance, since its announcement in 1823, of a tacit disavowal or disregard of the Monroe Doctrine."[37] Hay and Pauncefote had little choice but to go back to the drawing board. The second Hay-Pauncefote Treaty, which the Senate promptly ratified in late 1901, forced Britain explicitly to abrogate the Clayton-Bulwer Treaty, as well as allowing the United States to fortify the future canal. After more than fifty troubled years, the experiment in joint Anglo-American control of an isthmian canal officially ended.

Given the green light by the British, the Roosevelt administration next sought to clear the way with Colombia, whose province of Panama had become the favored canal route. Hay and Colombian minister Tomás Herrán agreed on a deal in 1903 in which the United States would get a hundred-year lease on a six-mile strip of territory in Panama for $10 million up front and an annual rent of $250,000. The U.S. Senate quickly ratified the agreement; its Colombian counterpart did not. Roosevelt interpreted the action as an unpardonable breach of faith on the part of Colombia. "I do not think," he wrote, "that the Bogota lot of jack rabbits should be allowed permanently to bar one of the future highways of civilization."[38] It was quite a view for the president of a nation notorious for rejecting treaties to take. "A treaty entering the Senate," John Hay once wrote, "is like a bull going into the arena: no one can say just how or when the blow will fall—but one thing is certain—it will never leave the arena alive."[39] Like the U.S. Senate's numerous rejections of treaties in this era, the Colombian senate's action reflected the hope that better terms could be negotiated in a second agreement. Many Colombians had their eye on the $40 million charter of the New Panama Canal Company, which the United States would have to purchase from them rather than from a French consortium once the company's charter expired in 1904. Opposition to the treaty in Colombia also grew out of domestic political turmoil. Emerging from a bitter three-year civil war at the very moment the

Hay-Herrán deal was debated, Colombian president José Manuel Marroquín exploited the treaty issue to consolidate his grip on power in the war-torn nation.

Roosevelt refused to return to the negotiating table with the Colombians. The administration considered seizing the land required for the canal on the grounds of an international conception of eminent domain. But the actions of Panamanian revolutionaries spared Roosevelt from ordering an outright colonial annexation. Philippe Bunau-Varilla, a lobbyist for the New Panama Canal Company, informed the Roosevelt administration that conditions in Panama were ripe for a revolution to free the province from Colombian rule. Roosevelt seized the opportunity to foster relations with what promised to be a more tractable negotiating partner on the canal issue. The President dispatched warships to Panama to prevent the landing of Colombian troops and secure the success of the revolutionaries. After a few minor hiccups, the scheme unfolded surprisingly well on November 3, 1903, creating the new state of Panama. Barely two weeks passed before Hay and Bunau-Varilla, now operating as Panama's envoy to Washington, hammered out an agreement that ceded a strip of the new nation's territory, as well as aspects of its sovereignty, to the United States. The digging started in 1906, and the American-controlled canal opened in 1914.[40]

In Cuba and Panama, American imperialists pursued interventionist policies in ways that were acceptable to a domestic political audience that was suspicious of further colonial ventures in the 1898 mold. These two episodes foreshadowed a new, hybrid Monroe Doctrine: one that was explicitly interventionist but stopped short of outright colonial expansion. With the notable exceptions of Guantánamo Bay and the leasing of the ten-mile-wide Panama Canal Zone, the United States did not formally annex territories or peoples in these episodes. Rather, American officials secured their strategic interests in the Caribbean by establishing protectorates and cultivating relations with collaborating elites. American commercial interests soon flourished in both places: a 1903 reciprocity treaty brought Cuba into the economic orbit of the United States, and the American presence in Panama paved the way for the American United Fruit Company to assume a dominant position there.

In both episodes, American statesmen sought to maximize benefits while minimizing costs. They aimed to balance international objectives with the imperatives of domestic politics; they searched for a suitable compromise between pursuing overseas interests and maintaining the perception at home that they adhered to national traditions. They shrewdly articulated their imperialist actions in the anticolonial terms of the promotion of independence (in Cuba) and the defense of self-determination (in Panama). They presented the Monroe Doctrine as a benefit both to the United States and to the imagined global constituency of "civilization." "It was a good thing for Egypt and the Sudan, and for the world, when England took Egypt and the Sudan," Roosevelt wrote. "And so it is a good thing, a very good thing, for Cuba and for Panama and for the world that the United States has acted as it has actually done."[41]

To be sure, there were critics of the Platt Amendment and the Panama episode, particularly in the Democratic Party. "Under the McKinley-Roosevelt regime," Richard Olney lamented in 1903, "our character as a nation has been greatly, if not irreparably injured, and we now stand before the world as a bullying, land-grabbing, treaty-breaking, unscrupulous power, all the more offensive for the unctuous and pharisaical professions of the public functionaries who represent us."[42] But there were no national debates on the scale of those in 1898. The alleged anticolonial and humanitarian objectives in Cuba and Panama, when combined with an emerging consensus on the strategic and economic rationale for action in those places, soothed enough consciences to preempt major domestic opposition.

Though this approach worked reasonably well in the realm of

domestic politics, it proved a flawed tactic for stabilizing the Caribbean. The fact that ultimate political power in Cuba resided in Washington destabilized politics on the island. American officials found themselves more and more involved in Cuban affairs and administration despite their efforts to minimize their presence on the island. The imperialist structure established by the Platt Amendment proved counterproductive: it led not to Cuban independence, but to dependence on the United States. Rival political groupings in Cuba competed to secure the support of Washington, thus further involving the United States in Cuban affairs. Intervention "was a self-perpetuating process," the Cuban historian Louis A. Pérez, Jr., has written; "more intervention required more intervention." The U.S. withdrawal from the island in 1902 would prove short-lived. Political unrest in 1906 led Roosevelt to order the troops back, a process that would repeat itself several more times in the next two decades.[43]

Though the construction of the Panama Canal was a technological triumph (indeed, it opened two years ahead of schedule), it, too, raised questions regarding future foreign policy in the region. The strategic and economic importance of the canal paradoxically heightened the anxiety and insecurity of the power that controlled it. "The inevitable effect of our building the Canal must be to require us to police the surrounding premises," Roosevelt informed Root in 1905. "In the nature of things, trade and control, and the obligation to keep order which go with them, must come our way."[44]

The Compromise of the Roosevelt Corollary

At the turn of the century, Americans perceived a new threat to their goals in the Western Hemisphere: Germany. After more than a century in which the British dominated the nightmares of American statesmen, the Germans now assumed the role of bogeyman. Even the most diehard Anglophobe recognized a diminished threat from America's former colonial master after the British backed down in Venezuela and in the Hay-Pauncefote treaties. But Germany was another matter. Like the United States, it underwent a violent process of national consolidation in the mid-nineteenth century and rapidly ascended the global pecking order thereafter.

The similarities between the two nations went further. Thanks in part to protectionist tariffs, the economies and industrial output of both grew rapidly. By 1914, both the United States and Germany would surpass Britain in most tables of economic production. The two nations boasted two of the world's greatest railway systems; both asserted themselves in new ways in international affairs; both began programs of naval buildup (indeed, U.S. Navy officials were so impressed with the upstart German navy that they began to look to it as well as to the Royal Navy for inspiration[45]). Observers in the United States became concerned as they watched Germans increase their commercial presence in Latin America. Also on the increase was the presence of actual Germans, who immigrated to South America, particularly Brazil, in large numbers. It was not long before leaders in each nation identified the other as a potential rival. The Monroe Doctrine, German Chancellor Otto von Bismarck remarked, was a "special manifestation of American arrogance." German activities in the Caribbean and South America, Roosevelt countered, "will make us either put up or shut up on the Monroe Doctrine."[46]

Yet, as in the case of earlier fears of Britain, American statesmen greatly overestimated the German threat. To be sure, German officials sought to promote their interests in the Western Hemisphere. But they moved delicately, careful not to step on the hypersensitive toes of Uncle Sam. There was no plot hatched in Berlin to destroy the Monroe Doctrine.[47] That many American statesmen at the time so misread and misrepresented the German threat reveals two important points. First, they recognized its political utility. It is not a coincidence that those who cried wolf the loudest were those who sought to mobilize support at home for naval buildup and an expansionist foreign policy. Second, the prominence of the German threat reflected the way American statesmen perceived threat through the lens of their fixed policy objectives. Seeking to establish unchallenged supremacy of the Western Hemisphere, it is no wonder that American statesmen were sensitive to every move of a rising Germany.

Another crisis in Venezuela illustrated how the cocktail of threat perception and international ambition laid the foundation for the Roosevelt Corollary to the Monroe Doctrine. In the years after the border dispute with Britain, that unstable country under the thumb of the nationalist Cipriano Castro defaulted on its foreign debts. The Germans and British opted for gunboat diplomacy to press their claims in 1902. In an act of deference to the United States, the Old World powers first ran their plans past Washington. "If any South American State misbehaves towards any European country," Roosevelt responded, "let the European country spank it." But attitudes in the United States soon changed. When the blockade of Venezuela resulted in the sinking of ships and the bombardment of coastal forts, public opinion in the United States denounced the intervention as a violation of the Monroe Doctrine. Though a joint action, the Germans were singled out as the bête noire. Roosevelt soon acted, pressing the intervening parties behind the scenes to refer the matter to the Hague arbitration tribunal. When they consented, Roosevelt patted himself on the back. "The Venezuela business," he wrote, was a "striking enforcement of the Monroe Doctrine and its acquiescence in by great foreign powers, while at the same time a great step forward was taken in the cause of international peace by securing The Hague Tribunal as the arbitrator."[48]

Roosevelt's triumph was short-lived. The Hague Tribunal had little sympathy for defaulting nations. It ruled in early 1904 that the claims of governments that had participated in the intervention in Venezuela would be given priority for repayment. The ruling, one State Department official put it, placed "a premium on violence" and encouraged future European interventions.[49] The Roosevelt administration feared a repeat intervention in Venezuela. It also turned its attention to the crumbling state of Santo Domingo.

The situation there reached a crisis point just as the Hague tribunal issued its ruling. Despite the failure of Ulysses S. Grant's attempt at annexation back in 1870, that Caribbean state came under the de facto control of an American consortium, the Santo Domingo Improvement Company. A creation of the early 1890s (which received the blessing of then secretary of state James Blaine), the SDIC represented the extended economic reach of the United States in Central America and the Caribbean. Though still trailing behind Britain in the race for the markets of South America, the United States had established commercial ascendancy in the Caribbean and Central America (so much so that by 1920 the United States would receive 79 percent of the region's exports and American goods would account for 74 percent of its imports[50]). But like other and more successful enterprises such as the United Fruit Company, the SDIC proved better at pursuing its own interests than it did at bringing political stability to the Caribbean. When the company fell out of favor with a new Dominican government after the assassination of President Ulises Heureaux in 1899, it used its influence in Washington to secure through arbitration a preferential debt repayment schedule. Dominican president Carlos Morales, however, denied the legitimacy of the arbitration. Meanwhile, European creditors objected to any preferential treatment of the SDIC, and their governments threatened to pursue their claims through intervention. By early 1904, the prospect of European intervention led the Morales government to appeal to the Roosevelt administration to prevent such a violation of the Monroe Doctrine.[51]

These circumstances ultimately led Roosevelt to issue his "corollary" to the Monroe Doctrine. Yet unilateral intervention was not the only option on the table. Back in 1902 during the Venezuela debt crisis, the Argentine foreign minister Luis María Drago proposed a hemispheric policy of dealing with the threat of European intervention for debt repayment. The so-called Drago Doctrine called for the governments of the Western Hemisphere to announce jointly their opposition to any intervention in the New World aimed at collecting debts. In his correspondence with Secretary of State John Hay, Drago shrewdly presented his proposal as a logical outgrowth of the Monroe Doctrine in that it would forestall European intervention in the New World. Drago was not the only statesman to propose multilateral action to resolve the troublesome issue of defaulting American governments. The French, Italians, and Belgians floated an idea that would have the United States and Europeans share the burden of sorting out the financial problems of the Dominican Republic. Modeled after joint European ventures in Greece and Turkey, this plan assigned each intervening party its own Dominican customs house to manage.

One can imagine statesmen other than Roosevelt being receptive to these alternatives to unilateral intervention. But neither of these options appealed to the American president, who viewed the Dominican crisis as a test of his nation's commitment to promote civilization in its sphere of influence. Though he had some sympathy with Drago's proposal, Roosevelt rejected a total ban on intervention for debt collection. He preferred the unilateralism of the Monroe Doctrine to the multilateralism of the Drago Doctrine. Roosevelt wanted to preserve the freedom to act in the future, particularly in Venezuela, where Castro continued to be uncooperative to American interests. The European proposal had even less traction, for it would be a dishonorable dereliction of the nation's duty to uphold the Monroe Doctrine and maintain order in its own backyard. A multilateral intervention would only open the door to the strategically vital Caribbean to the grasping designs of Europeans. In Roosevelt's eyes, the policy the United States should pursue "is the simplest common sense, and only the fool or the coward can treat it as aught else . . . if we intend to say 'Hands off' to the powers of Europe, then sooner or later we must keep order ourselves."[52]

Roosevelt chose the same forum used by Monroe in 1823 and Polk in 1845 to announce his corollary to the Doctrine: the President's annual message to Congress in December 1904. "Chronic wrongdoing, or an impotence which results in a general loosening of the ties of civilized society," Roosevelt declared, "may in America, as elsewhere, ultimately require intervention by some civilized nation, and in the Western Hemisphere the adherence of the United States to the Monroe Doctrine may force the United States, however reluctantly, in flagrant cases of such wrongdoing or impotence, to the exercise of an international police power." The message articulated the themes Roosevelt had come to associate with the Doctrine: inevitable conflict between the civilized and uncivilized peoples of the world (or between the manly and the impotent, as the former "Rough Rider" often put it); the United States as the rightful judge and guardian of civilization in the Western Hemisphere; and strict opposition to imperial rivalry in geographic proximity to the United States. Shortly after delivering his annual message, Roosevelt announced his intention to assume control of Dominican customs houses, the central source of revenue in the unstable republic. This act would preempt European intervention by giving the United States the capacity and authority to repay the foreign creditors of the Dominican Republic.[53]

This new "Corollary of the Monroe Doctrine," as the Roosevelt administration called it, explicitly transformed the negatively framed and noninterventionist message of 1823 into a proactive call for intervention. Its logic was rich with irony. Roosevelt sought to intervene in the Caribbean on behalf of Western civilization to preempt European powers from advancing that same civilization in the same place.[54] The European threat to Santo Domingo provided the pretext, rather than the rationale, for the Roosevelt Corollary. Throughout his political career, Roosevelt campaigned for an assertive and interventionist foreign policy. He called for war against Chile in 1891; he rattled the saber during the Venezuela crisis of 1895–96; he repeatedly made the case for naval buildup; he beat the war drum in 1898 and helped formulate the "large policy" of colonial expansion; he sought to control Cuba under the Platt regime; he helped pry Panama out of the hands of Colombia. Roosevelt believed that such actions advanced national interests, promoted "civilization" where it needed to be promoted, and furthered the cause of world peace by preempting great-power rivalry. "It is our duty," the President declared, "to police these countries in the interest of order and civilization."[55]

But Roosevelt was an astute enough politician to know that not all of his compatriots saw things in the same light. Rather than declare a "Roosevelt Doctrine"—a recommendation made by Philippe Bunau-Varilla a year earlier[56]—the President sought political cover by packaging his policy as an outgrowth of a revered tradition. Like President Polk before him, TR used an anticolonial symbol to extend legitimacy to an interventionist policy. "This in reality entails no new obligation upon us," Roosevelt said of his Dominican intervention, "for the Monroe doctrine means precisely such a guaranty on our part."[57] Roosevelt feared that the political coalition that opposed the "large policy" in 1898 and had grumbled about his actions in Panama the previous year would object to his Santo Domingo intervention.

Roosevelt shrewdly waited until after his 1904 election victory to announce his policy in full, delegating the public relations in the meantime to his new secretary of state, Elihu Root. In May 1904, Roosevelt and Root chose a dinner celebrating Cuba's 1902 independence as the occasion to announce the administration's new policy of intervention. Root walked the tightrope of speaking loudly enough so that European governments could hear, but not so loudly as to provoke critics at home before the November election. Root also became the point man after Roosevelt's annual message. In a speech in New York aimed at undermining domestic opposition, Root argued that Roosevelt's 1904 message was less imperialist than Richard Olney's "extreme declaration" back in 1895, which proclaimed that "the United States is sovereign to-day upon this continent, and its fiat is law." Roosevelt's message, Root argued, "is a disclaimer of all that we ought not to arrogate to ourselves in that broad and somewhat rhetorical statement of Mr. Olney."[58] The formulators of a nakedly interventionist policy hustled to present themselves as guardians of America's anticolonial tradition.

Opponents of Roosevelt recognized what the administration was up to. "Root undertakes to make you in part responsible for the Rooseveltian extension of the Monroe doctrine," Olney's perplexed brother informed the former secretary of state. "Don't you think you ought to repudiate the assertion?"[59] Democrats soon got their chance to strike back. Roosevelt submitted to the Senate the protocol arranged with the Dominicans that gave the United States control of the nation's customs houses. The President once again presented the agreement as a test of the nation's commitment to the Monroe Doctrine: "either we must abandon our duty under our traditional policy . . . or else we must ourselves take seasonable and appropriate action . . . This protocol affords a practical test of the efficiency of the United States Government in maintaining the Monroe doctrine." When the opposition mobilized, TR went further, informing a correspondent that "every man who votes against this treaty by his vote invites foreign nations to violate the Monroe Doctrine."[60]

Senate Democrats refused to be browbeaten. "I subscribe to every sentiment of the Monroe doctrine," the Maryland Democrat Isidor Rayner declared in the Senate, "that is, the genuine doctrine, the old text and not the revised edition; the original document and not the counterfeit presentment."[61] Some of this opposition can be attributed to simple party politics and a desire to embarrass the Roosevelt administration. But there were substantive objections to the treaty, which many thought involved the United States too deeply in the affairs of an unstable Caribbean nation. The protocol pledged the United States to respect Dominican territorial integrity, a clause uncomfortably close to a security guarantee. The agreement also put Washington in the position of adjusting the Dominican debt, thus placing itself in the middle of a potential scramble for Dominican funds.

Roosevelt was outraged when the special session of the Senate adjourned early in 1905 without ratifying the agreement. He lambasted the "mischievous monkeys" (a nomenclature he normally reserved for Latin Americans) and "the average yahoo among the Democratic Senators, [who] are wholly indifferent to national honor or national welfare." The President refused to allow the Senate's inaction to derail his plans in the Dominican Republic. Roosevelt ordered by executive fiat the takeover of Dominican customs houses, as well as encouraging private American financiers to consolidate the troubled nation's debt. "The Constitution did not explicitly give me power to bring about the necessary agreement with Santo Domingo," he later wrote. "But the Constitution did not forbid my doing what I did." Paradoxically, it was the very weakness of the imperialist impulse in early-twentieth-century America that led Roosevelt to pursue this portentous act of what later became known as the "imperial presidency."[62]

Though some opponents of the administration cried foul, the limited nature of the U.S. government's role in the intervention soon appeased them. TR had no intention of annexing Dominican territory (in contrast, it should be pointed out, to his Republican predecessors such as Ulysses S. Grant and Frederick Douglass). "I have about the same desire to annex it," Roosevelt stated, "as a gorged boa constrictor might have to swallow a porcupine wrong-end to."[63] The President satisfied proponents of small government by limiting the government's intervention only to Dominican customs houses. The administration outsourced the messy details of internal Dominican finances to private American banks, which arranged a bailout loan for the troubled republic. In order to secure the Senate's approval of the intervention in 1907, Roosevelt proved willing to explicitly limit its scope. Unlike its earlier version, the 1907 agreement eliminated the sections that might compel the United States to defend Dominican territory or to adjust the Dominican debt. The 1907 protocol also included the symbolic concession of deleting all references to the Monroe Doctrine, thus ensuring that future administrations could not point to it as an example of legislative support for the Roosevelt Corollary. Indeed, Roosevelt learned that the Doctrine had become a political lightning rod—both at home and in Latin America—and rarely referred to it in public during his second term as president.

The Roosevelt Corollary boldly announced the United States' intention to exercise an interventionist "international police power" in the Caribbean. Yet it did not launch the United States into a program of formal colonialism or territorial expansion. Constrained by domestic opponents and its commitments in the Philippines and Cuba, the Roosevelt administration sought to limit its ventures in the Caribbean without abandoning its overall goal of establishing hegemony. The administration restricted the intervention to a customs receivership; it trained a Frontier Customs Guard so that Dominicans could one day assume control of the customs houses themselves; and it delegated to private banks on Wall Street the administration and consolidation of the Dominican debt.[64] The implementation of the corollary also necessitated the prioritization of strategic interests. When Roosevelt delivered his 1904 message, many commentators thought it portended multiple interventions (indeed, the message never singled out Santo Domingo by name). Roosevelt appears seriously to have considered a similar action in Venezuela, but chose to spend his political capital on the Santo Domingo intervention. "In Cuba, Santo Domingo and Panama we have interfered in various different ways," Roosevelt wrote at the end of his presidency. "I would have interfered in some similar fashion in Venezuela, in at least one Central American State, and in Haiti already, simply in the interest of civilization, if I could have waked up our people so that they would back a reasonable and intelligent foreign policy."[65]

In the coming decades, American statesmen would be less inhibited about intervening under the Roosevelt Corollary. As instability in the Caribbean and Central America increased, domestic constraints decreased. Indeed, it would be none other than a Democratic president and apostle of self-determination, Woodrow Wilson, who ordered the most interventions of the era. Between 1898 and 1934 (when Franklin Delano Roosevelt's "good neighbor" policy distanced his administration from the right of intervention proclaimed by his distant relative back in 1904), the United States repeatedly intervened in the Caribbean: in Cuba, in Panama, in the Dominican Republic, in Honduras, in Mexico, in Nicaragua, in Haiti. In the wake of the marines came the "dollar diplomacy" contingent of American businessmen, financial experts, and investment capital.

In Theodore Roosevelt's second administration, however, most of these interventions lay in the future. Indeed, the combination of domestic constraints and rising anti-Americanism in Latin America led the Roosevelt administration to distance itself from its new corollary. The key figure here was Secretary of State Root, who feared that repeated interventions would prove both costly and detrimental to the standing of the United States in Latin America. Root's public addresses on the Monroe Doctrine made clear that he viewed intervention as a measure of last resort. He reiterated this theme during his goodwill tour of Latin

America in 1906 (the first time a sitting secretary of state had traveled there). Hiram Bingham, perhaps America's greatest critic of the 1823 shibboleth in the early twentieth century, conceded that Root's address in Rio de Janeiro was "the Monroe Doctrine at its best."[66] Even Roosevelt took part in this public diplomacy counteroffensive. "In many parts of South America," Roosevelt asserted in his 1906 annual message, "there has been much misunderstanding of the attitude and purposes of the United States toward the other American republics. An idea had become prevalent that our assertion of the Monroe Doctrine implied or carried with it an assumption of superiority and of a right to exercise some sort of a protectorate over the countries to whose territory over that doctrine applies. Nothing could be farther from the truth." Roosevelt here was disingenuous, for his Monroe Doctrine manifestly did carry with it assumptions of cultural superiority, and he certainly had considered establishing protectorates in troubled regions. But his remarks demonstrated newfound recognition of the importance of Latin American perceptions of the United States.[67]

This shift in rhetoric did bring with it some changes in policy. Root sought to construct U.S.-led legal processes and institutions to nip in the bud troublesome political situations in the Caribbean before they required all-out intervention. At a 1907 conference with Central American governments in Washington, the Secretary of State helped establish a Central American Court to arbitrate future disputes in this region. Root also sought to avert the need for the United States to engage in costly interventions by embedding a process of arbitration into the structure of international law. When the Russians organized a second international conference at The Hague in 1906, Root seized the opportunity to use it to the United States' advantage. At the conference, Root advocated a variant of the Drago Doctrine. He proposed that disputes over public debts, such as those that lay behind the recent crises in Venezuela and Santo Domingo, be sent to a newly empowered international claims tribunal. But his proposal carefully left the door open to the Roosevelt Corollary by allowing intervention in cases in which the arbitration process proved inadequate. The Hague convention approved Root's plan, despite the no votes of Latin American delegates who objected to the interventionist loophole that had not been part of the original Drago Doctrine (indeed, Drago himself, who represented Argentina at the conference, voted against the U.S. proposal).[68]

Though Latin Americans voted against Root's proposal at The Hague, their view of the Roosevelt administration was not unremittingly adversarial. Here one must distinguish between states in the Caribbean region, which were the actual or threatened targets of American intervention, and those in South America, whose relationship with the United States actually improved as a result of Root's diplomatic initiatives. American interventionism did not go down well in Mexico, where Porfirio Díaz had begun to view his northern neighbor as a threat to Mexican sovereignty and his own political position. Roosevelt's actions in the Caribbean and Central America tightened the U.S. grip around Mexico. "It is unpleasant, to say the least, to hear the knock of the officious policeman on the front door," stated the traditionally pro-American *Mexican Herald*.[69] The so-called Díaz Doctrine, which called for the states of the Americas to collectively enforce the Monroe Doctrine, reflected the Mexican leader's attempt to moderate Yankee imperialism while still capitalizing upon close economic relations with his northern neighbor. Little came of this multilateral vision of the Monroe Doctrine, not least because of Díaz's increasingly precarious position in Mexico.[70]

If the Roosevelt Corollary alienated an important neighbor, it did find support in quarters traditionally hostile to the United States. In stark contrast to the rivalries of the Washington Conference back in 1889–90, the United States found allies in South America. The Argentinians, whose economic interests and racialized thinking now allied them with the North Americans, became supporters of U.S.-led pan-Americanism. The Argentine minister to Washington, Epifanio Portela, went so far as to endorse the Roosevelt Corollary.[71] The 1906 pan-American conference assembled at a new building in Rio de Janeiro, the Palácio Monroe. Roosevelt reciprocated, proclaiming that some South American nations had attained "civilized" status. The American president stated in 1901 that he viewed the Monroe Doctrine "as being the equivalent to an open door in South America." Argentina, Brazil, and Chile, Roosevelt asserted, were "guarantors of the doctrine so far as America south of the Equator is concerned." (In contrast, to ask the same of states in the Caribbean and Central America "would be about like asking the Apaches and Utes to guarantee it.")[72]

The reaction to the Roosevelt Corollary across the Atlantic was largely acquiescent. Unlike the 1823 message, which divided the globe longitudinally into New World and Old World, the Roosevelt Corollary made the opposite bifurcation: latitudinally, between the "civilized" powers of the north and the "uncivilized" powers of the south. The 1823 message challenged the international order espoused by European powers; the 1904 message embraced it. There were, of course, grumbles in European capitals about the pretensions of the Americans, not least because Roosevelt's 1904 message asserted that the United States might have a "manifest duty" to intervene in extreme humanitarian disasters, whether or not they occurred inside America's sphere of influence. Despite this moralistic assertion, the Roosevelt Corollary advanced the interests of the European order both in legitimating the imperialist spread of "civilization" and in the more hardheaded sense of helping European creditors to recover their loans in the Caribbean. "Whatever the American people might think or say about it, they would sooner or later have to police those islands, not against Europe, but for Europe," wrote Henry Adams, the grandson of the primary author of the Monroe Doctrine.[73]

No power applauded the Roosevelt Corollary more than did Britain. Statesmen in London long had waited for the United

States to relieve the Royal Navy of the burden of upholding the Monroe Doctrine. Soon after Roosevelt announced his corollary, British naval planners relocated major naval units from Atlantic waters. "The rest of the world, and this country in particular," the London *Economist* asserted, "cannot fail to regard with satisfaction the [message of] the President of the United States." Many observers viewed the episode as the final act in the prolonged transfer of hemispheric supremacy from Britain to her former colonies. This process entailed not just a shift in the balance of power, but also the transfer of imperialist methods and tactics. Even if American imperialists reconfigured British practices to comport with their distinctive national tastes, there was no hiding the influence of the British Empire on its nascent American counterpart. "The process indicated by the President," the London *Times* wrote of the Roosevelt Corollary, "is one that has been carried out again and again—in Turkey, in Egypt, in China, in Cuba, in Asia by ourselves and others."[74]

American statesmen acknowledged their gratitude to the empire they had once rebelled against. "Its strength will be our strength, and the weakening it injury to us," Alfred Thayer Mahan wrote. "The downfall of the British Empire," Roosevelt asserted, "I should regard as a calamity to the race, and especially to this country."[75] Though British power had long benefited the United States, few American statesmen acknowledged this fact until the turn of the century. They did so only after the British had bowed before the Monroe Doctrine in the Venezuela crisis, had twice consented to revise the hated Clayton-Bulwer Treaty, and had applauded the Roosevelt Corollary. With an empire to call their own, Americans finally saw themselves as the equals of their former colonial master.

The Roosevelt Corollary marked an important development in American strategic thinking. It explicitly announced the United

States' intention to project its power in the Caribbean and Central America, where the sight of U.S. marines, and the business interests that so often accompanied them, would become commonplace in the coming decades.

Just as important were the conceptual innovations of the corollary. Roosevelt's corollary to the Monroe Doctrine was a statement of a self-confident nation concerned more with the great game of imperial rivalry than with the internal dynamics of its once fragile union of states. "We have become a great nation," Roosevelt stated in his inaugural address in 1905, "and we must behave as beseems a people with such responsibilities." His version of the Monroe Doctrine differed in this regard from the message of 1823. Even Olney's 1895 "twenty-inch gun," despite its bombast, was a deeply anxious document. In contrast to previous major statements on the Monroe Doctrine, Roosevelt's 1904 message did not mention the threat of European monarchy, which was no longer the glue holding the American nation together. Nor did the 1904 message seek to insulate the United States from the turbulent world of European power politics by dividing the globe into the separate spheres of the New World and the Old World.

Rather, the Roosevelt Corollary announced a new international role for the United States. Roosevelt drew strength from the nation, accommodated its anticolonial tradition, and went about building its empire.

Conclusion

L ike most of his nineteenth-century predecessors, President Woodrow Wilson believed that American principles would transform global politics. Unlike many of his predecessors, Wilson presided over a nation that was no longer subordinate to British power. Indeed, the roles of the two English-speaking states were quickly reversed during the course of the Great War that began in 1914: it was now the British who were in need of American capital, commerce, and support. Wilson hoped to use his nation's newfound power as leverage for the construction of a new world order. A cosmopolitan who considered William Gladstone a political hero, Wilson sought to embed anti-imperialism, self-determination, open diplomacy, economic liberalism, freedom of the seas, and international cooperation into the fabric of international relations. He aimed to replace the defunct European "balance of power" with a new "community of power" premised upon American principles. "I am proposing, as it were," Wilson asserted to Congress in January 1917, "that the nations should with one accord adopt the doctrine of President Monroe as the doctrine of the world; that no nation should seek to extend its polity over any other nation or people, but that every people should be left free to determine its own polity, its own way of development, unhindered, unthreatened, unafraid, the little along with the great and powerful."[1]

Wilson's rhetoric made him an instant global celebrity. Anticolonial nationalists within Old World empires were particularly drawn to his promise of a new world order. "It is impossible that the noble truths uttered by President Wilson in his War Message could be limited in their application," proclaimed the Indian nationalist Lala Lajpat Rai in 1918. "Henceforth, his words are going to be the war cry of all small and subject and oppressed nationalities in the world." A compatriot of Rai called for a "Monroe Doctrine for India."[2] Yet these high hopes were disappointed when Wilson negotiated a peace treaty to conclude the Great War that upheld the old colonial order. Despite America's newfound power, Wilson could not impose his views upon the Allied powers, who were intent upon justifying the appalling costs of the war through an advantageous peace treaty. Wilson thus accepted a flawed treaty at the Paris peace conference, holding out hope that the new League of Nations would right its wrongs and advance American principles in the future.

Wilson also found it impossible to live up to his anti-imperial rhetoric in the United States' sphere of influence. He came into office in 1913 hoping to improve relations with Latin America. "We must prove ourselves their friends and champions upon terms of equality and honor," he declared to an audience of businessmen in Mobile, Alabama.[3] He told a group of Mexican newspaper editors that the problem with the Monroe Doctrine was that it "was adopted without your consent . . . We did not ask whether it was agreeable to you that we should be your big brother."[4] Yet Wilson's administration soon acted like a bullying big brother. Fearful that disorder in the Caribbean endangered America's strategic and economic interests, Wilson resorted to forcible intervention—in Mexico, Cuba, Haiti, and the Dominican Republic. To Latin Americans, Wilson's Monroe Doctrine was not new at all, but simply a vigorous implementation of the Roosevelt Corollary.

This juxtaposition of anticolonial ambitions and imperial actions was characteristic of the first century of the Monroe Doctrine. Wilson's invocation of the Doctrine also drew from earlier traditions in that it was in large part intended for domestic audiences. Fully aware that his internationalist foreign policy would leave him exposed to charges that he violated the American tradition of nonentanglement in Europe, Wilson sought the cover of the old dogma of 1823. He went so far as to acquire explicit international acquiescence to the Monroe Doctrine in the covenant of the League of Nations.[5] Wilson's domestic political opponents were not appeased. "If we are to abandon the Monroe Doctrine," his archrival Henry Cabot Lodge asserted, "this is the one way of doing it."[6] The Republican-led opposition argued that the League of Nations was a British plot that would trap the United States into maintaining the imperiled British Empire. Wilson's opponents carried the day, thwarting the entry of the United States into the League of Nations. It would take another world war before Americans embraced Wilson's global conception of the Monroe Doctrine.

By the early twentieth century, the Monroe Doctrine had become a national myth that stood alongside the other foundational symbols of American history. The "statesmen of 1823" became the diplomatic counterparts to the "Founding Fathers" of the 1787 Constitution. "I believe strictly in the Monroe Doctrine, in our Constitution, and in the laws of God," asserted Mary Baker Eddy on the occasion of the centenary of the 1823 message. "Few persons can define it," wrote the historian Dexter Perkins, who authored a magisterial three-volume history of the Doctrine in the 1920s and '30s, "but that does not matter. One does not have to analyze in order to believe." The power of the mythic

Monroe Doctrine was so great that objective attempts to assess its origins and growth, such as that of Perkins, only reinforced its status as a national dogma. Critics of the "obsolete shibboleth," as Hiram Bingham called it, were bewildered by its ability to absorb criticism and persist as a symbol of American statecraft when its invocation counterproductively antagonized Latin Americans. "Hoary with age, it has defied the advance of commerce, the increase of transportation facilities," Bingham wrote in 1913. "Old ideas, proverbs, catchwords, national shibboleths die hard."[7]

The iconic stature of the Monroe Doctrine in later times obscured its complex and protean nature in the nineteenth century. Twentieth-century Americans viewed the Doctrine as a symbol of the rising power of the United States. The acquiescence of Old World powers to the Doctrine, they argued, served as evidence of the increased authority of the United States. The unraveling of European empires and the ascendancy of American political and economic principles served as further evidence of the centrality of the Doctrine to the emergence of the so-called American century. On one level, such an interpretation is absolutely correct: the United States transformed itself from a weak collection of former colonies into a global power that peoples around the world respected and, at times, feared. The transformation of the Monroe Doctrine from a limited, reactive statement of anticolonialism to an imperialist instrument that asserted the right of intervention symbolized this development.

Yet the Monroe Doctrine of the twentieth-century popular imagination airbrushed the larger geopolitical context in which the young United States operated, one far different from that of the "American century." It was British naval power and diplomacy, combined with the power of the states of Latin America, that prevented the recolonization of territories in the Western Hemisphere in the nineteenth century. George Canning hedged in 1823 that Britain's interests would best be advanced through opposition to European intervention in the Western Hemisphere and cooperation with the United States. The implication of this policy, however, was that the subsequent job of containing an expansionist United States would fall upon the shoulders of Britain. It was a task that Canning's successors would not be interested in taking up. It was in this hospitable environment that the American empire took root.

British power served as midwife to the rising American empire in a number of other ways. Americans exploited the wealth of their former colonial master, using British capital to integrate their vast territory and to help construct an economy that would become the world's largest in terms of overall output by the turn of the century. Britain's global economic system— its banks, communication networks, political connections, and other structures—benefited American businessmen, traders, and shippers, who labored to supplant their British rivals. To be sure, Britain constituted the greatest external threat to the United States in the nineteenth century. The specter of British power exacerbated internal divisions within the union, particularly those regarding slavery, thus contributing to the great sectional conflict that would result in civil war in 1861. Yet even here, the British menace at times cut the other way. The existence of the American union itself owed something to the lingering threat of Britain after 1783. If British antislavery helped pull the union apart in the mid-nineteenth century by leading Southerners to demand controversial safeguards for slavery, it should not be overlooked that it played an important role in binding together the states and sections of the early republic. Moreover, Britain declined the opportunity to help divide the American republic when the Confederacy begged it to do so during the Civil War. The Anglophobic card also helped politicians curry favor for the nationalist foreign and economic policies that were instrumental to the construction of the American empire.

The Monroe Doctrine proclaimed national exceptionalism.

Yet it emerged and evolved in relation to the foreign policies of other expansionist powers. The British Empire most often provided a model—both positive and negative—for nineteenth-century Americans. Its diverse forms allowed Americans to find in it what they wanted. Anticolonialists scored political points at home by condemning British practices in Ireland and India; proponents of nonintervention pointed to the state papers of Lord Castlereagh, which articulated this principle before the 1823 message; naval theorists such as Alfred Thayer Mahan marveled at the triumphs of the Royal Navy; businessmen and exporters mimicked the strategies employed by their British counterparts; American statesmen found inspiration in the tactics of "informal imperialism" employed by the British in Latin America and East Asia. Though the Monroe Doctrine aimed to supplant British power in the Western Hemisphere, it drew deeply from the practices of the British Empire in Latin America. Imperial influence in the nineteenth century was not unidirectional. The federal and anticolonial model of the American empire intrigued British leaders—one thinks here of the British North America Act of 1867, which recalled the territorial governments of the Northwest Ordinance in how it aimed to satisfy the demands of white settlers for home rule (in this case, in Canada) while at the same time securing the strategic and economic interests of the metropolitan government.

The Monroe Doctrine imagined by later Americans glossed over another of its defining features: its contested meaning and controversial application. Nineteenth-century Americans attached an array of policies and worldviews to the Monroe Doctrine. Indeed, it is misleading to refer to the Monroe Doctrine in the singular. There were as many Monroe Doctrines as there were perspectives on nineteenth-century statecraft: an isolationist one and an internationalist one; pro- and antislavery interpretations; expansionist and antiannexationist ones; interventionist and noninterventionist; one concerned exclusively with ideology and another interested only with interests. An "Anglo-Saxonist" Monroe Doctrine existed, as did one that celebrated "pan-Americanism." Peoples outside the United States articulated their own interpretations of the Monroe Doctrine, often in an attempt to direct American power on behalf of their own ends. Latin American statesmen exploited Yankee insecurities with ever more deftness as the nineteenth century progressed, even as they denounced the pretensions of the Monroe Doctrine. British leaders came to recognize that swallowing the bitter pill of accepting American hemispheric preeminence was sweetened by the fact that the United States would have to assume the burdens that came with its imperialist claims.

The nineteenth-century Monroe Doctrine was the product of the rivalry, interaction, and, at times, synthesis between competing interpretations of the role the United States should play in international affairs. The scramble between different politicians to claim the Monroe Doctrine fueled the rising nationalism of nineteenth-century America. The race to appropriate the dogma of 1823 stigmatized certain ideas and policies, thus leading to a convergence of political and diplomatic views. Debates about the Monroe Doctrine also contributed to the ascendency of an imperialist mind-set that, as the nineteenth century progressed, increasingly regarded Latin Americans as the racial inferiors of "Anglo-Saxons" in the United States.

Two moments of compromise and consensus provide bookends for the nineteenth-century Monroe Doctrine. The first was the compromise of 1823, in which the members of the Monroe cabinet formulated an extensive conception of national security even as they agreed on a limited and noncommittal course of action with regard to the perceived threat of the intervention of the Holy Allies. The second was the Roosevelt Corollary of 1904, which bridged the gap between those on either side of the great debate of 1898 by embracing an openly interventionist policy in the Caribbean, but one that stopped short of full colonial annexation. Though packaged as an extension of traditional anti-colonialism, the Roosevelt Corollary revealed how much had changed since 1823. No longer an insecure grouping of former colonies, the United States was now a great power with self-imposed imperial "duties." Herein lay the great paradox of the Monroe Doctrine: its anticolonialism and idealism—its enlightened call for a new world order premised upon nonintervention, republican self-government, and an open world economy—justified and empowered an imperialist role for the United States in international affairs.

Notes

Suggestions for Further Reading

Acknowledgments

Index

Notes

Abbreviations
CG   *Congressional Globe*
FRUS   *Foreign Relations of the United States*
JA, JQA   John Adams, John Quincy Adams
LC   Library of Congress
TR   Theodore Roosevelt

Introduction
 1. William Appleman Williams, *The Tragedy of American Diplomacy* (New York: W. W. Norton, 1972), pp. 18–58; Frank Ninkovich, *The United States and Imperialism* (Oxford: Blackwell's, 2001).
 2. Quoted in Walter LaFeber, *The New Empire: An Interpretation of American Expansion, 1860–1898* (Ithaca, N.Y.: Cornell University Press, 1963), p. 53.
 3. Rogan Kersh, *Dreams of a More Perfect Union* (Ithaca, N.Y.: Cornell University Press, 2001); Elizabeth R. Varon, *Disunion! The Coming of the American Civil War, 1789–1859* (Chapel Hill: University of North Carolina Press, 2008).
 4. Mary D. McFeely and William S. McFeely (eds.), *Memoirs and Selected Letters: Personal Memoirs of U. S. Grant, Selected Letters 1839–1865* (Library of America, 1990), p. 774; David C. Hendrickson, *Peace Pact: The Lost World of the American Founding* (Lawrence: University Press of Kansas, 2003).

1: Independence
 1. Lester D. Langley, *The Americas in the Age of Revolution, 1750–1850* (New Haven, Conn.: Yale University Press, 1996).
 2. Richard W. Van Alstyne, *The Rising American Empire* (New York: Oxford University Press, 1960); David M. Fitzsimmons, "Tom Paine's New World Order: Idealistic Internationalism in the Ideology of Early American Foreign Relations," *Diplomatic History* 19:4 (Fall 1995), pp. 568–82.

3. James Belich, *Replenishing the Earth: The Settler Revolution and the Rise of the Anglo-World, 1783–1939* (New York: Oxford University Press, 2009).
4. John Darwin, *The Empire Project: The Rise and Fall of the British World-System, 1830–1970* (Cambridge: Cambridge University Press, 2009).
5. Henry Cabot Lodge, "Colonialism in the United States," *Atlantic Monthly* (May 1883), pp. 612–27.
6. Quoted in Kinley Brauer, "The United States and British Imperial Expansion, 1815–1860," *Diplomatic History* 12 (Winter 1988), pp. 19-37.
7. Quoted in Peter Onuf, *Jefferson's Empire: The Language of American Nationhood* (Charlottesville: University Press of Virginia, 2000), p. 90.
8. Jefferson to Livingston, April 18, 1802, in Jefferson, *The Writings of Thomas Jefferson* (Washington, D.C.: Taylor & Maury, 1853–54), p. 432.
9. Bradford Perkins, *The First Rapprochement: England and the United States, 1795–1805* (Berkeley: University of California Press, 1967); Samuel Flagg Bemis, *Pinckney's Treaty: America's Advantage from Europe's Distress, 1783–1800* (Baltimore: Johns Hopkins Press, 1926).
10. George Washington, "Farewell Address," September 17, 1796; Alexander DeConde, "Washington's Farewell, the French Alliance, and the Election of 1796," in Burton Ira Kaufman (ed.), *Washington's Farewell Address: The View from the 20th Century* (Chicago: Quadrangle Books, 1969).
11. Quoted in Frank Prochaska, *The Eagle and the Crown: Americans and the British Monarchy* (New Haven, Conn.: Yale University Press, 2008), p. 82.
12. This discussion draws from David C. Hendrickson, *Peace Pact: The Lost World of the American Founding* (Lawrence: University Press of Kansas, 2003) and *Union, Nation, or Empire: The American Debate over International Relations, 1789–1941* (Lawrence: University Press of Kansas, 2009), and Peter Onuf, "A Declaration of Independence for Diplomatic Historians," *Diplomatic History* 22:1 (January 1998), pp. 71–83.
13. Jay quote from Peter Onuf, "The Expanding Union," in David T. Konig (ed.), *Devising Liberty: Preserving and Creating Freedom in the New American Republic* (Stanford, Calif.: Stanford University Press, 1995), pp. 50–80; Lawrence Goldman (ed.), *The Federalist Papers* (Oxford: Oxford University Press, 2008), pp. 26, 67.
14. Hendrickson, *Peace Pact*, p. 21.
15. Quoted in James E. Lewis, *John Quincy Adams: Policymaker for the Union* (Wilmington, Del.: SR Books, 2001), p. 7.
16. George Washington, "Farewell Address," September 17, 1796; Thomas Jefferson, "Inaugural Address," March 4, 1801.
17. Quoted in Hendrickson, *Peace Pact*, p. 174.
18. Belich, *Replenishing the Earth*, p. 224.
19. Thomas Jefferson, "Second Inaugural Address," March 4, 1805.
20. Quoted in Brian Balogh, *A Government Out of Sight: The Mystery of National Authority in Nineteenth-Century America* (New York: Cambridge University Press, 2009), p. 168.
21. John Craig Hammond, *Slavery, Freedom, and Expansion in the Early American West* (Charlottesville: University of Virginia Press, 2008), pp. 30–50; Adam

Rothman, *Slave Country: American Expansion and the Origins of the Deep South* (Cambridge, Mass.: Harvard University Press, 2005).

22. Quoted in Hendrickson, *Union, Nation, or Empire*, p. 65.

23. Hammond, *Slavery, Freedom, and Expansion in the Early American West*, pp. 150–68; Robert Pierce Forbes, *The Missouri Compromise and Its Aftermath* (Chapel Hill: University of North Carolina Press, 2007).

24. Monroe to Jefferson, May 1820, Stanislaus Murray Hamilton (ed.), *Writings of James Monroe* (New York: G. P. Putnams Sons, 1898–1903), vol. 6, pp. 119–23; Charles Francies Adams (ed.), *Memoirs of John Quincy Adams*, 12 volumes (Philadelphia, JB Lippincott), vol. 4, pp. 437–39; William Earl Weeks, *John Quincy Adams and American Global Empire* (Lexington: University of Kentucky Press, 1992), pp. 123–24, 167–68.

25. Clay, "Toast and Response at Public Dinner," May 19, 1821, in James Hopkins (ed.), *Papers of Henry Clay* (Lexington: University Press of Kentucky, 1959–1992), vol. 3, pp. 79–82; Hendrickson, *Union, Nation, or Empire*, pp. 118–23; Donald Ratcliffe, "The State of the Union, 1776–1860," in Susan-Mary Grant and Brian Holden Reid (eds.), *The American Civil War: Explorations and Reconsiderations* (London: Longman, 2000), pp. 3–38.

26. Rafe Blaufarb, "The Western Question: The Geopolitics of Latin American Independence," *American Historical Review* 112:3 (June 2007), pp. 712–41.

27. Zoltán Vajda, "Thomas Jefferson on the Character of an Unfree People: The Case of Spanish America," *American Nineteenth Century History* 8:3 (September 2007), pp. 273–92.

28. Tim Matthewson, *A Proslavery Foreign Policy: Haitian-American Relations During the Early Republic* (Westport, Conn.: Praeger, 2003); Robin Blackburn, "Haiti, Slavery, and the Age of the Democratic Revolution," *William and Mary Quarterly* 63:4 (2006).

29. Clay, "The Independence of Latin America," March 24, 25, 28, 1818, in Hopkins (ed.), *Papers of Henry Clay*, vol. 2, pp. 508–62; Clay, "Toast and Response at Public Dinner," May 19, 1821, in Hopkins (ed.), *Papers of Henry Clay*, vol. 3, pp. 79–82; Randolph Campbell, "The Spanish American Aspect of Henry Clay's American System," *The Americas* 24:1 (July 1967), pp. 3–17.

30. Weeks, *John Quincy Adams and American Global Empire*, pp. 91–94.

31. Quoted in Arthur Whitaker, *The United States and the Independence of Latin America, 1800–1830* (Baltimore: Johns Hopkins Press, 1941), p. 183.

32. Quoted in Lars Schoultz, *Beneath the United States: A History of U.S. Policy Toward Latin America* (Cambridge, Mass.: Harvard University Press, 1998), p. 5.

33. JQA diary, September 19, 1820, in C. F. Adams (ed.), *Memoirs of John Quincy Adams*, vol. 5, p. 176.

34. *North American Review* 3.2 (April 1821), p. 432.

35. JQA to Caesar Rodney, May 17, 1823, in Worthington C. Ford (ed.), *The Writings of John Quincy Adams* (New York: Macmillan, 1913–17), vol. 7, pp. 424–41.

36. JQA, *Niles' Weekly Register*, July 21, 1821.

37. Whitaker, *United States and the Independence of Latin America*, pp. 344–69.

38. James E. Lewis, Jr., *The American Union and the Problem of Neighborhood: The United States and the Collapse of the Spanish Empire* (Chapel Hill: University of North Carolina Press, 1998), pp. 157–78.

39. Quotes from Lewis, *American Union and the Problem of Neighborhood*, pp. 157–78; Monroe to Madison, May 10, 1822, in Stanislaus Murray Hamilton (ed.), *Writings of James Monroe* (New York: G. P. Putnam's Sons, 1898–1903), vol. 6, pp. 284–91.

40. Lewis, *American Union and the Problem of Neighborhood*, pp. 177–78.

41. JQA to Caesar A. Rodney, May 17, 1823, in JQA, *Writings*, vol. 7, pp. 424–41.

42. JQA to JA, August 1, 1816, in Walter LaFeber (ed.), *John Quincy Adams and American Continental Empire* (Chicago: Quadrangle Books, 1965), pp. 139–40.

43. Quoted in Weeks, *John Quincy Adams and American Global Empire*, p. 191.

2: American Systems

1. William Manning (ed.), *Diplomatic Correspondence of the United States Concerning the Independence of the Latin American Nations* (New York: Oxford University Press, 1925), vol. 3, pp. 1478–1507; Richard Rush, *A Residence at the Court of London* (London, 1845).

2. JQA to Hugh Nelson, April 28, 1823, in Worthington C. Ford (ed.), *The Writings of John Quincy Adams* (New York: Macmillan, 1913–17), vol. 7, pp. 369–70.

3. Quoted in David Hendrickson, *Union, Nation, or Empire: The American Debate over International Relations, 1789–1941* (Lawrence: University Press of Kansas, 2009), p. 87; Bradford Perkins, *Castlereagh and Adams: England and the United States, 1812–1823* (Los Angeles: University of California Press, 1964).

4. Dexter Perkins, *The Monroe Doctrine, 1823–1826* (Cambridge, Mass: Harvard University Press, 1927). Ernest May, *The Making of the Monroe Doctrine* (Cambridge, Mass.: Belknap Press, 1975), argues that the Monroe cabinet could have known that there was no threat.

5. Jefferson to Monroe, October 24, 1823, in Merrill Peterson (ed.), *Thomas Jefferson, Writings* (New York: Viking Press, 1985), pp. 481–83; Madison to Jefferson, November 1, 1823, in Stanislaus Murray Hamilton (ed.), *Writings of James Monroe* (New York: G. P. Putnam's Sons, 1898–1903), vol. 6, pp. 395–96.

6. Quoted in Bradford Perkins, "The Suppressed Dispatch of H. U. Addington Washington, November 3, 1823," *Hispanic American Historical Review* 37:4 (November 1957), pp. 480–85.

7. JQA diary, November 15, 1823, in Charles Francis Adams (ed.), *Memoirs of John Quincy Adams* (Philadelphia: J. B. Lippincott, 1874–77), vol. 6, p. 186. The Chimborazo is Ecuador's highest summit.

8. JQA diary, November 7 to December 2, 1823, *Memoirs*, vol. 6, pp. 177–235; quotes pp. 177–79.

9. JQA diary, November 26, 1823, *Memoirs*, vol. 6, pp. 204–10.

10. Arthur Whitaker, *The United States and the Independence of Latin America, 1800–1830* (New York: Norton, 1941), pp. 464–91.

11. Quoted in Edward Crapol, "John Quincy Adams and the Monroe Doctrine: Some New Evidence," *Pacific Historical Review* 48 (August 1979), pp. 413–18.

12. Henry Cabot Lodge, "Colonialism in the United States," *Atlantic Monthly* (May 1883), pp. 612–27; Henry Ammon, *James Monroe: The Quest for National Identity* (Charlottesville: University Press of Virginia, 1990), pp. 491–92; Bradford Perkins, *The Cambridge History of American Foreign Relations, Volume 1: The Creation of a Republican Empire, 1776–1865* (Cambridge: Cambridge University Press, 1993), p. 169.

13. JQA diary, November 16, 1823, *Memoirs*, vol. 6, p. 187; Monroe to Jefferson, December 4, 1823, in Hamilton (ed.), *Writings of James Monroe*, vol. 6, p. 342.

14. JQA diary, November 26, 1823, *Memoirs*, vol. 6, p. 210.

15. Gale W. McGee, "The Monroe Doctrine—A Stopgap Measure," *Mississippi Valley Historical Review* 38:2 (September 1951), pp. 233–50; JQA to Rush, December 8, 1823, reprinted in Samuel Flagg Bemis, *John Quincy Adams and the Foundation of American Foreign Policy* (New York: Knopf, 1949), pp. 577–79.

16. JQA, *Writings*, vol. 7, p. 488.

17. JQA diary, November 26, 1823, *Memoirs*, vol. 6, p. 207.

18. Ibid., p. 206.

19. Ibid.

20. Quoted in May, *Making of the Monroe Doctrine*, p. 48.

21. JQA diary, November 22 and December 2, 1823, *Memoirs*, vol. 6, pp. 197, 223–25.

22. JQA diary, November 21 and 26, 1823, *Memoirs*, vol. 6, pp. 192–96, 204–10.

23. James Monroe, "Seventh Annual Message," December 2, 1823.

24. JQA diary, November 26, 1823, *Memoirs*, vol. 6, p. 205.

25. Quoted in Perkins, *Creation of a Republican Empire*, p. 160. One historian who does consider this paragraph part of the "Monroe Doctrine" is Walter LaFeber (ed.), *John Quincy Adams and American Continental Empire* (Chicago: Quadrangle Books, 1965), pp. 109–15.

26. Quoted in Perkins, *History of the Monroe Doctrine*, pp. 56–57.

27. *Times*, January 6, 1824; *Economist*, November 14, 1863; "Polignac Memorandum," in Harold Temperley and Lillian Penson (eds.), *Foundations of British Foreign Policy: From Pitt (1792) to Salisbury (1902)* (Cambridge: Cambridge University Press, 1938), pp. 70–76.

28. Quoted in Harold Temperley, *The Foreign Policy of Canning, 1822–1827* (London: Frank Cass, 1966), pp. 43, 159.

29. JQA diary, November 29, 1823, *Memoirs*, vol. 6, p. 220; James Monroe, "Eighth Annual Message to Congress," December 7, 1824; Thomas B. Davis, Jr., "Carlos de Alvear and James Monroe: New Light on the Origin of the Monroe Doctrine," *Hispanic American Historical Review* 23:4 (November 1943), pp. 232–49.

30. Temperley, *Foreign Policy of Canning*, pp. 297–316, 307.
31. Wendy Hinde, *George Canning* (London, 1973), p. 355; Temperley, *Foreign Policy of Canning*, pp. 127–29; Charles Webster, *Britain and the Independence of Latin America* (London: Oxford University Press, 1938), p. 50; *Hansard*, 2nd ser., XII, p. 1209.
32. J. Fred Rippy, *Rivalry of the United States and Great Britain over Latin America, 1808–1830* (Baltimore: Johns Hopkins Press, 1929), pp. 247–302; Edward Moseley, "The United States and Mexico, 1810–1850," in Shurbutt (ed.), *United States–Latin American Relations*, pp. 122–96.
33. *Annals of Congress*, 18th Cong., 1st sess., pp. 1182–90.
34. William R. Manning (ed.), *Diplomatic Correspondence of the United States Concerning the Independence of the Latin American Nations*, 3 vols. (New York, 1925), vol. I, pp. 224–26, and vol. II, pp. 1281–82; JQA, *Memoirs*, vol. 7, p. 399.
35. Quoted in Rippy, *Rivalry of the United States and Great Britain over Latin America*, p. 115.
36. Allen to Clay, April 4, 1826, in Manning (ed.), *Diplomatic Correspondence*, vol. II, p. 1112; Forbes to JQA, April 30, 1823, in Manning (ed.), *Diplomatic Correspondence*, vol. I, pp. 620–21; David Bushnell and Neill Macaulay, *The Emergence of Latin America in the Nineteenth Century* (New York: Oxford University Press, 1988), pp. 21, 109; Thomas F. McGann, *Argentina, the United States, and the Inter-American System, 1880–1914* (Cambridge, Mass.: Harvard University Press, 1957), pp. 48–49.
37. John Lynch, *Simón Bolívar: A Life* (New Haven: Yale University Press, 2006), pp. 216-17; Rippy, *Rivalry of the United States and Great Britain over Latin America*, p. 152; Bolívar, "Views of General Simón Bolívar on the Congress of Panama," in Alejandro Alvarez, *The Monroe Doctrine: Its Importance in the International Life of the States of the New World* (New York: Oxford University Press, 1924), pp. 154–55.
38. R. A. Humphreys, *Tradition and Revolt in Latin America and Other Essays* (London: Weidenfeld and Nicolson, 1969), pp. 130–53.
39. Clay to Everett, April 27, 1825, in James Hopkins et al. (eds.), *Papers of Henry Clay*, vol. 4, pp. 292–300; Clay to Anderson and Sergeant, May 8, 1826, *Papers of Henry Clay*, vol. 5, pp. 313–44.
40. Clay to Poinsett, March 26, 1825, in James Hopkins et al. (eds.), *Papers of Henry Clay*, vol. 4, pp. 166–77.
41. Clay to Anderson and Sergeant, May 8, 1826, *Papers of Clay*, vol. 5, pp. 313–44.
42. José Martí (edited by Philip S. Foner), *Inside the Monster: Writings on the United States and American Imperialism* (New York: Monthly Review Press, 1975), p. 342.
43. Clay, "Toast," March 29, 1823, in Hopkins (ed.), *Papers of Henry Clay*, vol. 3, pp. 405.
44. JQA, *Memoirs*, vol. VI, April 23 and May 7, 1825, pp. 531, 542.
45. JQA, "First Annual Message to Congress," December 6, 1825; "Message to the Senate of the United States," December 26, 1825; "To the House of Representatives of the United States," March 15, 1826. The objective of the

"advancement of religious liberty" appeared only in Adams's message to the Senate.

46. Quoted in Randolph Campbell, "The Spanish American Aspect of Henry Clay's American System," *The Americas* 24:1 (July 1967), p. 8.

47. Kinley Brauer, "The United States and British Imperial Expansion, 1815–1860," *Diplomatic History* 12 (Winter 1988), pp. 19–37.

48. *Register of Debates*, 19th Cong., 1st sess., pp. 165–66.

49. Andrew Cayton, "The Debate over the Panama Congress and the Origins of the Second American Party System," *Historian* 47:2 (February 1985), pp. 219–38.

50. Jeffrey J. Malanson, "The Congressional Debate over U.S. Participation in the Congress of Panama, 1825–1826: Washington's Farewell Address, Monroe's Doctrine, and the Fundamental Principles of U.S. Foreign Policy," *Diplomatic History* 30:5 (November 2006), pp. 813–38.

51. Quoted in Robert Remini, *Daniel Webster: The Man and His Time* (New York: Norton, 1997), p. 255.

52. *Congressional Globe*, April 21, 1826, House of Representatives, p. 2490; Charles Sellers, *James Polk: Jacksonian* (Princeton: Princeton University Press, 1957), pp. 108–10.

53. *Register of Debates*, 19th Cong., 1st sess., II, part 1, pp. 166–67, 2276–77; JQA, *Memoirs*, vol. 7, pp. 75, 111, 117.

54. *Register of Debates*, 19th Cong., 1st sess., p. 2086; Piero Gleijeses, "The Limits of Sympathy: The United States and the Independence of Spanish America," *Journal of Latin American Studies* 24:3 (October 1992), pp. 481–505.

55. A searchable edition of Webster's dictionary is available at http://1828 .mshaffer.com/ (accessed September 2009).

56. Dawkins to Canning, October 15, 1826, in C. K. Webster (ed.), *Britain and the Independence of Latin America, 1812–1830* (London: Oxford University Press, 1938), vol. 1, pp. 422–24.

57. Andrew Jackson, "Second Inaugural Address," March 4, 1833.

58. John M. Belohlavek, *"Let the Eagle Soar!": The Foreign Policy of Andrew Jackson* (Lincoln: University of Nebraska Press, 1985), pp. 10, 191, 192–96, 254–56.

59. Christian J. Maisch, "The Falkland/Malvinas Islands Clash of 1831–32: U.S. and British Diplomacy in the South Atlantic," *Diplomatic History* 24:2 (Spring 2000), pp. 185–209.

3: A Declaration, a Doctrine, and a Disavowal

1. Quoted in John Niven, *John C. Calhoun and the Price of Union* (Baton Rouge: Louisiana State University Press, 1988), p. 115.

2. Edward B. Rugemer, *The Problem of Emancipation: The Caribbean Roots of the American Civil War* (Baton Rouge: Louisiana State University Press, 2008); Steven Heath Mitton, "The Free World Confronted: The Problem of Slavery and Progress in American Foreign Relations, 1833–1844," Ph.D. disser-

tation, Louisiana State University, 2005; Van Gosse, "'As a Nation, the English are our Friends': The Emergence of African American Politics in the British Atlantic World, 1772–1861," *American Historical Review* 113:4 (October 2008), pp. 1003–28.

3. Tyler to Calhoun, June 5, 1848, in Robert Meriwether (ed.), *Papers of John C. Calhoun* (Columbia: University of South Carolina Press, 1959–2003), vol. XXI, pp. 463–64.

4. Steven Heath Mitton, "The Upshur Inquiry: Lost Lessons of the Great Experiment," *Slavery and Abolition* 27:1 (April 2006), pp. 89–124; Frederick Merk, *The Monroe Doctrine and American Expansionism, 1843–1849* (New York: Knopf, 1966), pp. 18–20.

5. Quoted in William Freehling, *The Road to Disunion, Volume 1: Secessionists at Bay, 1776–1854* (New York: Oxford University Press, 1991), p. 399.

6. Ephraim Douglass Adams, *British Interests in Texas, 1838–46* (Baltimore: Johns Hopkins Press, 1910); Sam W. Haynes, "Anglophobia and the Annexation of Texas: The Quest for National Security," in Sam W. Haynes and Christopher Morris (eds.), *Manifest Destiny and Empire: American Antebellum Expansionism* (College Station: Texas A&M University Press, 1997), pp. 115–45.

7. Pickens to Polk, October 11, 1844, in Wayne Cutler (ed.), *Correspondence of James K. Polk*, vol. VIII, September–December 1844 (Knoxville: University of Tennessee Press, 1993), pp. 173–74.

8. Calhoun to Pakenham, April 18, 1844, *Papers of John C. Calhoun*, vol. 18, pp. 273–81; David Dykstra, *The Shifting Balance of Power* (New York: University Press of America, 1999), p. 48.

9. JQA, *Memoirs*, vol. 12, p. 171; vol. 11, p. 380.

10. Ernest McPherson Lander, Jr., *Reluctant Imperialists: Calhoun, the South Carolinians, and the Mexican War* (Baton Rouge: Louisiana State University Press, 1980), p. 161.

11. Sierra to Buchanan, April 3, 1848, in William R. Manning (ed.), *Diplomatic Correspondence of the United States: Inter-American Affairs, 1831–1860* (Washington, D.C., 1932–39), vol. 8, pp. 1075–78.

12. Polk, "To the Senate and House," April 29, 1848.

13. Polk diary, April 25 and 27, 1848, in Quaife (ed.), *The Diary of James K. Polk* (Chicago: A. C. McClurg & Co., 1910), vol. III, pp. 433–37; Merk, *Monroe Doctrine and American Expansionism*, pp. 194–232.

14. For Calhoun's speech, see *Papers of John C. Calhoun*, vol. xxv, pp. 401–21.

15. "Ostend Manifesto," in Henry Steele Commager and Milton Cantor (eds.), *Documents of American History*, 10th ed., vol. 1 (Englewood Cliffs, N.J., 1988), pp. 333–35; Robert May, *The Southern Dream of a Caribbean Empire, 1854–1861* (Athens: University of Georgia Press, 1989).

16. William Dusinberre, *Slavemaster President: The Double Career of James Polk* (New York: Oxford University Press, 2003), p. 19.

17. Thomas Hietala, *Manifest Design: American Exceptionalism and Empire* (Ithaca, N.Y.: Cornell University Press, 2003); Reginald Horsman, *Race and Manifest Destiny: The Origins of American Racial Anglo-Saxonism* (Cambridge, Mass.: Harvard University Press, 1981).

18. Norman Graebner, *Empire on the Pacific: A Study in American Continental Expansion* (New York: Ronald Press, 1955).

19. Larkin to Buchanan, July 10, 1845, in Manning (ed.), *Diplomatic Correspondence of the United States: Inter-American Affairs, 1831–1860*, vol. 8, pp. 735–36; Buchanan to Larkin, October 17, 1845, ibid., pp. 169–71; Buchanan to Slidell, November 10, 1845, ibid., pp. 172–82; Pletcher, *Diplomacy of Annexation*, pp. 420–26, 592–97; Dykstra, *Shifting Balance of Power*, esp. p. 99.

20. Bancroft's recollections in John Charles Frémont, "The Conquest of California," *Century Magazine* 41 (April 1891), pp. 923–24.

21. Henry Clay, "To the Editors of the Washington *Daily National Intelligencer*," April 17, 1844, in Melba P. Hay (ed.), *The Papers of Henry Clay*, vol. 10 (Lexington: University Press of Kentucky, 1991), pp. 41–46; "The Whig Party, Its Position, and Duties," *American Review* 2.6 (December 1845), pp. 547–60; Webster quoted in Daniel Walker Howe, *Political Culture of the American Whigs* (Chicago: University of Chicago Press, 1979), p. 143.

22. Bancroft to Sumner, January 13, 1846, in M. A. DeWolfe Howe, *The Life and Letters of George Bancroft* (New York: Scribner, 1908), vol. 1, p. 266.

23. James K. Polk Papers, "Draft of Inaugural 1845," reel 59; Polk diary, May 9, 1846, in Quaife (ed.), *Diary of Polk*, vol. I, p. 385; Pletcher, *Diplomacy of Annexation*, pp. 236–37.

24. Bancroft's draft can be found in "Messages and Speeches, 1845," James K. Polk Papers, microfilm reel 59, LC.

25. For Buchanan's views, see Polk diary, November 20 and 24, 1845, in Quaife (ed.), *Diary of Polk*, vol. I, pp. 99–102.

26. Polk diary, October 21 and 24, 1845, in Quaife (ed.), *Diary of Polk*, vol. I, pp. 67–72.

27. JQA, *Memoirs*, vol. 12, December 6, 1845, p. 218.

28. Polk, "First Annual Message to Congress," December 2, 1845.

29. Prevost to Buchanan, February 1, 1847; Clay to Buchanan, January 12, 1848, in Manning (ed.), *Diplomatic Correspondence*, vol. 10, pp. 550–52, 561–62.

30. Polk diary, January 19 and 20, 1848, in Quaife (ed.), *Diary of Polk*, vol. III, p. 306–7.

31. Cass speech in Senate on January 26, 1846, in *Niles' National Register*, February 7, 1846; Merk, *Monroe Doctrine and American Expansionism*, pp. 40–64.

32. Webster's 1828 dictionary accessed online at http://1828.mshaffer.com, February 2008.

33. Yonatan Eyal, *The Young America Movement and the Transformation of the Democratic Party, 1828–1861* (New York: Cambridge University Press, 2007), pp. 118–21.

34. George Tucker, *The Monroe Doctrine* (Boston: George B. Reed, 1885), p. 131.

35. Polk, "Third Annual Message to Congress," December 7, 1847.

36. Daniel Walker Howe, *What Hath God Wrought: The Transformation of America, 1815–1848* (New York: Oxford University Press, 2007), pp. 809–11.

37. Polk, "Fourth Annual Message to Congress," December 5, 1848.

38. Gary Kornblith, "Rethinking the Coming of the Civil War: A Counterfactual Exercise," *Journal of American History* 90:1 (June 2003).

39. Michael F. Holt, *The Rise and Fall of the American Whig Party: Jacksonian Poli-*

tics and the Onset of the Civil War (New York: Oxford University Press, 1999); Piero Gleijeses, "A Brush with Mexico," *Diplomatic History* 29:2 (April 2005).

40. Tyler message to Congress, December 30, 1842; Webster to Timoteo Haalilio and William Richards, December 19, 1842, DP I, 870–71; Webster to George Brown (U.S. commissioner), March 15, 1843, 873–76; Edward P. Crapol, *John Tyler: The Accidental President* (Chapel Hill: University of North Carolina Press, 2006), pp. 130–73.

41. Webster to Hulseman, December 21, 1850; Webster to George Ticknor, January 16, 1851, in Kenneth Shewmaker (ed.), *The Papers of Daniel Webster: Diplomatic Papers*, vol. 2 (Hanover, N.H.: University Press of New England, 1987), pp. 49–61, 64.

42. Quoted in Howard Jones, *Blue and Gray Diplomacy: A History of Union and Confederate Foreign Relations* (Chapel Hill: University of North Carolina Press, 2009), p. 22.

43. Clayton to Bulwer, February 15, 1850, John M. Clayton Papers, Library of Congress; Reginald Horsman, *Race and Manifest Destiny: The Origins of American Racial Anglo-Saxonism* (Cambridge, Mass.: Harvard University Press, 1981).

44. Jay Sexton, *Debtor Diplomacy: Finance and American Foreign Relations in the Civil War Era, 1837–1873* (Oxford: Oxford University Press, 2005), pp. 31–40.

45. Quoted in Richard Carwardine, "Lincoln's Horizons," in Carwardine and Sexton (eds.), *The Global Lincoln* (New York: Oxford University Press, 2011).

46. Crapol, *John Tyler*, p. 173; Macabe Keliher, "Anglo-American Rivalry and the Origins of U.S. China Policy," *Diplomatic History* 31.2 (April 2007), pp. 227–58.

47. Howe, *Political Culture of the American Whigs*, p. 146.

48. Henry Wheaton, *Elements of International Law* (London, 1836); William Ladd, *An Essay on a Congress of Nations* (London: Thomas Ward and Co., 1840); Robert Sampson, *John O'Sullivan and His Times* (Kent, Ohio: Kent State University Press, 2003), pp. 92–93.

49. Taylor, "First Annual Message," December 4, 1849; William Malloy, *Treaties, Conventions, International Acts, Protocols and Agreements Between the United States of America and Other Powers* (Washington, D.C., 1910), vol. 1, pp. 659–63.

50. Taylor, "To the Senate of the United States," April 22, 1850.

51. Lawrence to Palmerston, December 14, 1849, RG59, M30, National Archives, College Park, Maryland.

52. Crampton to Palmerston, October 15, 1849, in "Correspondence with United States Respecting Central America," 1856 session, vol. LX.1, *House of Commons Parliamentary Papers*, p. 5. Clayton here was responding to Squier's invocation of the Monroe Doctrine to the Nicaraguan government, which Clayton contended was unauthorized.

53. Bulwer quoted in Richard Van Alstyne, *The Rising American Empire* (New York: W. W. Norton, 1974), p. 160.

54. Taylor, "To the Senate of the United States," April 22, 1850; Taylor, "First Annual Message," December 4, 1849.

55. Buchanan to John A. McClernand, April 2, 1850, in "Letters of Bancroft and Buchanan on the Clayton-Bulwer Treaty, 1849, 1850," *American Historical Review* 5:1 (October 1899), pp. 95–102.
56. Bulwer to Clayton, April 21, 1850, Clayton Papers, LC.
57. Abraham Lincoln, "Address to the Young Men's Lyceum of Springfield, Illinois," 1838.
58. A. E. Campbell, "An Excess of Isolation: Isolation and the American Civil War," *Journal of Southern History* 29:2 (May 1963), pp. 161–74.
59. Jonathan Earle, *Jacksonian Antislavery and the Politics of Free Soil, 1824–1854* (Chapel Hill: University of North Carolina Press, 2004).
60. Polk, "Fourth Annual Message to Congress," December 5, 1848.

4: Civil Wars

1. Quoted in David Hendrickson, *Union, Nation, or Empire: The American Debate over International Relations, 1789–1941* (Lawrence: University Press of Kansas, 2008), p. 225.
2. Joshua Leavitt, *The Monroe Doctrine* (New York: Sinclair Tousey, 1863); *Harper's Weekly*, June 11, 1864; Ulysses S. Grant, "To the Senate of the United States," May 31, 1870.
3. *Congressional Globe*, 32nd Cong., 2nd sess., App., pp. 90–92.
4. This is the phrase of the Tennessee congressman John Savage. *CG*, 31st Cong., 1st sess., p. 1441.
5. London *Times*, February 7, 1853.
6. James J. Barnes (ed.), *Private and Confidential: Letters from British Ministers in Washington to the Foreign Secretaries in London, 1844–67* (Selinsgrove, Pa.: Susquehanna University Press, 1993), p. 69.
7. Roy P. Basler (ed.), *The Collected Works of Abraham Lincoln* (New Brunswick, N.J.: Rutgers University Press, 1953–55), vol. 3, p. 54.
8. *CG*, 32nd Cong., 2nd sess., App., 170–73, and Special Session, 32nd Cong., pp. 271–74.
9. *CG*, 34th Cong., 1st sess., App., p. 114.
10. *North American Review* 82:2 (April 1856), pp. 478–512.
11. Clayton to Marcy, June 4, 1853, in John Bassett Moore Papers, box 134, folder "Panama Affair," LC.
12. *CG*, 32nd Cong., 2nd sess., App., p. 126.
13. Seward's eulogy of John Clayton, December 3, 1856, Seward Papers, microfilm reel 186, 6382, Vere Harmsworth Library, University of Oxford.
14. *CG*, 32nd Cong., 2nd sess., App., p. 127.
15. Barnes (ed.), *Private and Confidential*, p. 66.
16. Quoted in R. W. Van Alstyne, "British Diplomacy and the Clayton-Bulwer Treaty, 1850–1860," *Journal of Modern History* XI (1939), p. 179.
17. Seward to Howard, March 23, 1853, Seward Papers, Additions, box 1, Rush Rhees Library, Rochester, New York.
18. *CG*, 32nd Cong., 2nd sess., App., p. 126.
19. Sumner to the Duchess of Argyll, February 10, 1859, Sumner-Argyll Col-

lections, 1857–64, HM25934–HM25990, Huntington Library, Pasadena, California.

20. Perkins, *The Monroe Doctrine: 1826–1867* (Baltimore: Johns Hopkins Press, 1933), pp. 193–252; Palmerston quote from Kenneth Bourne, *Britain and the Balance of Power in North America, 1815–1908* (London: Longmans, 1967), p. 182.

21. Bourne, *Britain and the Balance of Power in North America*, p. 203.

22. Aims McGuinness, *Path of Empire: Panama and the California Gold Rush* (Ithaca, N.Y.: Cornell University Press, 2008).

23. Donathon Olliff, *Reforma Mexico and the United States: A Search for Alternatives to Annexation, 1854–1861* (Tuscaloosa: University of Alabama Press, 1981).

24. Pearl T. Ponce, "'As Dead as Julius Caesar': The Rejection of the McLane-Ocampo Treaty," *Civil War History* 53:4 (December 2007), pp. 342–78.

25. *CG*, 34th Cong., 1st sess., App., p. 114.

26. Robert Bonner, *Mastering America: Southern Slaveholders and the Crisis of American Nationhood* (Cambridge: Cambridge University Press, 2009), p. 300; Brian Schoen, *The Fragile Fabric of Union: Cotton, Federal Politics, and the Global Origins of the Civil War* (Baltimore: Johns Hopkins University Press, 2009).

27. Frank Owsley, *King Cotton Diplomacy: Foreign Relations of the Confederate States of America* (Chicago: University of Chicago Press, 1931); Charles Hubbard, *The Burden of Confederate Diplomacy* (Knoxville: University of Tennessee Press, 1998).

28. Seward to JQA, June 19, 1861, *FRUS*, 1861, p. 108; Howard Jones, *Blue and Gray Diplomacy: A History of Union and Confederate Foreign Relations* (Chapel Hill: University of North Carolina Press, 2009), p. 154; Phillip E. Myers, *Caution and Cooperation: The American Civil War in British-American Relations* (Kent, Ohio: Kent State University Press, 2008).

29. Quoted in D. P. Crook, *The North, the South, and the Powers, 1861–1865* (London: John Wiley & Sons, 1974), p. 262.

30. Mary D. McFeely and William S. McFeely (eds.), *Memoirs and Selected Letters: Personal Memoirs of U. S. Grant, Selected Letters 1839–1865* (Library of America, 1990), p. 775.

31. Joshua Leavitt, *The Monroe Doctrine* (New York: Sinclair Tousey, 1863).

32. Seward quoted in Dean Mahin, *One War at a Time* (Washington, D.C.: Brassey's, 1999), p. 110; Lieber to Sumner, February 24, 1863, box 43, Lieber Papers, Huntington Library.

33. In the Seward papers, there is a draft acceptance of the European offer authored by Caleb Cushing. See "Draft of Message on Mexican Affairs, 1862," drawer 32, Seward Papers, Rush Rhees Library, Rochester. For the rejection of the offer, see United States, *Correspondence Relative to the Present Condition of Mexico* (Washington, D.C.: Government Printing Office, 1862), pp. 185–90.

34. Corwin quotes from Thomas D. Schoonover, *Dollars over Dominion: The Triumph of Liberalism in Mexican–United States Relations, 1861–1867* (Baton

Rouge: Louisiana State University Press, 1978), p. 57; and Andrew N. Cleven (ed.), "The Corwin-Doblado Treaty, April 6, 1862," *Hispanic American Historical Review* 17:4 (November 1937), pp. 499–506.

35. Schoonover, *Dollars over Dominion*, pp. 48–77; Jones, *Blue and Gray Diplomacy*, p. 76.
36. Thomas D. Schoonover (ed.), *Mexican Lobby: Matías Romero in Washington 1861–1867* (Lexington: University Press of Kentucky, 1986), pp. 7–9.
37. Romero quotes from Schoonover, *Dollars over Dominion*, p. 19; Schoonover (ed.), *Mexican Lobby*, pp. 151–52.
38. Quotes from Allison William Bunkley (ed.), *A Sarmiento Anthology* (Princeton, N.J.: Princeton University Press, 1948), pp. 10, 315–32.
39. Robert Burr and Roland Hussey (eds.), *Documents on Inter-American Cooperation, Volume 1, 1810–1881* (Philadelphia: University of Pennsylvania Press, 1955), p. 149.
40. Matías Romero (ed.), *Correspondencia de la Legación Mexicana en Washington Durante la Intervención Extranjera, 1860–1868* (México, 1870–92), vol. 2, p. 153; Howard K. Beale (ed.), *Diary of Gideon Welles, Secretary of the Navy Under Lincoln and Johnson*, vol. 1 (New York: W. W. Norton, 1960), p. 385.
41. Lyons to Russell, August 3, 1863, in James J. Barnes and Patience P. Barnes (eds.), *The American Civil War Through British Eyes: Dispatches from British Diplomats*, vol. 3 (Kent, Ohio: Kent State University Press, 2005), pp. 86–88; *FRUS*, 1862, vol. 1, pp. 131–33, 164; Myers, *Caution and Cooperation*; Phillip Magness and Sebastian N. Page, *Colonization After Emancipation: Lincoln and the Movement for Black Resettlement* (Columbia: University of Missouri Press, 2010).
42. Lieber to Sumner, October 10, 1865, box 46, and Lieber to Sumner, June 20, 1864, box 43, Lieber Papers, Huntington Library.
43. Mary D. McFeely and William S. McFeely (eds.), *Memoirs and Selected Letters: Personal Memoirs of U. S. Grant, Selected Letters 1839–1865* (Library of America, 1990), p. 777.
44. Quoted in Norman Graebner, "Northern Diplomacy and European Neutrality," in David Herbert Donald (ed.), *Why the North Won the Civil War* (New York: Simon & Schuster, 1996), p. 59.
45. This exchange is reproduced in Basler (ed.), *The Collected Works of Abraham Lincoln*, vol. 4, pp. 316–20.
46. Adam I. P. Smith, *No Party Now: Politics in the Civil War North* (New York: Oxford University Press, 2006).
47. Henry Winter Davis, *The War of Ormuzd and Ahriman in the Nineteenth Century* (Baltimore: James S. Waters, 1852).
48. Chase to Leavitt, January 24, 1864, in John Niven (ed.), *The Salmon P. Chase Papers*, 5 vols. (Kent, Ohio: Kent State University Press, 1993–98), vol. 4, pp. 261–62.
49. *FRUS*, 1864, part III, pp. 216–20; no author, *Arguments in Favor of the Enforcement of the Monroe Doctrine* (New Orleans, 1864).
50. Lincoln to Dennison, June 27, 1864, Basler (ed.), *The Collected Works of Abraham Lincoln*, vol. 7, p. 411.

51. Wallace to Seward, July 10, 1865, Seward Papers, microfilm reel 90, Vere Harmsworth Library, University of Oxford.
52. London *Times*, November 2, 1865; Beale (ed.), *Diary of Gideon Welles*, vol. 1, p. 623.
53. William E. Hardy, "South of the Border: Ulysses S. Grant and the French Intervention," *Civil War History* 54:1 (2008), pp. 63–86.
54. Lieber to Sumner, September 20, 1863, Lieber Papers, box 43, Huntington Library.
55. Ruth Elson, *Guardians of Faith: American Schoolbooks of the Nineteenth Century* (Lincoln: University of Nebraska Press, 1964), p. 160.
56. Leavitt, *Monroe Doctrine*; Leavitt to Seward, August 22, 1862, Seward Papers; Leavitt to Chase, January 9, 1864, Chase Papers microfilm, Vere Harmsworth Library, University of Oxford. Leavitt used the term "Americanize" in another one of his articles, "Poland," *New Englander and Yale Review* 23:87 (April 1864), p. 290.

5: Control

1. Patricia Nelson Limerick, *The Legacy of Conquest* (New York: Norton, 1987); Jeffrey Ostler, *The Plains Sioux and U.S. Colonialism from Lewis and Clark to Wounded Knee* (Cambridge: Cambridge University Press, 2004); Heather Cox Richardson, *West from Appomattox: The Reconstruction of America after the Civil War* (New Haven, Conn.: Yale University Press, 2007).
2. Frank Ninkovich, *Global Dawn: The Cultural Foundation of American Internationalism, 1865–1890* (Cambridge, Mass.: Harvard University Press, 2009).
3. Kevin H. O'Rourke and Jeffrey G. Williamson, *Globalization and History: The Evolution of a Nineteenth-Century Atlantic Economy* (Cambridge, Mass.: MIT Press, 1999).
4. Quoted in Gillian Cookson, *The Cable: The Wire That Changed the World* (Stroud, U.K.: Tempus Publishing, 2003), p. 151.
5. John Kasson, "The Monroe Declaration" and "The Monroe Doctrine in 1881," *North American Review* (September–October 1881).
6. Quoted in Fred Harvey Harrington, *Fighting Politician: Major General N. P. Banks* (Philadelphia: University of Pennsylvania Press, 1948), p. 186.
7. Frederick Douglass, "Address on Santo Domingo," January 13, 1873, in John Blassingame and John McKivigan (eds.), *The Frederick Douglass Papers*, series 1, vol. 4 (London, 1979–), pp. 342–55.
8. Eric T. L. Love, *Race over Empire: Racism and U.S. Imperialism, 1865–1900* (Chapel Hill: University of North Carolina Press, 2004), pp. 27–72.
9. Grant, "Annual Message to Congress," December 5, 1870.
10. Quoted in Ernest May, *American Imperialism: A Speculative Essay* (Chicago: Imprint Publications, 1968), p. 197.
11. Quoted in Allan Nevins, *Hamilton Fish: The Inner History of the Grant Administration* (New York: Dodd, Mead and Co., 1936), p. 494; Jay Sexton, "The Funded Loan and the *Alabama* Claims," *Diplomatic History* 27:4 (September 2003), 449–78.
12. Unless otherwise indicated, the following Fish quotes can be found in

Hamilton Fish, "Circular to Ministers and Consuls in Spanish-American States and Brazil," *FRUS, 1870–1871*, July 14, 1870, 254–61.

13. Fish diary, July 15, 1875, Fish Papers, LC.

14. Quoted in Charles Campbell, *The Transformation of American Foreign Relations, 1865–1900* (New York: Harper, 1976), p. 61.

15. For this episode, see the exchanges between Fish and Cárdenas in Fish Papers, container 251, folder "Central America, Nicaragua, Interoceanic Canal." See also Fish diary, January–February 1877, Fish Papers, LC.

16. Ada Ferrer, *Insurgent Cuba: Race, Nation, and Revolution, 1868–1898* (Chapel Hill: University of North Carolina Press, 1999).

17. *New York Tribune*, November 21, 1873.

18. Quoted in Philip S. Foner, *A History of Cuba and Its Relations with the United States* (New York: International Publishers, 1962), vol. 2, p. 200.

19. Fish diary, October 26, 1869, Fish Papers, LC.

20. Walter LaFeber, *The New Empire: An Interpretation of American Expansion, 1865–1898* (Ithaca, N.Y.: Cornell University Press, 1963), pp. 37–38.

21. Fish to Robert Schneck, January 15, 1876, Fish letterbooks, LC; Fish diary, November 29, 1875, Fish Papers, LC; Fish to Caleb Cushing, January 5, 1876, Cushing Papers, LC.

22. Senate Executive Document 885, 55th Cong., 2nd sess., April 1898, 43–179.

23. *Times*, February 1, 1876.

24. *The World* (New York City), January 19, 1876; Fish Papers, container 251, folder "Monroe Doctrine," LC.

25. Caleb Cushing to Fish, March 23, 1876, Sen. Ex. Doc. 885, 55th Cong., 2nd sess., 118.

26. Fish to Schneck, January 15, 1876, Fish letterbooks, LC.

27. Eric Hobsbawm, *The Age of Empire: 1875–1914* (London: Weidenfeld and Nicolson, 1987); May, *American Imperialism*, pp. 116–64; Mark F. Proudman, "Words for Scholars: The Semantics of 'Imperialism,'" *Journal of the Historical Society* 8:3 (September 2008), pp. 395–433.

28. José Martí (edited by Philip S. Foner), *Inside the Monster: Writings on the United States and American Imperialism* (New York: Monthly Review Press, 1975), p. 336.

29. Edward Crapol, *James G. Blaine: Architect of Empire* (Wilmington, Del.: Scholarly Resources, 2000); Mike Sewell, "Political Rhetoric and Policy-Making: James G. Blaine and Britain," *Journal of American Studies* 24 (April 1990), pp. 61–84; Lester D. Langley, "The Ideologue as Diplomatist," in Frank J. Merli and Theodore A. Wilson (eds.), *Makers of American Diplomacy: From Benjamin Franklin to Henry Kissinger* (New York: Scribner, 1974), pp. 253–78; Democratic Party Platform, 1884.

30. Serial set no. 2070, session vol. no. 6, 47th Cong., 1st sess., H. Rpt. 1790.

31. Quoted in David Healy, *James G. Blaine and Latin America* (Columbia: University of Missouri Press, 2001), p. 108.

32. Ferdinand de Lesseps, "The Panama Canal," *North American Review*, July 1880, pp. 75–78; Joseph Smith, *Illusions of Conflict: Anglo-American Diplomacy Toward Latin America, 1865–1896* (Pittsburgh: University of Pittsburgh Press, 1979), pp. 104–5.

33. Serial 1982, session vol. no. 1, 46th Cong., 3rd sess., H. Rpt. 224, "Inter-oceanic Canal and the Monroe Doctrine"; "The Monroe Doctrine and the Isthmian Canal," *North American Review*, May 1880.

34. Rutherford B. Hayes, "To the Senate," March 8, 1880.

35. Blaine to Lowell, November 19, 1881, *FRUS*, 1882, pp. 554–59. *FRUS* reprinted the entire exchange in the 1882 and 1883 volumes.

36. *The Economist*, December 24, 1881, p. 3.

37. Quoted in Smith, *Illusions of Conflict*, p. 103.

38. David Pletcher, *The Diplomacy of Trade and Investment: American Economic Expansion in the Hemisphere, 1865–1900* (Columbia: University of Missouri Press, 1998), pp. 132–33.

39. Quoted in Healy, *James G. Blaine and Latin America*, p. 116.

40. James G. Blaine, "Garfield's Administration; James G. Blaine's Defense of Its Foreign Policy," *Daily Evening Bulletin* (San Francisco), September 14, 1882.

41. Pletcher, *Diplomacy of Trade and Investment*, pp. 41, 180; LaFeber, *New Empire*.

42. House Ex. Doc. 48th Cong., 2nd sess., vol. 29, no. 1, serial no. 2304.

43. Quoted in Joseph Smith, "The First Conference of American States (1889–1890) and the Early Pan American Policy of the United States," in David Sheinin, *Beyond the Ideal: Pan-Americanism in Inter-American Affairs* (Westport, Conn: Praeger, 2000), pp. 19–32.

44. Matías Romero, "The Pan-American Conference," *North American Review* (September–October 1890), pp. 354–66, 402–21.

45. Thomas Schoonover, *The United States in Central America, 1860–1911: Episodes in Social Imperialism and International Rivalry in the World System* (Durham, N.C.: Duke University Press, 1991), p. 78; J. Valerie Fifer, *United States Perceptions of Latin America, 1850–1930: A "New West" South of Capricorn?* (Manchester: Manchester University Press, 1991).

46. Pletcher, *Diplomacy of Trade and Investment*, pp. 77–113.

47. Quoted in LaFeber, *New Empire*, p. 105.

48. The Dominican Republic refused the invitation because the U.S. Senate refused to ratify a bilateral commercial deal negotiated back in 1884.

49. *Chileno* (Valparaiso) quoted in Pletcher, *Diplomacy of Trade and Investment*, p. 238.

50. James Bryce, *South America: Observations and Impressions* (London, 1929), p. 510.

51. José Martí, *Nuestra América* (Caracas: Fundación Biblioteca Ayacucho, 2005), pp. 51–56; *The Nation*, September 4, 1890, p. 183.

52. Thomas F. McGann, *Argentina, the United States, and the Inter-American System, 1880–1914* (Cambridge, Mass.: Harvard University Press, 1957), pp. 59, 98.

53. Ibid., p. 137.

54. William Whatley Pierson, Jr., "Alberdi's Views on the Monroe Doctrine," *Hispanic American Review* 3:3 (August 1920), pp. 373–74; Sáenz Peña quote from McGann, *Argentina, the United States, and the Inter-American System*, pp. 157–58.

55. Quoted in Samuel Guy Inman and Harold Eugene Davis, *Inter-American*

Conferences, 1826–1954: History and Problems (Washington, D.C.: University Press, 1965), p. 38.
56. McGann, *Argentina, the United States, and the Inter-American System*, p. 141.
57. Smith, *Illusions of Conflict*, p. 144.
58. Romero, "The Pan-American Conference."
59. Smith, "The First Conference of American States (1889–1890)."
60. Harrison, "To the Senate and House," January 25, 1892.
61. Quoted in Mark Peterson, "The *Baltimore* Affair and the Question of American Neutrality During the Chilean Revolution of 1891," University of Oxford thesis, 2009.
62. Martí, *Inside the Monster*, p. 355.
63. Joyce S. Goldberg, *The* Baltimore *Affair* (Lincoln: University of Nebraska Press, 1986), pp. 110, 116; Theodore Roosevelt, "The Foreign Policy of President Harrison," *The Independent*, August 11, 1892.

6: Intervention
1. Ulysses S. Grant, *Personal Memoirs*, vol. 1 (New York: Charles L. Webster & Co., 1885), p. 53.
2. Grover Cleveland, "To the House of Representatives," February 16, 1887.
3. Democratic Party Platform, 1884.
4. Cleveland to Bayard, December 29, 1895, Olney Papers, reel 14, LC.
5. Olney to Bayard, July 20, 1895, *FRUS*, 1895, I, pp. 545–62.
6. Cleveland to Olney, July 7, 1895, in Robert McElroy, *Grover Cleveland: The Man and the Statesman*, vol. 2 (New York: Harper & Brothers, 1923), pp. 180–81.
7. Olney to Knox, January 29, 1912, Olney Papers, reel 41, LC.
8. Gerald Eggert, *Richard Olney: Evolution of a Statesman* (University Park, Pa.: Penn State University Press, 1974); Robert Kagan, *Dangerous Nation: America and the World, 1600–1898* (London: Atlantic Books, 2006), pp. 368–74.
9. Olney to Bayard, July 20, 1895, *FRUS*, 1895, I, pp. 545–62.
10. Olney to Keet, January 15, 1897, Olney Papers, reel 26, LC.
11. Quoted in Bradford Perkins, *The Great Rapprochement: England and the United States, 1895–1914* (London: Victor Gollancz, 1969), p. 15.
12. Cleveland to Bayard, December 29, 1895, Olney Papers, reel 14, LC.
13. Cleveland, "Special Message to the Congress," December 17, 1895.
14. *The Economist*, April 4, 1891.
15. Cleveland to Bayard, December 29, 1895, Olney Papers, reel 14, LC.
16. Olney to Peter Olney, December 27, 1904, Olney Papers, reel 55, LC.
17. TR to Olney, December 20, 1895, Olney Papers, reel 14, LC.
18. TR, "The Monroe Doctrine," March 1896, in Theodore Roosevelt, *The Works of Theodore Roosevelt*, vol. 13 (New York, 1926), pp. 168–81; TR to Henry C. Lodge, December 27, 1895, in Elting E. Morison, *The Letters of Theodore Roosevelt*, vol. 1 (Cambridge, Mass.: Harvard University Press, 1951), pp. 503–4; Henry Cabot Lodge, "Colonialism in the United States," *Atlantic Monthly* (May 1883), pp. 612–27.

19. Walter LaFeber, "That 'Splendid Little War,' in Historical Perspective," *Texas Quarterly* 11 (1968), pp. 89–98.
20. Julius Pratt, "The 'Large Policy' of 1898," *Mississippi Valley Historical Review* 19 (September 1932), pp. 219–42.
21. Paul A. Kramer, "Empires, Exceptions, and Anglo-Saxons: Race and Rule Between the British and United States Empires, 1880–1910," *Journal of American History* 88:4 (March 2002); TR to Cecil Spring-Rice, December 2, 1899, Morison, *Letters of Theodore Roosevelt*, vol. 2, pp. 1103–5.
22. May, *American Imperialism: A Speculative Essay*, pp. 221–22; Henry Cabot Lodge, "Our Blundering Foreign Policy," *Forum* XIX (March 1895), 12–15.
23. Walter L. Williams, "United States Indian Policy and the Debate over Philippine Annexation: Implications for the Origins of American Imperialism," *Journal of American History* 66:4 (March 1980), pp. 810–31.
24. Robert Beisner, *Twelve Against Empire: The Anti-Imperialists, 1898–1900* (New York: McGraw-Hill, 1968), p. 228.
25. John Chetwood, *Manila, or Monroe Doctrine?* (New York: Robert Lewis Weed Co., 1898).
26. William Graham Sumner, *Conquest of the United States by Spain* (Boston: Dana Estes and Co., 1899).
27. Hoar quote from Beisner, *Twelve Against Empire*, p. 162.
28. Frank Ninkovich, "Theodore Roosevelt: Civilization as Ideology," *Diplomatic History* 10 (Summer 1986), pp. 221–45; TR, "The Monroe Doctrine."
29. Wood to Root, January 13, 1900, January 19, 1901, and March 23, 1901, Root Papers, container 168, LC.
30. Wood to Root, January 19, 1901, Root Papers, container 168, LC.
31. Root to Hay, January 11, 1901, Root Papers, container 168, LC.
32. Wood to Root, May 26, 1901, Root Papers, container 168; Philip S. Foner, *The Spanish-Cuban-American War and the Birth of American Imperialism*, vol. II (New York: Monthly Review Press, 1972), p. 615.
33. *Congressional Record*, 56th Cong., 2nd sess., p. 3145.
34. TR to Root, February 16, 1904, Root Papers, container 163, LC.
35. Quoted in Foner, *Spanish-Cuban-American War*, p. 632.
36. Quoted in Perkins, *Great Rapprochement*, p. 178.
37. John W. Foster, *A Century of American Diplomacy* (Boston, 1900), p. 457.
38. TR to Hay, August 19, 1903, Morison, *Letters of Theodore Roosevelt*, vol. 3, pp. 566–67.
39. Quoted in W. Stull Holt, *Treaties Defeated by the Senate* (Baltimore: Johns Hopkins Press, 1933), p. 209.
40. For two different angles on this episode, see Richard H. Collins, *Theodore Roosevelt's Caribbean: The Panama Canal, the Monroe Doctrine, and the Latin American Context* (Baton Rouge: Louisiana State University Press, 1990), pp. 186-305, and Thomas Schoonover, "Morality and Political Purpose in Theodore Roosevelt's Actions in Panama in 1903," in Schoonover, *The United States in Central America, 1860–1911: Episodes in Social Imperialism and International Rivalry in the World System* (Durham, N.C.: Duke University Press, 1991), pp. 97–110.

41. TR to Spring-Rice, January 18, 1904, Morison, *Letters of Theodore Roosevelt*, vol. 3, p. 699; Thomas McCormick, "From Old Empire to New: The Changing Dynamics and Tactics of American Empire," in Alfred McCoy and Francisco Scarano (eds.), *Colonial Crucible: Empire in the Making of the Modern American State* (Madison: University of Wisconsin Press, 2009), pp. 63–82.

42. Olney to Peter Olney, November 11, 1903, Olney Papers, reel 54, LC.

43. Louis A. Pérez, Jr., *Cuba Under the Platt Amendment, 1902–1934* (Pittsburgh: University of Pittsburgh Press, 1991), p. 337.

44. Quoted in Walter LaFeber, *Inevitable Revolutions: The United States in Central America* (New York: W. W. Norton, 1984), p. 37.

45. Dirk Bönker, "Admiration, Enmity, and Cooperation: U.S. Navalism and the British and German Empires Before the Great War," *Journal of Colonialism and Colonial History* 2:1 (Spring 2001).

46. Nancy Mitchell, *The Danger of Dreams: German and American Imperialism in Latin America* (Chapel Hill: University of North Carolina Press, 1999), pp. 3, 41.

47. This is the central theme of Mitchell, *Danger of Dreams*.

48. TR to Root, June 2, 1904, Morison, *Letters of Theodore Roosevelt*, vol. 4, pp. 810–13; Mitchell, *Danger of Dreams*, p. 76.

49. Dexter Perkins, *The Monroe Doctrine, 1867–1907* (Baltimore: Johns Hopkins Press, 1937), p. 420.

50. David Healy, *Drive to Hegemony: The United States in the Caribbean, 1898–1917* (Madison: University of Wisconsin Press, 1988), p. 261.

51. Cyrus Veeser, *A World Safe for Capitalism: Dollar Diplomacy and America's Rise to Global Power* (New York: Columbia University Press, 2002).

52. TR to Root, June 7, 1904, Morison, *Letters of Theodore Roosevelt*, vol. 4, pp. 821–23.

53. Roosevelt, "Annual Message to Congress," December 6, 1904; Serge Ricard, "The Roosevelt Corollary," *Presidential Studies Quarterly*, 36:1 (March 2006).

54. Frank Ninkovich, *The United States and Imperialism* (Oxford: Blackwell Publishers, 2001), p. 91.

55. TR to Hale, February 26, 1904, Morison, *Letters of Theodore Roosevelt*, vol. 4, pp. 740–1.

56. Bunau-Varilla to Moore, October 3, 1903, Papers of John Bassett Moore, box 134, folder "Panama Affair," LC.

57. "Protocol of an Agreement Between the United States and the Dominican Republic," February 15, 1905, *FRUS*.

58. *New York Times*, December 23, 1904.

59. Peter Olney to Olney, December 24, 1904, Olney Papers, reel 37, LC.

60. "Protocol of an Agreement Between the United States and the Dominican Republic," February 15, 1905, *FRUS*; TR to William George Tiffany, March 14, 1905, Morison, *Letters of Theodore Roosevelt*, vol. 4, p. 1139.

61. *Congressional Record*, 59th cong., 1st sess., p. 793.

62. Holt, Treaties Defeated by the Senate, p. 221; Theodore Roosevelt, *An Autobiography* (New York: Scribner, 1926), pp. 506–31; Arthur M. Schlesinger, Jr., *The Imperial Presidency* (Boston: Houghton Mifflin, 1973).

63. Quoted in Lester D. Langley, *The Banana Wars: United States Intervention in the Caribbean, 1898–1934,* 2nd edition (Lanham, Md.: Rowman & Littlefield, 2002), p. 23.
64. Emily Rosenberg, *Financial Missionaries to the World: The Politics and Culture of Dollar Diplomacy, 1900–1930* (Durham, N.C.: Duke University Press, 2003), pp. 31–60.
65. TR to Hale, December 3, 1908, Morison, *Letters of Theodore Roosevelt,* vol. 6, pp. 1407–8.
66. Hiram Bingham, *The Monroe Doctrine: An Obsolete Shibboleth* (New Haven, Conn.: Yale University Press, 1913), p. 134.
67. James Holmes, *Theodore Roosevelt and World Order: Police Power in International Relations* (Washington, D.C.: Potomac Books, 2006), pp. 113–18.
68. Healy, *Drive to Hegemony,* pp. 135–44; Arthur P. Whitaker, *The Western Hemisphere Idea: Its Rise and Decline* (Ithaca, N.Y.: Cornell University Press, 1954), pp. 86–107.
69. *Mexican Herald,* June 7, 1904.
70. Paul Garner, *Porfirio Díaz* (London: Pearson Education, 2001), pp. 149–53.
71. David M. K. Sheinin, *Argentina and the United States: An Alliance Contained* (Athens: University of Georgia Press, 2006), p. 35.
72. TR to Archibald Bulloch Roosevelt, December 2, 1914, Morison, *Letters of Theodore Roosevelt,* vol. 8, pp. 851–52; Walter LaFeber, *The American Search for Opportunity, 1965–1913* (Cambridge: Cambridge University Press, 1993), pp. 195–96.
73. Quoted in Ninkovich, *United States and Imperialism,* p. 209.
74. *Economist,* December 10, 1904; London *Times,* May 26, 1904.
75. Mahan and Roosevelt quoted in Howard K. Beale, *Theodore Roosevelt and the Rise of America to World Power* (Baltimore: Johns Hopkins University Press, 1956), pp. 96, 134.

Conclusion

1. Woodrow Wilson, "Peace Without Victory," January 22, 1917.
2. Erez Manela, *The Wilsonian Moment: Self-Determination and the International Origins of Anticolonial Nationalism* (New York: Oxford University Press, 2007), pp. 90, 164.
3. Woodrow Wilson, "Address Before the Southern Commercial Congress at Mobile, Alabama," October 27, 1913.
4. Thomas Knock, *To End All Wars: Woodrow Wilson and the Quest for a New World Order* (Princeton, N.J.: Princeton University Press, 1995), p. 84.
5. Article 21, League of Nations Covenant.
6. Quoted in Dexter Perkins, *A History of the Monroe Doctrine* (Boston: Little, Brown, 1963), p. 285.
7. Quotes from Perkins, *A History of the Monroe Doctrine,* p. ix; Hiram Bingham, *The Monroe Doctrine: An Obsolete Shibboleth* (New Haven, Conn.: Yale University Press, 1913), p. 111.

Suggestions for Further Reading

The beginning place for the history of the Monroe Doctrine remains Dexter Perkins's classic trilogy: *The Monroe Doctrine, 1823–1826* (Cambridge, Mass.: Harvard University Press, 1927); *The Monroe Doctrine, 1826–1867* (Baltimore: Johns Hopkins Press, 1933); and *The Monroe Doctrine, 1867–1907* (Baltimore: Johns Hopkins Press, 1937). Perkins later synthesized these works in the single volume *A History of the Monroe Doctrine* (Boston: Little, Brown, 1963). In formulating a coherent narrative of the Doctrine's evolution, Perkins is both its foundational historian and a central figure in its history. Two other works of the early twentieth century are indispensable. For a compilation of key official documents, see J. Reuben Clark, *Memorandum on the Monroe Doctrine* (Washington, D.C.: Government Printing Office, 1930). The Latin American perspective is emphasized in Alejandro Alvarez, *The Monroe Doctrine: Its Importance in the International Life of the States of the New World* (New York: Oxford University Press, 1924).

More recent interpretations of the Monroe Doctrine include Richard Van Alstyne, "The Monroe Doctrine," in Alexander DeConde, *Encyclopedia of American Foreign Policy*, vol. 2 (New York: Scribner, 1978); Kenneth M. Coleman, "The Political Mythology of the Monroe Doctrine," in John D. Martz and Lars Schoultz (eds.), *Latin America, the United States and the Inter-American System* (Boulder, Colo.: Westview Press, 1980); Walter LaFeber, "The Evolution of the Monroe Doctrine from Monroe to Reagan," in Lloyd C. Gardner, *Redefining the Past: Essays in Diplomatic History in Honor of William Appleman Williams* (Corvallis: Oregon State University Press, 1986); David W. Dent, *The Legacy of the Monroe Doctrine* (London: Greenwood Press, 1999); and Mark T. Gilderhus, "The Monroe Doctrine: Meanings and Implications," *Presidential Studies Quarterly* 36:1 (March 2006). For a cultural and literary study, see Gretchen Murphy, *Hemispheric Imaginings: The Monroe Doctrine and Narratives of U.S. Empire* (Durham, N.C.: Duke University Press, 2005).

Two important recent studies provide fresh interpretations of nineteenth-century American foreign relations. David C. Hendrickson, *Union, Nation, or Empire: The American Debate over International Relations, 1789–1941* (Lawrence: University Press of Kansas, 2009), examines Americans' competing conceptions of statecraft, as well as the interrelationship between internal and external affairs. For a work that emphasizes ideology, see Robert Kagan, *Dangerous Nation: America and the World, 1600–1898* (London: Atlantic Books, 2006). For overviews of American statecraft that are particularly strong on the nineteenth century, see Richard Van Alstyne, *The Rising American Empire* (New York: W. W. Norton, 1974); D. W. Meinig, *The Shaping of America: A Geographical Perspective on 500 Years of History*, vols. 1–4, (New Haven, Conn.: Yale University Press, 1986–2004); Fred Anderson and Andrew Cayton, *The Dominion of War: Empire and Liberty in North America, 1500–2000* (New York: Penguin, 2005); and Brian Balogh, *A Government Out of Sight: The Mystery of National Authority in Nineteenth-Century America* (New York: Cambridge University Press, 2009). A very engaging overview of U.S.-Latin American relations is Lars Schoultz, *Beneath the United States: A History of U.S. Policy Toward Latin America* (Cambridge, Mass.: Harvard University Press, 1998). The United States' bilateral relations with other nations of the Western Hemisphere are examined in "The United States and the Americas," a series from the University of Georgia Press edited by Lester Langley.

For the global context of the nineteenth century, see C. A. Bayly, *The Birth of the Modern World 1780–1914* (Oxford: Blackwell Publishing, 2004), and, of course, the work of Eric Hobsbawm. The place to start for the British Empire is the five-volume (plus a growing number of companion volumes) *Oxford History of the British Empire* (Oxford: Oxford University Press, 1998–). Three other recent studies must be read: P. J. Cain and A. G. Hopkins, *British Imperialism: 1688–2000*, 2nd ed. (London: Longman, 2001); James Belich, *Replenishing the Earth: The Settler Revolution and the Rise of the Anglo World, 1783–1939* (New York: Oxford University Press, 2009); and John Darwin, *The Empire Project: The Rise and Fall of the British World-System, 1830–1970* (Cambridge: Cambridge University Press, 2009). For an introduction to the Western Hemisphere in the nineteenth century, see Arthur P. Whitaker, *The Western Hemisphere Idea: Its Rise and Decline* (Ithaca, N.Y.: Cornell University Press, 1954); Lester D. Langley, *The Americas in the Age of Revolution, 1750–1850* (New Haven, Conn.: Yale University Press, 1996); R. A. Humphreys, *Tradition and Revolt in Latin America and Other Essays* (London: Weidenfeld and Nicolson, 1969); and David Bushnell and Neill Macaulay, *The Emergence of Latin America in the Nineteenth Century* (New York: Oxford University Press, 1988).

Early American statecraft has been the subject of several important recent studies. For the international dimensions of the origins of the United States, see David C. Hendrickson, *Peace Pact: The Lost World of the American Founding* (Lawrence: University Press of Kansas, 2003), and Peter Onuf, "A Declaration of Independence for Diplomatic Historians," *Diplomatic History* 22:1 (January 1998). Felix Gilbert, *To the Farewell Address* (Princeton, N.J.: Princeton University Press, 1961), examines the ideas of early American diplomacy. The forms and nature of early territorial expansion are examined in Peter Onuf, "The

Expanding Union," in David T. Konig (ed.), *Devising Liberty: Preserving and Creating Freedom in the New American Republic* (Stanford, Calif.: Stanford Unversity Press, 1995); John Craig Hammond, *Slavery, Freedom, and Expansion in the Early American West* (Charlottesville: University of Virginia Press, 2008); J.C.A. Stagg, *Borderlines in Borderlands: James Madison and the Spanish-American Frontier, 1776–1821* (New Haven, Conn.: Yale University Press, 2009); Reginald Horsman, "The Dimension of an 'Empire for Liberty': Expansion and Republicanism, 1775–1825," *Journal of the Early Republic* 9 (Spring 1989); Drew R. McCoy, *The Elusive Republic: Political Economy in Jeffersonian America* (Chapel Hill: University of North Carolina Press, 1980); and William Earl Weeks, *Building the Continental Empire* (Chicago: Ivan R. Dee, 1996).

The place to begin for the U.S. response to the Latin American revolutions is James E. Lewis, Jr., *The American Union and the Problem of Neighborhood: The United States and the Collapse of the Spanish Empire* (Chapel Hill: University of North Carolina Press, 1998). For the broad context of the dissolution of the Spanish Empire, see Rafe Blaufarb, "The Western Question: The Geopolitics of Latin American Independence," *American Historical Review* 112:3 (June 2007); John Lynch, *The Spanish American Revolutions, 1808–1826* (New York: W. W. Norton and Co., 1986); and Arthur Whitaker, *The United States and the Independence of Latin America, 1800–1830* (Baltimore: Johns Hopkins Press, 1941). Piero Gleijesses, "The Limits of Sympathy: The United States and the Independence of Spanish America," *Journal of Latin American Studies* 24:3 (October 1992), makes the case for the limited nature of U.S. support for the Latin American revolutions. The role of John Quincy Adams has rightly attracted much attention. Two key works that approach his statecraft from different perspectives are Samuel Flagg Bemis, *John Quincy Adams and the Foundation of American Foreign Policy* (New York: Knopf, 1949), and William Earl Weeks, *John Quincy Adams and American Global Empire* (Lexington: University of Kentucky Press, 1992). For a debate concerning the importance of domestic politics to the drafting of the 1823 message, see the exchange between Ernest May, *The Making of the Monroe Doctrine* (Cambridge, Mass.: Belknap Press, 1975), and Harry Ammon, "The Monroe Doctrine: Domestic Politics or National Decision?" *Diplomatic History* 5 (1981). An underappreciated article that emphasizes the limited scope of the 1823 message is Gale W. McGee, "The Monroe Doctrine—A Stopgap Measure," *Mississippi Valley Historical Review* 38:2 (September 1951). Jacksonian foreign policy is in need of more scholarship, though we are fortunate to have John M. Belohlavek, *"Let the Eagle Soar!": The Foreign Policy of Andrew Jackson* (Lincoln: University of Nebraska Press, 1985).

The expansion of the 1840s is the subject of several important studies. The key works here are Thomas Hietala, *Manifest Design: American Exceptionalism and Empire* (Ithaca, N.Y.: Cornell University Press, 2003); Reginald Horsman, *Race and Manifest Destiny: The Origins of American Racial Anglo-Saxonism* (Cambridge: Mass.: Harvard University Press, 1981); David Pletcher, *The Diplomacy of Annexation: Texas, Oregon, and the Mexican War* (Columbia: University of Missouri Press, 1973); Howard Jones and Donald Rakestraw, *Prologue to Manifest Destiny: Anglo-American Relations in the 1840s* (Wilmington, Del.: Scholarly Resources, 1997);

and Norman Graebner, *Empire on the Pacific: A Study in American Continental Expansion* (New York: Ronald Press Co., 1955). Frederick Merk, *The Monroe Doctrine and American Expansionism, 1843–1849* (New York: Knopf, 1966), examines Polk's reinterpretation of the 1823 message. The expansionism of John Tyler is made clear in Edward P. Crapol, *John Tyler: The Accidental President* (Chapel Hill: University of North Carolina Press, 2006). The importance of British imperialism to U.S. policy is the subject of a landmark article, Kinley Brauer, "The United States and British Imperial Expansion, 1815–1860," *Diplomatic History* 12 (Winter 1988). Another work that emphasizes the British angle in this period is Sam Haynes, "Anglophobia and the Annexation of Texas: The Quest for National Security," in Sam Haynes and Christopher Morris (eds.), *Manifest Destiny and Empire: American Antebellum Expansionism* (College Station: Texas A&M University Press, 1997). Aims McGuinness, *Path of Empire: Panama and the California Gold Rush* (Ithaca, N.Y.: Cornell University Press, 2008), shows how the acquisition of California drew the United States into the affairs of Panama in the 1850s. Whig foreign policy needs more research. The best place to begin for this, as well as an overview of the period, is Daniel Walker Howe, *What Hath God Wrought: The Transformation of America, 1815–1848* (New York: Oxford University Press, 2007).

The Civil War period continues to attract much scholarly attention. For the international roots of the sectional conflict, see Edward B. Rugemer, *The Problem of Emancipation: The Caribbean Roots of the American Civil War* (Baton Rouge: Louisiana State University Press, 2008); Brian Schoen, *The Fragile Fabric of Union: Cotton, Federal Politics, and the Global Origins of the Civil War* (Baltimore: Johns Hopkins University Press, 2009); and Steven Heath Mitton, "The Free World Confronted: The Problem of Slavery and Progress in American Foreign Relations, 1833–1844," Ph.D. dissertation, Louisiana State University, 2005. Southern expansion and filibustering are the subjects of two important works by Robert May: *The Southern Dream of a Caribbean Empire, 1854–1861* (Athens: University of Georgia Press, 1989), and *Manifest Destiny's Underworld: Filibustering in Antebellum America* (Chapel Hill: University of North Carolina Press, 2002). International finance is examined in Jay Sexton, *Debtor Diplomacy: Finance and American Foreign Relations in the Civil War Era, 1837–1873* (Oxford: Oxford University Press, 2005). Confederate foreign policy is the subject of Frank Owsley, *King Cotton Diplomacy: Foreign Relations of the Confederate States of America* (Chicago: University of Chicago Press, 1931), and Charles Hubbard, *The Burden of Confederate Diplomacy* (Knoxville: University of Tennessee Press, 1998). For Civil War diplomacy, see Howard Jones, *Blue and Gray Diplomacy: A History of Union and Confederate Foreign Relations* (Chapel Hill: University of North Carolina Press, 2009); Philip Myers, *Caution and Cooperation: The American Civil War in British-American Relations* (Kent, Ohio: Kent State University Press, 2008); Brian Jenkins, *Britain and the War for the Union*, 2 vols. (Montreal: McGill-Queen's University Press, 1974 and 1980); and, D. P. Crook, *The North, the South and the Powers, 1861–1865* (London: John Wiley & Sons, 1974). U.S.-Mexican relations during the French intervention are best examined in Thomas D. Schoonover, *Dollars over Dominion: The Triumph of Liberalism in Mexican–United*

States Relations, 1861–1867 (Baton Rouge: Louisiana State University Press, 1978).

Walter LaFeber's *The New Empire: An Interpretation of American Expansion, 1860–1898* (Ithaca, N.Y.: Cornell University Press, 1963), has stood the test of time and remains the most cogent interpretation of late-nineteenth-century foreign policy. An important counterpoise is David Pletcher, *The Diplomacy of Trade and Investment: American Economic Expansion in the Hemisphere, 1865–1900* (Columbia: University of Missouri Press, 1998). Other illuminating overviews include Charles Campbell, *The Transformation of American Foreign Relations, 1865–1900* (New York: Harper & Row, 1976); Robert Beisner, *From the Old Diplomacy to the New, 1865–1900* (New York: Thomas Y. Crowell, 1975); and Joseph Smith, *Illusions of Conflict: Anglo-American Diplomacy Toward Latin America, 1865–1896* (Pittsburgh: University of Pittsburgh Press, 1979). For a study of how racism functioned as a deterrent to expansion, see Eric T. L. Love, *Race over Empire: Racism and U.S. Imperialism, 1865–1900* (Chapel Hill: University of North Carolina Press, 2004). For the underappreciated cosmopolitanism of the era, see Ernest May, *American Imperialism: A Speculative Essay* (Chicago: Imprint Publications, 1968), and Frank Ninkovich, *Global Dawn: The Cultural Foundation of American Internationalism, 1865–1890* (Cambridge, Mass.: Harvard University Press, 2009). James Blaine has been the focus of two important studies in the past decade: Edward P. Crapol, *James G. Blaine: Architect of Empire* (Wilmington, Del.: Scholarly Resources, 2000), and David Healy, *James G. Blaine and Latin America* (Columbia: University of Missouri Press, 2001). Other important studies of individual statesmen, which are in need of updating, are Allan Nevins, *Hamilton Fish: The Inner History of the Grant Administration* (New York: Dodd, Mead and Co., 1936), and Gerald Eggert, *Richard Olney: Evolution of a Statesman* (University Park, Pa.: Penn State University Press, 1974). The writings of José Martí on the United States have been translated in the collection edited by Philip S. Foner, *Inside the Monster: Writings on the United States and American Imperialism* (New York: Monthly Review Press, 1975).

A rich literature examines the War of 1898 and its aftermath. A great starting point is Frank Ninkovich, *The United States and Imperialism* (Oxford: Blackwell Publishing, 2001). Two provocative studies of the War of 1898 are Louis A. Pérez, Jr., *The War of 1898: The United States and Cuba in History and Historiography* (Chapel Hill: University of North Carolina Press, 1998), and Thomas Schoonover, *Uncle Sam's War of 1898 and the Origins of Globalization* (Lexington: University Press of Kentucky, 2003). For a gender interpretation, see Kristin Hoganson, *Fighting for American Manhood: How Gender Politics Provoked the Spanish-American and Philippine-American Wars* (New Haven, Conn.: Yale University Press, 1998). Anglo-American dimensions are examined in Bradford Perkins, *The Great Rapprochement: England and the United States, 1895–1914* (London: Victor Gollancz, 1969), and Paul A. Kramer, "Empires, Exceptions, and Anglo-Saxons: Race and Rule Between the British and United States Empires, 1880–1910," *Journal of American History* 88:4 (March 2002). The connection between Indian policy and the overseas colonialism of the post-1898 period is made clear in Walter L. Williams, "United States Indian Policy and the Debate over Philippine Annexation: Implications for the Origins of American Imperialism," *Journal of American History* 66:4 (March 1980). For the anti-imperialists, see Robert Beisner, *Twelve Against Empire: The Anti-Imperialists, 1898–1900* (New York: McGraw-Hill, 1968), and David Mayers, *Dissenting Voices in America's Rise to Power* (Cambridge: Cambridge University Press, 2007).

The literature on Theodore Roosevelt is vast and varied. An important conceptualization of his worldview is Frank Ninkovich, "Theodore Roosevelt: Civilization as Ideology," *Diplomatic History* 10 (Summer 1986). Two contrasting interpretations of TR are Richard H. Collins in *Theodore Roosevelt's Caribbean: The Panama Canal, the Monroe Doctrine, and the Latin American Context* (Baton Rouge: Louisiana State University Press, 1990) and Thomas Schoonover, *The United States in Central America, 1860–1911: Episodes in Social Imperialism and International Rivalry in the World System* (Durham, N.C.: Duke University Press, 1991). TR's foreign policy is examined in relation to great power dynamics in Howard K. Beale, *Theodore Roosevelt and the Rise of America to World Power* (Baltimore: Johns Hopkins University Press, 1956), and William N. Tilchin, *Theodore Roosevelt and the British Empire: A Study in Presidential Statecraft* (New York: St. Martin's Press, 1997). The Roosevelt Corollary is the subject of two important recent studies: Cyrus Veeser, *A World Safe for Capitalism: Dollar Diplomacy and America's Rise to Global Power* (New York: Columbia University Press, 2002), and Serge Ricard, "The Roosevelt Corollary," *Presidential Studies Quarterly* 36:1 (March 2006). The significance of the perceived German threat is the subject of Nancy Mitchell, *The Danger of Dreams: German and American Imperialism in Latin America* (Chapel Hill: University of North Carolina Press, 1999). U.S. interventionism in the Caribbean is examined in Louis A. Pérez, Jr., *Cuba Under the Platt Amendment, 1902–1934* (Pittsburgh: University of Pittsburgh Press, 1991); David Healy, *Drive to Hegemony: The United States in the Caribbean, 1898–1917* (Madison: University of Wisconsin Press, 1988); and Emily Rosenberg, *Financial Missionaries to the World: The Politics and Culture of Dollar Diplomacy, 1900–1930* (Durham, N.C.: Duke University Press, 2003).

Acknowledgments

It is a great pleasure to extend my warm thanks to those who assisted in the making of this book. Thomas LeBien, Dan Crissman, and June Kim at Hill and Wang all provided sage advice, as did the copy editor, Emily DeHuff. They also helped me relearn American English. Several colleagues took the time to read drafts of the manuscript: Eric Rauchway, Richard Carwardine, Gareth Davies, and John Watts (whose claims of ignorance about American history are belied by the value of his comments). I am grateful to them for their many helpful suggestions and am in their debt. Natalia Bas helped to broaden the scope of the project by giving me countless tutorials on Latin American history. David Sim provided essential research assistance early in the project, as well as invaluable conversations toward its end. Several other colleagues generously shared thoughts that have shaped the book: Peter Onuf, Daniel Walker Howe, Ian Tyrell, Martin Crawford, John Thompson, Don Ratcliffe, Lawrence Goldman, Seb Page, Peter Thompson, Stephen Tuck, Will Pettigrew, Wendy Warren, Joe Fronczak, Tamson Pietsch, Joseph Smith, Heath Mitton, Richard Huzzey, and all the folks that make BrANCH the best conference of the year.

This project was an outgrowth of a paper I teach at Oxford on the nineteenth-century American empire. Many of the ideas in this book have their origin in tutorial discussions with Oxford undergraduates. A number of students and grad students are owed individual thanks: Steve Tuffnell, Andrew Boxer, Justin Marquardt, Sally Bagwell, Tom Gover, and Alex Edmiston. Funds from the Zvi Meitar/Vice-Chancellor Oxford University Research Prize provided the time away from tutoring required for translating the ideas onto paper. I extend a special thanks to Zvi Meitar for his generosity. I am also grateful for the research support I received from the Andrew W. Mellon Foundation, the Oxford History Faculty, and Corpus Christi College. Sophie and the Chrises generously took me in during my many trips to Washington. Finally, and most of all, I'd like to thank Julie and Georgia for helping to put the nineteenth-century Monroe Doctrine in its appropriate context. This book is dedicated to my parents, who continue to inspire.

Index